ANALYZING SHORT STORIES

Fourth Edition

Joseph Lostracco
George Wilkerson

Austin Community College

KENDALL/HUNT PUBLISHING COMPANY
4050 Westmark Drive Dubuque, Iowa 52002

ISBN 0-7872-7376-7

Library of Congress Catalog Card Number: 98-67719

Printed in the United States of America
10 9 8 7 6 5 4 3 2

Contents

FOREWORD

The Philosophy Behind This Book

The approach in this book is classic. We take a tried-and-true approach to the study of literary narration that has the following characteristics:

- **A Special Use of Language**—How something is said is more important than what is said.
- **Probability**—The characters and events have the appearance of reality.
- **Entertainment Value**—The writing evokes an emotional response.

Our goal is to teach an approach to analyzing works of literature. We have chosen the short story as a basis for analysis because our teaching experience shows that it is the easiest place for students to begin learning the concepts of analysis and evaluation. The structure and elements are generally the same; each story contains a conflict, imaginary characters, a setting, an emphasis on language, and a clear distinctive voice.

While oral discussions of prose are valuable, the most common approach to evaluating one's understanding of a work of literature is through an analytical essay that discusses a story's elements and explains their interrelationship, especially as they work together to produce a single effect. The separate parts of an automobile engine can't make the car go; only by operating together can they accomplish that goal. To explain how an engine works we need to know how each piece of the engine works, in relation to each other piece. The same is true of analyzing literature. You need to understand how each of the elements works with the others to achieve the single effect that is central to the story.

Writing that performs that analytical function must be objective, present evidence, and draw conclusions that follow reasonably from the evidence. Emotional words are inappropriate, as well as are ambiguous, confusing, or exclamatory terms. Formal grammar and punctuation are important, especially as they contribute to the clarity of the writing, and the organization of the writing must conform to the traditional format for academic papers: an introduction (interpretation), body (evidence), and conclusion.

We present the basic information you need to understand literary writing. The following basic format for writing a paper about a short story is simple.

Part I

A brief summary of the story is followed by a statement of the central idea (your interpretation of the story's meaning).

Part II

A discussion of each element of the story as it relates to or supports your interpretation.

- Character
- Conflict
- Point of view
- Setting
- Language
- Tone

Part III

A brief review of the elements of the story and their contribution to the central idea.

Once you have mastered this basic approach, you can modify it to suit other needs. You can compare and contrast one story with another or, using your analysis as a basis, evaluate the story. We have found that mastering the analytical process enhances your appreciation of literature and increases your ability to judge a story's quality objectively. Ultimately, the skill can be generalized and extended to nonliterary subjects, providing you with a basic methodology for writing about subjects in science and the humanities.

Joseph Lostracco
George Wilkerson
Austin, Texas 1998

CHAPTER ONE

The Central Idea

"God has no need to justify His actions to man. He who built the universe can destroy it when He chooses. It is arrogance—it is perilously near blasphemy—for us to say what He may or may not do. This I could have accepted, hard though it is to look upon whole worlds and peoples thrown into the furnace. But there comes a point when even the deepest faith must falter, and now, as I look at the calculations lying before me, I know I have reached that point at last."

from "The Star," by Arthur C. Clarke

Literature provides a concentrated, imaginative vision of the world. The type of literature known as the short story deals with every conceivable subject. An author can dramatize any aspect of human nature or the human condition: youth, happiness, marriage, divorce, nonconformity, growing old, dying. The narrative gives life to the idea, but what an author wants to convey about some aspect of life is what makes the story significant and meaningful.

WHAT IS A CENTRAL IDEA?

A story's central idea (sometimes called the theme) is the implied comment on the subject of the story. It's what the story reveals about some aspect of existence as perceived by the author. When the story is done, the attitude we feel toward the subject of the story is derived from the central idea. Through that central idea, the story can give us insight into ourselves and increase our awareness of part of our world.

Kate Chopin's "Desiree's Baby" is about hatred and love. The author's comment on those conflicting human emotions gives the story significance: people who let hatred and bigotry rather than love guide their lives can invite tragic, self-destructive consequences. That central idea—and the way it is conveyed—causes this story to stick in the reader's mind.

THE CENTRAL IDEA AND THE ELEMENTS OF FICTION

The central idea, or theme, of a story is the motivating force that influences the author's choices. The writer chooses from a variety of techniques:

character, conflict, point of view, setting, and language. An author may not have an articulated central idea in mind when writing the story; he or she may not be consciously aware of the force behind it, but the central idea is there nonetheless. It may form during the writing process, or it may never be precisely conceived. In fact, a critical reader, in the process of analyzing a story, may develop a clearer sense of the central idea than the author did. That awareness results from the reader working after the fact with the story as a whole.

Analyzing fiction requires a thorough examination of how the elements of a story contribute to the whole, how they work together to achieve the central idea, and how they convey it. Each element influences the central idea and, in turn, is influenced by it. And each element may communicate the theme, especially when some change occurs as a result of (or within) one or more of the elements.

The only exception occurs when a particular element is so essential to the central idea that it dictates the form of one or more of the other elements.

INTERPRETATION

Interpretation is the process of deriving a generalization from specifics. Because our own experiences can give us a deeper understanding of ourselves, of other people, and of life in general, we can also gain insights vicariously through literature. In a well-written story, the central idea grows naturally out of the unique combination of narrative elements, and the idea is inseparable from the narrative that embodies it. The central idea is an organic part of the story and grows naturally from it.

A literary interpretation makes a general statement about the meaning of a story based on the specific evidence in it. That generalization is the statement of the story's central idea or theme; the evidence consists of the specifics of each element (character, conflict, point of view, setting, and language) as it reflects the central idea.

An essay analyzing a short story always contains an interpretation, a statement that functions as the thesis. An analysis of a story should always state the interpretation in the introductory paragraph. Furthermore, the introductory paragraph should include a brief summary of the plot (what happens in the story) for the benefit of someone who may not have read it. This summary should include only the events essential to understanding what the story is about. Subsequent paragraphs, analyzing each of the story's elements and the relationship between those elements and the central idea, should include more details and provide support for the interpretation.

During the analysis, some evidence may be found that requires a modification or revision of the central idea statement. Since a valid generalization must be supported by all of the available evidence, an accurate statement of the central idea must accommodate all elements of the story. There should be nothing out of place or extraneous. The central idea should be consistent with all the evidence.

Consider John Steinbeck's "The Chrysanthemums." If Steinbeck had been a scientist interested in human behavior, he might have conducted experiments, isolating people and misleading them to see how they respond. Eventually, he might report that nine out of the ten people who lived in an isolated area for an extended period of time were more apt to be misled than those who were given opportunities to mix with others. Then he might have used that evidence to make the general observation that isolation creates circumstances that make people vulnerable.

Instead, Steinbeck chose the literary method, an approach to the truth that is opposite that of the scientist. He relied on emotional response and the human tendency to generalize from insufficient evidence. Knowing that, he created a story that seems real. He created characters for whom we might feel emotions like those we feel toward real people. Then he simply allows us to make inferences based on the fictitious experience in the same way we make inferences based on real experiences.

So one way to determine the central idea of a story is to ask, "What is the story submitting as evidence?" But we must also remember that the main purpose of the story is to entertain us, and that's all that some stories do. They are simply meant to stir our emotions, but not to direct the emotional response toward some kind of statement about humanity. Most mystery stories are meant to arouse curiosity; adventure tales, excitement; horror stories, fear; and humorous stories, smiles and laughter. And that's all.

SOURCES FOR CENTRAL IDEAS

The central idea (or theme) of a story should be a general statement of the idea behind it. There are some central ideas commonly found in many stories. They're common because great writers deal with universal "truths." These are usually of the following types.

Psychological

Some stories make a statement about human behavior, our psychological makeup, and the way our minds work—"what makes us tick." These statements are not value judgments; the writers usually aren't saying that the behavior we're seeing is good or bad, right or wrong. They simply tell us that the behavior is part of the human condition; it's just the way some of us are.

Sociological

The sociological nature of humanity concerns the behavior of humans in groups (nationalities, small-town folk, city dwellers, rural life, those in regions like the American South or Northern Ireland, etc.) and is the domain of the sociological central idea. The aim is to point out a truth of groups as opposed to that of individuals.

Philosophical

Some stories point out the limitations of human perception, like our inability to distinguish fantasy from reality. (Is it a dream or is it real?) Others deal with the ultimate questions of existence: Why are we here? Is life worth living? Is there life after death? Usually, the story simply raises that type of question; it does not provide an answer.

Moral and Ethical

Some stories deal with moral and ethical issues. Those that take a clear position on an issue (e.g., abortion is wrong, capital punishment is right) and try to change the reader's view are called didactic (some might say "preachy.") Like the philosophical type, other stories simply raise these ethical or moral questions without proposing an answer: Does the end justify the means? When is it wrong to tell the truth? What is our duty to one another? Or to our country? Another way of looking at this matter of central idea, especially in relation to those central ideas that deal with issues of morality, is to recognize that some stories may have a persuasive aim. The writer may want the reader to accept a particular view of the world and/or life as he or she represents it in the story. In such cases, everything in the story is skewed toward promoting that view.

Entertainment

Some writing is aimed solely at entertaining the reader, generating an emotional response: laughter, sorrow, fear, anger, horror, repulsion, surprise, shock, unease for its own sake. Many of us enjoy experiencing those responses, and some stories exist to evoke such emotions. If some kind of meaning is inferred, it may be that the reader feels the need for it, not that the story was designed for it. (As children, we are often taught to look for the "moral" of a story, which can be a hard habit to break.)

A good story always evokes an emotional response. For example, Edgar Allen Poe's "The Cask of Amontillado," is primarily a horror story. The central idea is to entertain us by generating an emotional reaction: horror. If that's all a story does, then the central idea of the story is "to entertain," and the only issue should be what emotion the story arouses. But if, for example, the reader comes away from a story like Steinbeck's "The Chrysanthemums" with a feeling of sadness about Elisa's situation, that feeling goes beyond simple entertainment; it has been aroused to support the story's theme: how loneliness and isolation often make people easy prey for exploitation.

IF THE CENTRAL IDEA ISN'T A MORAL, WHAT IS IT?

There's a tendency on the part of many students to try to find a moral in the stories they read. Learning the difference between a central idea and a moral is critical. A moral tells us how to live (or not live) and it's often in the form of an "If...then..." statement. "If you don't think before you act, you'll get into trouble." A central idea, on the other hand, says, "Insensitive people who act without thinking sometimes get into trouble."

What's the difference? First, a moral is absolute. The moral says "If you don't think before you act, (then) you will get into trouble." No exceptions. But the central idea says "Insensitive people who act before they think sometimes get into trouble." Second, a moral tells us what to do: don't act without thinking; a central idea tells us something about "insensitive people who act without thinking."

John Updike, author of "A & P," may want us to see adolescence as an impulsive age. He created Sammy, an adolescent, who seems very real and, perhaps, reminds us of someone we know. He then lets us in on the way Sammy thinks and acts. He tells the story in such a way that when we have finished reading it, we don't just say, "That adolescent sure acted foolishly." Instead, we say, "Adolescents can be impulsive."

Notice the difference between the form of the word adolescent, which is a specific, singular statement, and adolescents, which is general and plural. The central idea of "A & P" lies in the general statement about adolescence: adolescents are often very impulsive. Sammy is simply a specific example, a piece of evidence (albeit fictional), to support the author's case.

SUMMARY AND CENTRAL IDEA

The basic method for introducing the central idea of a story is to use a brief summary, a single paragraph of about one hundred words or less that tells the reader the major details: the main characters, the setting, and the major events. This summary includes only highlights; the details are saved for later.

Keep in mind that we're defining a "standard approach" to the analytical essay. In this approach, the central idea is usually a single sentence and it appears at the end of the summary paragraph. When stating the central idea, a direct approach leaves no room for doubt, so a safe way to be sure it's clear is to begin the idea statement this way: "The central idea of this story is that ______."

SAMPLES

The following passages are examples of introductory paragraphs to analytical papers written by students.

The Central Idea in "A & P"

"A & P," by John Updike, is the story of a significant event in the life of Sammy, a nineteen-year-old grocery store checker. One summer day, three girls dressed in bathing suits come into the store. Before Sammy can ring up their purchase, Lengel, the store manager, sees the girls and informs them that their attire is inappropriate and that they must be decently dressed the next time they come in. Embarrassed for the girls, and in an attempt to impress them, Sammy tells Lengel that he is quitting. Lengel, recognizing Sammy's resignation for what it is, gives him an opportunity to change his mind, but Sammy is determined to follow through with his gesture even though he realizes "how hard the world was going to be to me hereafter." Updike suggests that youthfulness and immaturity contribute to impulsive decisions, and that the consequences of such decisions contribute to our growth.

The Central Idea in "I Want to Know Why"

"I Want to Know Why," by Sherwood Anderson, is a story about a young adolescent who has a passion for race horses, and the dilemma he faces when confronted with the shocking reality of his role-model horse trainer. The boy who narrates the story takes a trip with three friends to Saratoga to see a horse race. Before the race, the boy spots his favorite horse, Sunstreak, and Sunstreak's trainer, Jerry Tilford, whom the boy admires. The night after the race, the boy goes alone to search for his hero and is enraged to find him in a house full of prostitutes, leaving the boy to wonder how a man of such valor and beauty could be found with "bad women." Anderson's story reveals how the actions and morals of role models have a strong influence on those who admire them. It also touches on the pain associated with the loss of innocence.

The Central Idea in "Like a Bad Dream"

Heinrich Boll's "Like a Bad Dream" is the story of a dutiful husband striving to get ahead in the business world. The questionable ethics involved in negotiating a contract and the willingness of the participants (including his wife) to support these practices are somewhat shocking to the protagonist. When he sees how easily he becomes a willing participant in the affair, it all seems like a bad dream to him, leaving the reader and the protagonist wondering whether the pursuit of material gain is worth the agony of compromising one's moral convictions. Boll's theme suggests that there is an inherent conflict between moral values and material success.

The Central Idea in "A Worn Path"

"A Worn Path," by Eudora Welty, is the story of an aged black woman's difficult cross-country journey from her rural home to a distant town where she must go to get her grandson's medicine. In spite of her age and frailty, and because of her determination and courage, she overcomes physical and human obstacles to accomplish her task. Welty implies that dignity is its own reward and that, despite indignities, suffering, and prejudice, the nobility of the human spirit can prevail.

The Central Idea in "Miss Brill"

Katherine Mansfield's "Miss Brill" is the story of a shy schoolteacher who spends her Sundays sitting in a public park imagining herself and others around as actors in a stage play. A young couple's rude remarks shatter her illusion of belonging to the group in the park and put an end to her satisfying self-deception. The story reveals how lonely, shy people can be deeply hurt when their illusions of "belonging" are shattered and they must face the lonely singularity of their lives.

You may have noticed in these examples that while most of the central idea statements do not begin with the phrase "The central idea of the story is that...," you had no problem understanding the student's interpretation. We recommend that you don't deviate from the "formula" approach. Once you become comfortable with the central idea concept, however, you can begin to modify the way you state it. Notice in the following how each of these central ideas could be phrased using the formula approach.

"Updike suggests that youthfulness and immaturity contribute to impulsive decisions, and that the consequences of such decisions contribute to our growth."

The central idea of this story is that youthfulness and immaturity contribute to impulsive decisions, and that the consequences of such decisions contribute to our growth.

"Anderson's story reveals how the actions and morals of role models have a strong influence on those who admire them."

The central idea of this story is that the actions and morals of role models have a strong influence on those who admire them.

"Boll's theme suggests that there is an inherent conflict between moral values and material success.

The central idea of this story is that there is an inherent conflict between moral values and material success.

"Welty implies that dignity is its own reward and that, despite indignities, suffering, and prejudice, the nobility of the human spirit can prevail.

The central idea of this story is that dignity is its own reward and that, despite indignities, suffering, and prejudice, the nobility of the human spirit can prevail.

"The story reveals how lonely, shy people can be deeply hurt when their illusions of 'belonging' are shattered and they must face the lonely singularity of their lives.

The central idea of this story is that lonely, shy people can be deeply hurt when their illusions of "belonging" are shattered and they must face the lonely singularity of their lives.

COMMON INTERPRETATION PITFALLS

Whether you read for pleasure or as part of an assignment, you should remain aware of the guiding principles of interpretation. The goal is to identify the central idea and explain how you determined it without falling into traps like believing there's only one correct interpretation, or rejecting an obvious interpretation because it conflicts with your own values. Interpretations differ from one reader to the next; some central ideas are complex and some may conflict with your own view of the world. Those are some of the pitfalls you must face.

Differing Interpretations

Because everyone's experiences are unique, no two readers respond to and interpret a story in exactly the same way. Likewise, there is no one way to express the central idea of a story. There is only a range of ideas. The best stories have multiple levels of meaning, so they are open to various interpretations. Serious readers know that most stories require more than one reading before the central idea becomes clear.

Complex Ideas

Sometimes you may feel the central idea, but you're unable to explain it. Don't give up; analysis involves finding the words to express the felt meaning of a story. In other cases, the central idea may be too complex to reduce to a single-sentence statement, so you may need to use the entire analysis to elaborate and clarify your interpretation.

Ideas That Conflict with Your Own

You can't ignore or deny the theme of a story merely because you don't agree with it. And you can't bend the story to fit your own perspective. A story is the expression of an author's vision or experience. While that vision or experience may differ from yours, it cannot be ignored. After all, a major function of literature is to entertain, and one way an author may entertain us is to challenge our way of looking at life, at other people, or even at ourselves.

Meaning Beyond the Story

Because a story's theme is a generalization about people and life, you must not limit your interpretation to the specific characters and situations of the story. They represent something larger. Because a story's theme is rarely explicit, you must probe beneath the surface to discover what the story has to reveal. To interpret a story correctly, focus on what the action means, rather than on the action itself.

Reading Exercise:

See if you can determine the central idea in Arthur C. Clarke's "The Star." After you've read the story, try writing a central idea statement. Remember to begin the statement this way: The central idea of "The Star," by Arthur C. Clarke, is that....

CHAPTER TWO

Character

"Paul was tall for his age and very thin, with high, cramped shoulders and a narrow chest. His eyes were remarkable for a certain hysterical brilliancy, and he continually used them in a conscious, theatrical sort of way, peculiarly offensive in a boy. The pupils were abnormally large, as though he were addicted to belladonna, but there was a glassy glitter about them which that drug does not produce."

from "Paul's Case," by Willa Cather

Analyzing a short story requires a careful examination of the characters, the "who" of the story and the critical part they play in the execution of the story's central idea. This chapter examines various character types and the methods authors use to develop them. Once you can identify these types and recognize how and why the writer developed them as he or she did, you'll find analyzing the story much easier.

CHARACTER TYPES

The characters in a story are like the actors in a play. They're imaginary figures created by the author to advance the plot. They're usually human, but animals can be characters, too (read Liam O'Flaherty's "The Hawk"). But once in a great while a natural force, like nature or time, is just as much a character as a human being. Jack London did that in "To Build A Fire," and lately we've seen a spate of films (*Twister, Volcano, Typhoon*, etc.) where the main "character" is a natural force.

ROUND AND FLAT CHARACTERS

Flat characters have only one dimension. For example, there's the porter in "The Bride Comes to Yellow Sky" who "at times surveyed them from afar with an amused and superior grin. On other occasions he bullied them with skill in ways that did not make it exactly plain to them that they were being bullied. He subtly used all the manners of the most unconquerable kind of snobbery. He oppressed them; but of this oppression they had small knowledge...." That is all we know of the man and all we need to know. His job is to give the reader a sense of how others reacted to the couple on the train. He is one-sided.

But when we say that characters are round, we're saying they have many sides to their personality. The writer fills in a lot of details. And they usually have some of the following characteristics.

Details

The character is carefully drawn; physical and behavioral details make the character seem very human. Some of these details concern the character's physical appearance; others focus on how the character acts, behaviors that make the character unique. Notice the careful selection of details in this description of Paul, from "Paul's Case" by Willa Cather:

> "Once, when he had been making a synopsis of a paragraph at the blackboard, his English teacher had stepped to his side and attempted to guide his hand. Paul had started back with a shudder and thrust his hands violently behind him. The astonished woman could scarcely have been more hurt and embarrassed had he struck at her. The insult was so involuntary and definitely personal as to be unforgettable. In one way and another, he had made all his teachers, men and women alike, conscious of the same feeling of physical aversion. In one case he habitually sat with his hand shading his eyes; in another had made a running commentary on the lecture, with humorous intent."

Many Sides

Realistic characters have multifaceted personalities. They're neither all good nor all bad. A good story reveals the many sides of a character. An author creates a rich, complex, even ambiguous, personality to dramatize and vivify the story. (Read Katherine Mansfield's "Miss Brill" for a good example of a complex, concisely drawn character.)

Complexity

Rather than giving us simplistic descriptions (Everyone loved him or She was a warm and loving person), the writer usually spends some time telling us about the character so that we know him or her.

MAJOR CHARACTERS, MINOR CHARACTERS, AND STEREOTYPES

In the most common structure in a short story, the writer presents a major character and one or more minor characters.

Major Characters

Most short stories focus on a central or major character. That is usually who the story is about. He or she is crucial to the story and the action revolves around what this character says and does. Because this character is so important to the story's central idea, he or she is usually a round character.

Minor Characters

Not all characters in a short story can be fully developed. (Writers save that sort of development for novels.) Minor, supporting characters may contribute to the action, add to the story's meaning, and serve as either a complement or a contrast to the central character.

Because supporting characters are not as crucial to the story, they are usually flat. They lack complexity and are portrayed in broad strokes, with little attention to detail.

Stereotypes

A stereotype is a special type of flat character. The stereotype conforms to a pattern established in other stories. The personality is recognized easily and quickly. The personality can be summed up in a phrase: the miserly moneylender; the sweet, lovely heroine waiting to be rescued by her brave, handsome hero; the refined, but totally evil villain and his dim-witted, but loyal servant. (Read Richard Connell's "The Most Dangerous Game" for examples of those last two stereotypes.)

When a writer lacks the skill or imagination to invent a new, unique character, or when brevity is important, he or she may introduce a stereotype. While it's much easier to use characters that the reader already knows from other sources, stereotypes generally weaken a story's impact and deprive it of "newness." If we know the character type, we can anticipate what he or she will do, so there are no surprises. Nonetheless, even a skillful writer may occasionally use a stereotype. If it suits the central idea or produces a needed effect (especially if the effect is humor or satire), a stereotype may be called upon to play a trivial part but never to serve as the main character.

Sometimes an inexperienced reader may describe a character as a stereotype without realizing that the character is actually the source, not the result, of stereotyping. Stephen Crane's "The Bride Comes to Yellow Sky" includes Scratchy, the town drunk. His character is a type that has been repeated often in western stories. But Scratchy is not a stereotype, he's a prototype, an original from which others werecopied.

STATIC AND DYNAMIC CHARACTERS

Characters are defined as static or dynamic on the basis of whether or not they undergo some important personality or behavioral change. Those who change are considered dynamic; a character who remains the same is static.

The Static Character

A static character does not change in any basic way during the course of a story. He or she has the same values, attitudes, and behavior patterns at the end of the story as at the beginning. Because of their compactness and brevity, most short stories focus on the personalities of static characters.

Walter Mitty is the central character in James Thurber's "The Secret Life of Walter Mitty." He is an excellent example of a static character. He never changes from the beginning to the end of the story. Because Thurber's central idea revolves around that type of character, Mitty's static nature is essential. If he changes (say, from someone who is a meek daydreamer, to someone who is an active "go-getter"), the entire story changes.

The Dynamic Character

Dynamic characters undergo some fundamental change in their nature. The character's personality is altered in some significant way by the experiences depicted in the story. In John Updike's "A & P," Sammy, the main character, qualifies as a dynamic figure. While working in a grocery store, he behaves in an immature, foolish way; but by the end of the story, he realizes he can't act that way anymore. At the end of the story, we can tell that he has somewhat different values (than at the beginning) when he says, "My stomach kind of fell as I felt how hard the world was going to be to me hereafter." He had begun to mature.

With the exception of fantasies, we expect plausible motivations for changes in a character's personality. If a character is to be credible, changes in his or her behavior must also be credible.

METHODS OF CHARACTER PRESENTATION AND EXPOSITION

Presentation refers to the way the author defines a character for the reader. Character exposition refers to character development.

Character Presentation

Presentation can be direct or indirect. In a direct presentation, the author uses explicit statements to tell what a character is like. In an indirect presentation, the author shows a character's personality through actions, words, or thoughts. (This is also known as a dramatic presentation.)

Fiction that employs direct presentation to quickly introduce or physically describe a character often moves more rapidly than stories using indirect methods.

Character Exposition

Character exposition refers to character development. An author has four possible sources for character exposition: what the narrator says (in an omniscient point of view), and the words, actions, and thoughts of the character.

What the Narrator Says

What the narrator of the story says about a character in a direct, expository manner is usually reliable information. After all, it is the author's story and the characters are the author's creations. Notice how much the narrator of this passage from Sherwood Anderson's "Brother Death" reveals about the children in the story:

> "They were both children, but something had made them both in an odd way. Mary was fourteen and Ted eleven, but Ted wasn't strong and that rather evened things up. They were the children of a well-to-do Virginia farmer named John Grey in the Blue Ridge country in Southwestern Virginia. There was a wide valley called the Rich Valley with a railroad and a small river running through it and high mountains in sight, to the north and south. Ted had some kind of a heart disease, a lesion or something of the sort, the result of a severe attack of diphtheria when he was a child of eight. He was thin and not strong but curiously alive. The doctor said he might die at any moment, might just drop down dead. The fact had drawn him peculiarly close to his sister Mary. It had awakened a strong and determined maternalism in her."

What the Character Does

A character's actions help define the personality. Behavior under certain circumstances or in a given situation provides clues to the character's true self. In this and other dramatic methods of characterization, the author involves the reader by requiring inferences. We learn about the character by what the author shows rather than what the narrator tells us. Here's a description of the main character of John Steinbeck's "The Chrysanthemums" getting ready to go out with her husband. Notice what her actions tell us about her.

"In the kitchen she reached behind the stove and felt the water tank. It was full of hot water from the noonday cooking. In the bathroom she tore off her soiled clothes and flung them into the corner. And then she scrubbed herself with a little block of pumice, legs and thighs, loins and chest and arms, until her skin was scratched and red. When she had dried herself she stood in front of the mirror in her bedroom and looked at her body. She tightened her stomach and threw out her chest. She turned and looked over her shoulder at her back.

After a while she began to dress slowly. She put on her newest underclothing and her nicest stockings and the dress which was the symbol of her prettiness. She worked carefully on her hair, penciled her eyebrows, and rouged her lips."

What the Character Says

What characters say is often more revealing than their actions; however, to draw valid conclusions about a character's personality, the reader must consider the character's words in conjunction with these other factors.

The Character's Mood

Is the character saying one thing but meaning another, which may reveal the author's portrayal of the character's state of mind?

The Situation

Is there some irony about the circumstances, something that the character does not know, but the reader does?

The Relationship Between Characters

Is there an unspoken understanding between the characters that changes the nature of the remarks or affects the way they are to be taken?

The Consistency Between the Character's Words and Actions

What is the character doing while speaking; is that action consistent with the words?

Here's a passage from Kate Chopin's "Desiree's Baby." Notice how the author lets Desiree speak and how her own words tell us much about her.

"Oh, Armand is the proudest father in the parish, I believe, because it is a boy, to bear his name; though he says not, that he would have loved a girl as well. But I know it isn't true. I know he says that to please me. And mama," she added, drawing Madame Valmonde's head down to her, and speaking in a whisper, "he hasn't punished one of them not one of them since the baby is born. Even Negrillon, who pretended to have burnt his leg that he might rest from work he only laughed, and said Negrillon was a great scamp. Oh, mama, I'm so happy; it frightens me."

What the Character Thinks

What a character thinks can be the best clue to a personality. Because a character's thoughts constitute the most intimate part of his or her nature, they are the most revealing; a glimpse inside a character's mind provides a more reliable basis for making inferences about personality than actions or words alone. In this second passage from "Desiree's Baby," Kate Chopin makes us privy to one of the characters' thoughts:

"He thought Almighty God had dealt cruelly and unjustly with him; and felt, somehow, that he was paying Him back in kind when he stabbed thus into his wife's soul. Moreover he no longer loved her, because of the unconscious injury she had brought upon his home and name."

Without this "inside look" at what the character thinks, we would never know so much about Armand and never see that he does not even entertain the thought that the situation may have been caused by his genes, not hers.

Reading Exercise:

See if you can determine the central idea in Willa Cather's "Paul's Case." After you've read the story, try writing a central idea statement. Then look at what happens to the main character (for whom the story is named) and determine how that ties into the central idea.

CHAPTER THREE

Conflict

"The two men faced each other at a distance of three paces. He of the revolver smiled with a new and quiet ferocity. 'Tried to sneak up on me,' he said. 'Tried to sneak up on me!' His eyes grew more baleful. As Potter made a slight movement, the man thrust his revolver venomously forward. 'No; don't you do it, Jack Potter. Don't you move a finger toward a gun just yet. Don't you move an eyelash. The time has come for me to settle with you, and I'm goin' to do it my own way, and loaf along with no interferin'. So if you don't want a gun bent on you, just mind what I tell you.' "Potter looked at his enemy. 'I ain't got a gun on me, Scratchy,' he said. 'Honest, I ain't.'"

from "The Bride Comes to Yellow Sky," by Stephen Crane

The way the author arranges the story's events is called the "plot." It's the sequence in which the author tells the story. Chronological order is the most natural, so that's how most stories are told. In John Steinbeck's "The Chrysanthemums," for example, the narrative unfolds chronologically. The first thing we read about (Elisa Allen, working in her flower garden, looked down across the yard and saw Henry, her husband, talking to two men in business suits.) is the first thing that happened. The last event we read (She turned up her coat collar so he could not see she was crying weakly like an old woman.) is the last thing that happened.

Conflicts are derived from a story's plot. They're essentially a result of the cause-and-effect relationship between the events because they are IF/THEN situations. IF Jack had never traded the cow for the beans, THEN his mother would have never been angry and thrown the beans out the window, causing the beanstalk to grow and...well, you know the rest.

DEVIATING FROM THE CHRONOLOGICAL ORDER

When telling the story, the author may change the sequence. The writer can take the reader back and forth in time, tell the last event first and save the first event for last. That can be done for the surprise effect or for the suspense that's created when an event is concealed until the end of the story, even though it occurred earlier.

Here's the plot—the sequence of events—in Kate Chopin's "Desiree's Baby":

1. Armand's mother writes the letter that tells of Armand being Negro.
2. The Valmondes find Desiree, an orphan.
3. Desiree grows up into a beautiful girl.
4. Armand rides by and falls in love with her.
5. Armand and Desiree are married.
6. The baby is born.
7. Armand is proud; he does not punish his slaves.
8. Madame Valmonde comes to visit.
9. Armand's behavior changes (baby is about 3 months old).
10. Desiree recognizes that the baby is Negro.
11. She writes to Madame Valmonde.
12. Madame Valmonde replies, Come home.
13. Desiree goes to Armand with the letter.
14. He tells her to go.
15. Desiree takes the baby and leaves (commits suicide).
16. Armand burns all remnants of Desiree and the baby.
17. Armand finds the letter his mother wrote.

But when she tells the story, Kate Chopin changes the order; she begins with the eighth event. So, as you read it, the events are presented in the following sequence:

8. Madame Valmonde comes to visit.
2. The Valmondes find Desiree, an orphan.
3. Desiree grows up into a beautiful girl.
4. Armand rides by and falls in love with her.
5. Armand and Desiree are married.
6. The baby is born.
7. Armand is proud; he does not punish his slaves.
9. Armand's behavior changes (baby is about 3 months old).
10. Desiree recognizes that the baby is Negro.
11. She writes to Madame Valmonde.
12. Madame Valmonde replies, Come home.
13. Desiree goes to Armand with the letter.
14. He tells her to go.
15. Desiree takes the baby and leaves (some believe she commits suicide).
16. Armand burns all remnants of Desiree and the baby.
17. Armand finds the letter his mother wrote.
1. Armand's mother writes the letter that tells of Armand being Negro.

THE MAJOR ELEMENTS OF A PLOT

Most stories, whether plotted chronologically or not, have a cause-and-effect plot line with generally five stages. Of course, not all stories have these stages clearly defined. An author may present the exposition in piecemeal fashion as the story progresses, or the climax and resolution may occur in a single event.

If the author wants to shock us or suggest that some conflicts have no resolution, the story may end at the moment of climax. Some experimental fiction dispenses with the elements of plot altogether, forcing the reader to create a story out of a series of seemingly unrelated events.

CONFLICT AND PLOT

Of all of the elements of fiction, conflict is the most essential. The clash and resulting struggle between opposing forces is the force that drives the story. It stimulates our curiosity and helps us understand the significance of the story.

Most stories consist of characters who face or must work out a conflict. The conflict is the element that engages the reader. Regardless of the nature of the conflict, it can be classified as internal or external and it is always between two forces.

Conflicts: Internal and External

Conflicts can be internal or external or both. An external conflict involves some sort of struggle between characters, or between a character and the social or physical environment. An internal conflict involves a character's struggle with two elements within his or her psychological self.

A classic example of an internal conflict occurs in *The Adventures of Huckleberry Finn*. Huck is helping his friend Jim, a runaway slave, escape to the North. Jim is out of sight, inside a tiny structure on a raft they've built for his escape, when a boat filled with men looking for the runaway comes by. They ask Huck if he's seen anything of the slave. Huck has an internal conflict because of these two competing elements: he's been told that it's a sin to lie and if he lies he will go to hell; but he also knows what will happen to his friend Jim if he tells the truth. This conflict (to lie or to tell the truth) goes on for a while, but it's finally resolved when Huck reasons to himself that his Aunt Polly is going to heaven and he has enough trouble being around her now, when she's alive. He just couldn't stand having to put up with her after they're dead. So he lies. Usually, as with Huckleberry Finn, an internal conflict requires that a character resolve some kind of emotional or ethical dilemma.

Some stories can have more than one conflict. Very often, there is an internal conflict as well as an external one. In Harry Sylvester's "Going to Run All Night," for example, Pete Nilson, a former marathon runner now serving in the army, is selected to run through enemy lines to summon help for his besieged unit. The reader is interested in the obvious external conflict between Nilson and the enemy soldiers because it raises the question of his physical stamina: Can he make it through the enemy lines? Of equal interest, however, is Nilson's internal struggle to overcome his self-doubt: Does he believe he can make it?

Sometimes, as in Ring Lardner's "Haircut," an author creates a conflict between the values of a character in the story and those of the reader in order to make the reader a more active participant in the story.

For a story to succeed, the conflict should be plausible and the opposing forces must be balanced. Otherwise, the consequences of the conflict hold little interest or significance, and the reader cares little about the outcome or gains nothing from the story.

CONFLICT AND THE CENTRAL IDEA

Regardless of how many conflicts occur in a story, there is usually one that is central to the meaning. This central conflict is often the key to the central idea. In "Desiree's Baby," the central conflict involves an emotional dilemma: Armand is torn between his love for his wife and child and his hatred of blacks. How he decides to deal with this conflict and the results of his decision are crucial to the central idea of the story (that is, the potentially tragic and self-destructive power of hatred and bigotry).

In the following paragraph, a student describes the relationship between conflict and the central idea in Heinrich Boll's "Like a Bad Dream":

> The basic internal conflict in "Like a Bad Dream" involves moral values or choices of action. Even though both Bertha and her husband desire wealth and success, she senses his reluctance to indulge in bribery and graft in order to reach these goals. Determined to bring him around to her moral standards, Bertha places her husband in a dilemma; he can either admit to Bertha's autonomy and dominance or he can pretend to have given his consent and take credit for the action. Bertha knows that her husband's pride and strong ambition will not allow him to take the former course; therefore, she has manipulated him to act as her surrogate. Working his way through the dilemma, Bertha's husband thinks of the events as a bad dream or a nightmare, signifying his mental anguish. These events and the emotions they evoke are appropriate to the central idea that an im-

perceptive but ambitious person can be deceived and manipulated to act contrary to his moral convictions.

CONFLICT AND CHARACTER

The reaction of the story's central character to the conflict provides an important clue to the central idea. Whether he succeeds or fails; whether she lives or dies; whether the character's personality, values, or beliefs are reinforced or permanently altered point to the meaning of the story.

In the following example, a student illustrates how the relationship between character and conflict can form the basis for the central idea. The paper follows the basic analytical structure: a paragraph of summary (concluding with a statement of the central idea), a paragraph discussing character, and a paragraph discussing conflict. In the analysis of this particular story, that sequence is perfect for using the link between character and conflict to underscore the central idea.

"The Story of an Hour" by Kate Chopin tells of Louise Mallard, a woman who receives news that her husband has been killed in a train wreck. Her sister and a friend break the news gently, for she has a heart condition. Upon hearing of the tragedy, Louise weeps and then retires to the solitude of her room. While staring out her window, she comes to the conclusion that she has been freed. A wave of understanding overwhelms her, and she sees that she can now live on her own terms. She joins her sister and triumphantly heads downstairs. At this instant, her husband, who was not on the train that crashed, enters the house. Upon seeing him, Louise dies suddenly of a heart attack. Chopin's theme is that triumph and tragedy may be defined only in the mind of the beholder.

At the outset, Louise seems to be a passive person; however, she quickly deals with the grief caused by her husband's "death," which indicates that she has cared for him, but now accepts his death. She revels in the knowledge that, with him gone, she can now live life on her own terms. Her sudden realization suggests that her marriage was a veil concealing her true feelings from herself. The ending of the story is a classic example of life's irony: her husband dies, she achieves self-awareness; and when he arrives unharmed, she dies her heart unable to accept a lifetime with this man. The doctor's assertion that she died of "joy that kills" represents life's injustice; her true feelings will never be known.

The central conflict in "The Story of an Hour" is an internal one. Louise is torn between grief over her husband's death and joy over her new-found freedom. She has never considered living life for herself, but is suddenly presented with the chance to do so. This blinding realization shows that she has repressed her conflict for a long time, and the author's description of her internal change indicates that she has no control over it. She has always desired freedom but has allowed her marriage to triumph over her true sentiments. Now that her husband is gone, her long-suppressed desire possesses her and she experiences true joy. In fact, she is so elated to be "Body and soul free" that she dies when she discovers that she is not free at all. So, in a sense, her free-spirited side has won—choosing death over a dull, loveless lifetime.

Reading Exercise:

See if you can determine the central idea in Stephen Crane's "The Bride Comes to Yellow Sky." After you've read the story, try writing a central idea statement. Then look at the conflict and try to determine how it is a symbolic representation of the central idea of the story.

Chapter Four

Point of View

"'They're so damn cocky,' thought Walter Mitty, walking along Main Street; 'they think they know.' Once he had tried to take his chains off, outside New Milford, and he had got them wound around the axles. A man had to come out in a wrecking car and unwind them, a young, grinning garage man. Since then Mrs. Mitty always made him drive to a garage to have the chains taken off. 'The next time,' he thought, 'I'll wear my right arm in a sling; they won't grin at me then.'"

from "The Secret Life of Walter Mitty," by James Thurber

Since point of view refers to the position the writer takes to present the story, it is closely related to the methods of characterization. The narrative voice an author uses to tell the story determines how and what the reader sees, and that, has an impact on the reader's understanding and emotional response to the story.

The point of view takes one of three distinct forms: first person, omniscient, and dramatic (or objective). The author's choice of which to use depends on (and should be consistent with) the story's central idea. This chapter considers these different types of narrative voices, their advantages and disadvantages, and how they affect an interpretation.

FIRST PERSON NARRATION

When the story is told by a character within it, the narration is first person. The author uses the pronouns "I" and "me," and the narrator is most often the central character or an active participant in the action, as in Sherwood Anderson's "I'm a Fool" and John Updike's "A & P." Occasionally, the first person narrator is a minor character or a mere observer of the action. (Read William Faulkner's "A Rose for Emily" for an example of that.) Of the three types of narration, this point of view imposes the most restrictions on the author. It limits the presentation to the chosen character's knowledge and interpretation of the other characters and the events. It also prohibits comments from the author. Furthermore, the author must be careful to assure that the narrative voice (the character's awareness, speech, and attitudes) are consistent with the details of the character's personality and background.

The First Person Narrator's Perspective

Despite its limitations, the first person narrator has more variations than we might think. A common use of the first person has the narrator telling of a childhood experience from the perspective of an adult. That allows the author to show how the passage of time affects a person's attitudes, because the adult can reflect on the reactions he or she had as a child.

In this example from Poe's "The Cask of Amontillado," we can see how the first person narrative reveals the twisted mind of a man driven by revenge. Poe lets the main character speak and through his remarks reveals his tortured feelings. Notice in the sample portion from the story, how Poe not only reveals Montresor's feelings, but lets us see how he rationalizes them.

> "Fortunato!"
> No answer. I called again.
> "Fortunato!"
> No answer still. I thrust a torch through the remaining aperture and let it fall within. There came forth in return only a jingling of the bells. My heart grew sick; it was the dampness of the catacombs that made it so. I hastened to make an end of my labour. I forced the last stone into its position; I plastered it up."

"My heart grew sick" (Montresor's admission of his feelings) is immediately followed by "it was the dampness of the catacombs that made it so" (a denial). Because Montresor can describe what he thinks and feels as well as what he sees and hears, this first person narrator creates a sense of realism and immediacy (a you-are-there feeling). The first person viewpoint creates a personal bond with the reader. Consequently, an author can use the first person point of view to capture our interest and increase our involvement with the narrator.

In contrast to the sense of immediacy Poe's narrator gives us, some authors may use an ignorant, unreliable narrator for the irony it provides. (Read "Haircut" by Ring Lardner for a good example of that.) Instead of closeness, there's a distance that's created between the narrator's values and those of the reader. (See the chapters on Language and Tone.)

Avoiding the Narrator-as-Author Confusion

We should never confuse a first person narrator with the author of the story. Such confusion often leads to a misreading of the story. We should never lose sight of the fact that the narrator is fictional. If the author's attempts to involve us in the story are successful, we may believe, for a while at least, that the voice we're hearing is that of a real person; but that's an illusion created by a skillful writer. The story never really happened; the characters never existed; the narrator is not real. Poe never walled up his friend in the catacombs. The fictional character Montresor did that.

OMNISCIENT NARRATION

Most of us conceal our true thoughts and feelings. Even if someone tells us what he or she is thinking or feeling, we cannot be completely certain it's the truth. Fiction, on the other hand, allows us inside a character's mind. An omniscient (all-knowing) narrator can reveal the true thoughts and feelings of a character. This adds a dimension to characterization in fiction that goes beyond anything in reality.

Of the three points of view, a completely omniscient narration gives an author the greatest flexibility and freedom. The omniscient narrator is credible and reliable; the reader accepts the narrator's revelations as true and accurate. This allows an author to control the reader's attitude toward the story. If the author tells us that a character's thoughts are evil, we accept the premise that the character is evil, regardless of what the character says or how he or she acts toward others. We know what they really think.

In the following quote from "Desiree's Baby," we have no reason to doubt the omniscient narrator. When the narrator says that Armand's nature had softened and Desiree loved him desperately, we know it's true because the omniscient narrator knows a character's true feelings:

"What Desiree said was true. Marriage, and later the birth of his son, had softened Armand Aubigny's imperious and exacting nature greatly. This was what made the gentle Desiree so happy, for she loved him desperately."

Later in the story, Chopin reveals Armand's feelings again:

"He thought Almighty God had dealt cruelly and unjustly with him and felt, somehow, that he was paying Him back in kind when he stabbed thus into his wife's soul. Moreover he no longer loved her, because of the unconscious injury she had brought upon his home and his name."

Complete vs. Limited Omniscience

A completely omniscient narrator can reveal the thoughts and feelings of any of the story's characters, but a limited omniscient narrator reveals only the thoughts and feelings of one character, usually the main one. The completely omniscient point of view provides the reader with glimpses into the minds of each character.

In James Thurber's "The Secret Life of Walter Mitty," we only know what's going on in one character's mind. The limited omniscient narrator explains, interprets, and evaluates the actions of just one of the characters. The reader sees everything the author chooses to show, but sees only Mitty's thoughts, not those of any other character, because his thoughts are the only ones necessary for us to understand the central idea. This limited omniscience increases our understanding of the character and creates an intimacy with him. As a result, we share his senses and feelings more strongly and this makes the character the unifying element of the story. This is nearly true of all stories where the limited omniscient narrator is used.

Though it might seem the ideal choice, and the easiest, a writer faces certain disadvantages with an omniscient point of view. Because an all-knowing authority makes the reader conscious of the author's presence, it lacks subtlety and restricts reader involvement. The omniscient view lacks immediacy and may lead to an excessively direct presentation of characters; too much telling and not enough showing.

DRAMATIC NARRATION

The dramatic (also called objective) point of view presents only the words and actions of characters. We're never told the characters' thoughts and feelings. Consequently, we must interpret their thoughts and feelings by what they say and do (much as we do in real life). Dramatic narration is the simplest type. It is straightforward and often reads like a news story, which lends it a feeling of authenticity. The reader is forced to infer the meaning from the action without an authorial comment. The dramatic point of view creates a sense of realism because it requires an interpretation of the events and characters. It increases our involvement in the story because we're forced to do more work. The opinions we form as we read are based on what the characters say and do, giving the story a very realistic "feel." (Read Ernest Hemingway's "Hills Like White Elephants" or Shirley Jackson's "The Lottery" for good examples of dramatic narration.)

Ironically, the very features that give the dramatic point of view its strength also create risks for the author. Few stories are presented from a completely dramatic point of view because of that limitation. The objectivity of dramatic narration does not allow the author to comment on the action. Such narration is limited to reporting only that which is observable and nothing of what goes on in the minds of any of the characters. This severely limits the author's ability to influence the reader's attitude. Therefore, a writer using a dramatic narrative voice must carefully construct the story so that the possibilities for misinterpretation are minimal. The writer presents the events in a way that leads to a single interpretation.

In the following example of the dramatic point of view from John Steinbeck's "The Chrysanthemums," the author narrates what each of the characters says and does. The author's choice of words and tone of voice in describing the action are the clues that tell us what's going on in the characters' minds and hearts. Notice the descriptions tell us that "Her breast swelled passionately" and "He looked away self-consciously." And later, her voice "grew husky," and she almost touches him, but then "She crouched low like a fawning dog." Steinbeck does not have to tell us that the woman is sexually frustrated; his description makes it abundantly clear.

> She was kneeling on the ground looking up at him. Her breast swelled passionately.
>
> The man's eyes narrowed. He looked away self-consciously. "Maybe I know," he said. "Sometimes in the night in the wagon there"
>
> Elisa's voice grew husky. She broke in on him. "I've never lived as you do, but I know what you mean. When the night is dark why, the stars are sharp-pointed, and there's quiet. Why, you rise up and up! Every pointed star gets driven into your body. It's like that. Hot and sharp and lovely."
>
> Kneeling there, her hand went out toward his legs in the greasy black trousers. Her hesitant fingers almost touched the cloth. Then her hand dropped to the ground. She crouched low like a fawning dog.

CONSISTENCY OF VIEWPOINT

Short stories, because of their length, must have a single, consistent point of view. If an author shifts from one form of narration to another, there must be a valid reason. Such a shift must never attract attention or cause the reader to question why it occurred. If such a shift occurs perhaps from a completely dramatic to a limited omniscient viewpoint, the shift must be important to the meaning and tone of the story. It must be essential to make the story (and the central idea) successful.

READING EXERCISE:

See if you can determine the central idea in James Thurber's "The Secret Life of Walter Mitty." After you've read the story, try writing a central idea statement. Then identify the point of view and see if you can tell how important Thurber's choice was in the execution of the central idea.

CHAPTER FIVE

Setting

"It was about dusk, one evening during the supreme madness of the carnival season, that I encountered my friend... We came at length to the foot of the descent, and stood together upon the damp ground of the catacombs of the Montresors."

from "The Cask of Amontillado," by Edgar Allen Poe

The setting of a story is where and when the events happen, but the choice of a setting is rarely an arbitrary decision. The author often uses the setting to enrich the meaning. The setting includes the conditions, the total environment—physical, emotional, economic, political, social, and psychological—the characters inhabit.

Stories may describe the physical setting or provide references to the time and place, but more often our awareness of the setting evolves gradually. In a good story, the setting is revealed more subtly. As the story progresses, the author provides details and clues like the description of a character's clothing, the dialect the character speaks, or even the character's vehicle, a horse-drawn carriage, say, or a dune buggy. From those details we can infer the time and place.

SPECIFIC VS. GENERAL SETTINGS

A story's setting may be either specific or general. For example, if the story takes place in New York City in February 1940, it's specific. If the time and place are never specified and can't be inferred, the setting is general. Whether a story's setting is specific or general usually depends on the central idea.

The author can use the setting to show the effects of a particular period in history or of certain geographical or social conditions on people. By providing very specific and detailed information about the setting, the author can support a central idea that's related to changes in the social, moral, and religious environment of a region.

If an author wants to make a comment about the human condition or about humanity in general, the setting may be deliberately vague. Such a story takes on a universal, rather than a limited, significance. Similarly, when an author does not concentrate on setting, it is usually because he or she is interested almost exclusively in the characters and wants us to see them as humans, not as Americans in 1940 or Russians in 2010, but as people who are the same no matter where or when they live. We should be cautious, though, not to assume that a setting is always an intentional choice. A story must happen somewhere and sometimes the choice of time and place are driven by other elements

THE SETTING AND THE CENTRAL IDEA

If the setting is very general, it may not seem significant. It may not have any direct relation to the story; but if the meaning of the story would be drastically affected by a change to a specific time and place, then the choice of a general setting may have been intentional to show the universality of the theme.

Frequently, though, the setting supports the central idea of a story, so any changes in the setting would significantly change the story. For example, if the setting is a lonely house during a raging nighttime storm, it may be crucial to shaping a character's actions and attitudes.

Likewise, if the setting is the vast ocean surrounding four shipwrecked men, the theme may have to do with nature's indifference toward man's fate. For example, in "Paul's Case" by Willa Cather, the contrast between the environment Paul hates and the one he desires underscores the central conflict of the story.

Look at the setting in John Steinbeck's "The Chrysanthemums":

> "The high grey-flannel fog of winter closed off the Salinas Valley from the sky and from all the rest of the world. On every side it sat like a lid on the mountains and made of the great valley a closed pot. On the broad, level land floor the gang plows bit deep and left the black earth shining like metal where the share had cut. On the foothill ranches across the Salinas River, the yellow stubble fields seemed to be bathed in pale cold sunshine, but there was no sunshine in the valley now in December. The thick willow scrub along the river flamed with sharp and positive yellow leaves.
>
> It was a time of quiet and of waiting. The air was cold and tender. A light wind blew up from the southwest so that the farmers were mildly hopeful of a good rain before long; but fog and rain did not go together."

Steinbeck uses the image of the fog sitting "like a lid on the mountains" and making "a closed pot" of the valley to establish his meaning through the symbolism of the setting. We learn later in the story that this setting parallels the main character's restricted life and repressed emotional conflict. It is directly related to the central idea.

In this next passage, from Kate Chopin's "Desiree's Baby," Chopin describes L'Abri, the plantation home of the main characters:

> "It was a sad looking place, which for many years had not known the gentle presence of a mistress, old Monsieur Aubigny having married and buried his wife in France, and she having loved her own land too well ever to leave it. The roof came down steep and black like a cowl, reaching out beyond the wide galleries that encircled the yellow stuccoed house. Big, solemn oaks grew close to it, and their thick-leaved, far-reaching branches shadowed it like a pall."

The plantation is gloomy and foreboding, totally lacking light and happiness. (Light is generally associated with joy; darkness, with sorrow.) The setting mirrors the natural temperament of Armand, Desiree's husband. It also foreshadows the tragedy that befalls Armand, Desiree, and their baby. Chopin's choice of such a setting complements the characters and the conflict. Most importantly, the story is set in the antebellum South on a plantation. It's a time of strong and clear racial attitudes essential to the central idea of the story.

Reading Exercise:

See if you can determine the relationship between the setting and the central idea in Edgar Allen Poe's "The Cask of Amontillado." After you've read the story, try writing a central idea statement and identifying the aspects of the setting that relate to it.

CHAPTER SIX

Language

> *"Did you ever hear of planting hands?"*
>
> *'Can't say I have ma'am.'*
>
> *'Well, I can only tell you what it feels like. It's when you're picking off the buds you don't want. Everything goes right down into your fingertips. You watch your fingers work. They do it themselves. You can feel how it is. They pick and pick the buds. They never make a mistake. They're with the plant. Do you see? Your fingers and the plant. You can feel that, right up your arm. They know. They never make a mistake. You can feel it. When you're like that you can't do anything wrong. Do you see that? Can you understand that?'"*
>
> **from "The Chrysanthemums," by John Steinbeck**

The essence of any story is its language: its diction, images, symbolism, irony, dialog, and syntax. Joining words and sentences into a cohesive narrative is what drives the other elements. Understanding and interpreting a story fully is impossible without closely analyzing the aspects of its language. Only by reading, and rereading, can we reach a full appreciation of the story and the work that went into its creation.

DICTION

Diction refers to the writer's choice of words. Good writers search for "just the right word." This "word searching" focuses on the connotation and denotation of words.

Denotation and Connotation

The denotation of a word is its exact, dictionary definition. The connotation is the suggested or associated meaning. While the denotation of a word like "trash" may be "useless matter," its connotation suggests filth, slovenliness, and so on. The writer can imply a great deal about something by using a strongly connotative word. For example, when describing a character's clothing, the writer can choose any of the following nouns. Like the word clothing itself, these words refer to the way the character is dressed, but each has a different connotation.

Your choice of apparel is very interesting.

Where did you find that get-up?

His garb is unfamiliar to us.

I changed into my work gear.

He wore real fancy duds.

Is formal attire required?

His raiment bore the mark of a nobleman.

The formality of the word "apparel" suggests elegance, while the word "get-up" suggests a costume. "Garb" sounds medieval, like something a knight would wear, while "work gear" is more industrial. "Fancy duds" might be used to describe western wear. "Attire" sounds very polite, and like "apparel," it's associated with elegance. "Raiment," on the other hand, is an archaic word commonly associated with historical times.

The following adjectives may be used to describe a character who is slightly built: slender, slim, lean, gaunt, scrawny, skinny, thin, delicate, attenuated, or emaciated. The choice of which word to use depends on what the writer wants you to associate with the character.

The examples below illustrate the importance of diction and how the connotations of the words chosen for naming and describing things and actions imply the writer's attitude toward the subject and create a specific image for the reader.

"Paul was startled for a moment, and had the feeling of wanting to put her out; what business had she here among all these fine people and gay colors? He looked her over and decided that she was not appropriately dressed and must be a fool to sit downstairs in such togs."

In that example from Willa Cather's "Paul's Case," the connotative diction creates a contrast between the woman, who is wearing "togs," and the rest of the crowd, who are wearing "gay colors."

"A newly married pair had boarded this coach at San Antonio. The man's face was reddened from many days in the wind and sun, and a direct result of his new black clothes was that his brick-colored hands were constantly performing in a most conscious fashion. From time to time he looked down respectfully at his attire. He sat with a hand on each knee, like a man waiting in a barber's shop. The glances he devoted to other passengers were furtive and shy.

The bride was not pretty, nor was she very young. She wore a dress of blue cashmere, with small reservations of velvet here and there, and steel buttons abounding. She continually twisted her head to regard her puff sleeves, very stiff, straight, and high. They embarrassed her. It was quite apparent that she had cooked, and that she expected to cook, dutifully. The blushes caused by the careless scrutiny of some passengers as she had entered the car were strange to see upon this plain, under-class countenance, which was drawn in placid, almost emotionless lines."

Before the narrator in Stephen Crane's "The Bride Comes to Yellow Sky" reveals the direction this story will take, he has established the nature of his characters through the diction. The man has "brick-colored" hands. The diction connotes not only redness, but also hardness and strength. He looks down at his "attire," which supports the earlier suggestion of formal clothing: it's both "new" and "black."

The bride's dress has small "reservations of velvet." That is not a usual use of the word; it connotes a very conservative dress. And her "countenance" is "under-class." Crane carefully chose that word because it tells us that the bride is not from a wealthy or even middle-class background, but calling it "lower-class" would have prompted the negativity of that term.

IMAGERY

The mental impressions evoked by words and phrases are the imagery of a story. An effective description creates an image, a sensory impression, in the reader's mind. The image is more than visual. The author can appeal to any of the senses—hearing, sight, smell, touch, and taste—to vivify events, characters, settings, and the other elements.

Literal and Figurative Images

If a word or phrase can only be interpreted one way, it is said to be literal. A literal image is created by the use of such unambiguous words and phrases. A figurative image, on the other hand, relies on the associated meanings of a word or phrase. A statement like, "My mother entered the room" creates a simple, literal image. We have a mental picture of a woman entering the room. All we know is that the woman is the speaker's mother. The writer is not suggesting anything more.

But when the writer says, "The odor of tobacco preceded his mother's cold and haughty entrance"; figurative and literal meanings associated with "cold" and "haughty" come into play, as well as the implications of the smell of tobacco. These associations demand that the reader understand that the word "cold" is not meant literally. We not only know that the speaker's mother has entered the room, but we also have a feeling for the woman. It's a feeling that touches our senses, and if we correctly understand its meaning, "cold" tells us the woman is unfriendly and aloof. This is what figurative imagery contributes to the story.

"Haughty" means proud, arrogant, and snobbish, and adds to the image the perception of the woman as proud, arrogant, and snobbish. We don't need to be familiar with the associated meaning of the word because there is none. That is a literal use of imagery.

Similes and Metaphors

The most common forms of figurative imagery are the simile and the metaphor. A simile is a direct comparison introduced by the word "like" or "as." A metaphor is an implied comparison. The simile says "A is like B," whereas the metaphor says that "A is B." The metaphor is stronger, more emphatic, than the simile. It is one thing to say someone eats like a pig, but a stronger insult to say someone is a pig.

Steinbeck begins "The Chrysanthemums" this way: "On every side it sat like a lid on the mountains and made of the great valley a closed pot." This description begins with a simile: the fog is like a lid. It closes with a metaphor: the fog "made of the great valley a closed pot." The valley, with the fog over it, does not look like a pot; it is a pot, a closed pot. Steinbeck uses the simile and the metaphor to describe the valley, but there is more here than a simple physical description. The metaphor of the closed pot represents Elisa's situation. She is trapped. She is like something in a pot with a lid on it.

When an author uses figurative rather than literal language, the image is more vivid. For example:

Instead of a character's voice being harsh and screechy, it may sound like fingernails raking across a chalkboard.

Instead of someone leaving quickly, she may fly from the room.

Instead of a room being stale or musty, it may smell like an old pair of sneakers.

Instead of a man wandering aimlessly around town, he may be a rudderless craft at the mercy of wind and currents.

Those images are also more vivid because they involve the comparison of two dissimilar things: the voice and the chalkboard-raking sound, walking and flying, air and sneaker odor, walking and floating. By comparing one thing with something extremely different from itself, an author gives that thing more meaning.

The examples that follow illustrate the uses of imagery to create an immediate sense of character, setting, and tone.

Imagery and Character

"But as they approached Miss Dove's room their disorder began to vanish. They pulled their excitement in, like a proud but well-broken pony."

"The hat was summertime. It was deep and soft like summer. It caused deep soft scallops of shadow, like summer shadows under the densest trees, to fall across her face."

Imagery and Setting

"The buggy is mine—It is made of wicker, rather unraveled, and the wheels wobble like a drunkard's legs."

Imagery and Tone

"Possibly we doze; but the beginnings of dawn splash us like cold water: we're up, wide-eyed and wandering while we wait for others to waken."

"A cheery crunch, scraps of miniature thunder sound as the [pecan] shells collapse and the golden mound of sweet oily ivory meat mounts in the milk-glass bowl."

"Then Sam's horn rang in the wet gray woods and again and again; there was a boiling wave of dogs about them, with Tennie's Jim and Boon Hoggan whipping them back after each had had a taste of the blood—"

Allusions

An allusion is a type of imagery that uses a reference to a mythological, religious, historical, or literary figure, place, or event. For example, a character may be described as living in a place resembling the Augean stables, or he may be called a Hamlet of decision makers. These references to mythology (the Augean stables) and literature (Shakespeare's Hamlet) are effective only if the reader has some knowledge and understanding of them. An author who uses allusions runs the risk that a reader may not be familiar with them. Such references limit their understanding to those readers with a knowledge of the specific references.

Repetition

Repetition emphasizes an image and underscores its importance to the central idea of the story. Sometimes an author creates an image and refers to it later. In "The Chrysanthemums," Steinbeck makes frequent references to Elisa Allen's hands. They are repeatedly described as strong, vital, or full of energy. At the end of the story, the image of Elisa crying weakly is made more effective because it stands in sharp contrast to the repeated images of her strength.

SYMBOLISM

A symbol is something that represents or suggests something else. We live with and respond to symbols, and we take them for granted. For example, if we see a building with a cross on top, we assume it is a Christian church. In the U.S., if we form a circle with our thumb and forefinger and raise our hand for someone to see, we're indicating our approval that everything is "okay." If we're driving down a street and see a blinking red light, we recognize it as a signal to stop; red symbolizes danger. And if we see a gigantic pair of glasses above an office, we assume it's the office of an optometrist.

As those examples illustrate, a symbol represents or suggests something else. In each case, an object or action communicates a message. Some authors use symbols in their work to represent an idea. A character, an object, or an incident that embodies an idea or quality can be a symbol. Symbolism allows an author to imply things, to convey ideas without actually stating them; it is literary shorthand, which compresses several meanings into a single person, object, or event.

Universal Symbols

Some symbols are recognized quickly and universally. Because they are used so widely, an author can assume we'll understand them. Few symbols, however, are recognized worldwide. In the Euro/American culture, a dove represents peace; a long journey signifies life; a character's immersion in water suggests baptism or initiation into a way of life; springtime often symbolizes life or rebirth; and winter suggests death. But these symbols are not recognized in all parts of the world. The star in Arthur Clarke's story by that title is a Christian symbol associated with the birth of Christ.

Contextual Symbols

Some symbols derive meaning from their context in a particular work. The furniture and clothing burned by Armand at the end of "Desiree's Baby" by Kate Chopin become symbols of his marriage to Desiree.

Characters as Symbols

Characters may be symbolic because of what they do or even because of the name the author gives them. There is symbolism (as well as irony, which we discuss later) in the choice of Fortunato as one character's name in Poe's "The Cask of Amontillado." The character may have been fortunate, or he may have acquired a fortune before the story begins, but he soon becomes a symbol of someone very unfortunate.

Objects as Symbols

The symbolic use of objects is even more common than symbolic characters. In Crane's "The Bride Comes to Yellow Sky," the marshall does not have a gun. A gun, symbolic of manhood, is also symbolic of authority and, even more important to the central idea of this story, of the fact that the town is becoming civilized. Similarly, in John Steinbeck's "The Chrysanthemums," the flowers in Elisa's gardens become symbols of the children she has never borne. Therefore, the tinker's disregard for the flowers takes on a larger meaning.

Actions as Symbols

Symbolic action, like characters and objects, can embody ideas. Suicide may be one of the most symbolic actions anyone can take. In Willa Cather's "Paul's Case," Paul's suicide is an action that defines the entire story. The boy is trapped; death is the only escape. When Armand burns the furniture in Kate Chopin's "Desiree's Baby," his actions symbolize his feelings and, on a larger scale, the intensity of racism.

Symbolism, like imagery, is helpful in expressing various meanings or ideas concisely. Also, as the preceding examples demonstrate, symbols strengthen or completely carry the meaning of a story. An author chooses symbols that are more than apt; they add depth to the story and are appropriate to the central idea.

Allegory: The Symbolic Story

An allegory is a story in which symbolism is dominant; virtually every action, character, and place represents something—an abstraction—that usually promotes moral values or qualities. In an allegory, the idea conveyed is more important than the narrative itself. Allegory is rare in modern fiction, but "The White Knight" by Eric Nicol is one example; Nathaniel Hawthorne's "The Celestial Railroad," a wry modernization of "The Pilgrim's Progress," is another.

IRONY

Irony is the use of language to express a discrepancy between appearance and reality. It's useful to a writer because, like imagery and symbolism, irony compresses or implies meaning in a brief statement. There are three basic types of irony: verbal, dramatic, and situational.

Verbal Irony

Verbal irony involves an obvious discrepancy between what a speaker says and what the reader knows the character really means. In the following dialogue from Poe's "The Cask of Amontillado," verbal irony appears as Montresor and Fortunato discuss the latter's cough. Montresor, who is taking Fortunato into the catacombs to kill him, replies in a sarcastic way:

> "Come," I said, with decision, "we will go back; your health is precious. You are rich, respected, admired, beloved; you are happy, as once I was. You are a man to be missed. For me it is no matter. We will go back; you will be ill, and I cannot be responsible. Besides, there is Luchresi—"
>
> "Enough," he said; "the cough is a mere nothing; it will not kill me. I shall not die of a cough."
>
> "True true," I replied..."

From the context, we know that Montresor despises Fortunato and is not likely to let him turn back. We also appreciate the ironic significance of Montresor's reply that Fortunato "truly shall not die of a cough."

Dramatic Irony

When there is a discrepancy between what a character says or perceives and what the reader knows to be true, dramatic irony is at work. In Thurber's "The Secret Life of Walter Mitty," the reader knows things about Mitty that his wife does not realize. Because of Thurber's use of dramatic irony, our impression of Mitty is quite different from that of his wife.

> Something struck his shoulder. "I've been looking all over this hotel for you," said Mrs. Mitty. "Why do you have to hide in this old chair? How did you expect me to find you?"

"Things close in," said Walter Mitty vaguely.

"What?" Mrs. Mitty said. "Did you get the what's-its-name? The puppy biscuit? What's in that box?"

"Overshoes," said Mitty. "Couldn't you have put them on in the store?"

"I was thinking," said Walter Mitty. "Does it ever occur to you that I am sometimes thinking?"

She looked at him. "I'm going to take your temperature when I get you home," she said.

Mrs. Mitty thinks Walter is sick, but we know what's going on because we have been inside his mind.

Steinbeck uses dramatic irony in "The Chrysanthemums" when Elisa responds to her husband's offer to take her to the fights.

"Oh no," she says, "I don't want to go. I'm sure I don't—
It will be enough if we can have wine. It will be plenty."

The reader, unlike Elisa's husband, knows that she desperately wants to experience things she has never known; however, wine with dinner is the only excitement she seems prepared to risk.

Situational Irony

A more interesting and usually more important kind of irony is that which involves a discrepancy between what a character (or the reader) expects to happen and what actually does happen. The conflict and the central idea of a story may both turn on an ironic situation.

For example, it is ironic that Armand, the husband and father in "Desiree's Baby," finally discovers that he, not the loving wife he drove away, is black.

Bruno Bettelheim has said, "If the artist uses irony to achieve his goal, he presents his vision as if seen in a mirror that distorts, to make us aware of what would otherwise escape us, to force us to respond to that which we would rather avoid." The writer juxtaposes contrasting ideas so that a character (or the reader) must view the world in a new and different way. In that way, the writer uses irony to convey the central idea, the writer's view.

DIALOGUE

Dialogue refers to the words spoken between two or more characters. Dialogue, which is easy to spot because it is set off by quotation marks, serves a variety of purposes:

To inform (or misinform) the reader

To reveal or develop a conflict

To move the plot (story line) forward

To build suspense

To reveal character

Dialogue often provides indirect, less obvious clues to character, conflict, and other story elements, as in the following examples:

"Tried to sneak up on me," he said. "Tried to sneak up on me!" His eyes grew more baleful. As Potter made a slight movement, the man thrust his revolver venomously forward. "No; don't you do it, Jack Potter. Don't you move a finger toward a gun just yet. Don't you move an eyelash. The time has come for me to settle with you, and I'm goin' to do it my own way, and loaf along with no interferin'. So if you don't want a gun bent on you, just mind what I tell you."

Potter looked at his enemy. "I ain't got a gun on me, Scratchy," he said. "Honest, I ain't." He was stiffening and steadying, but yet somewhere at the back of his mind a vision of the Pullman floated: the sea-green figured velvet, the shining brass, silver, and glass, the wood that gleamed as darkly brilliant as the surface of a pool of oil all the glory of the marriage, the environment of the new estate. "You know I fight when it comes to fighting, Scratchy Wilson; but I ain't got a gun on me. You'll have to do all the shootin' yourself."

His enemy's face went livid. He stepped forward, and flashed his weapon to and fro before Potter's chest. "Don't you tell me you ain't got no gun on you, you whelp. Don't tell me no lie like that. There ain't a man in Texas ever seen you without no gun. Don't take me for no kid." His eyes blazed with light, and his throat worked like a pump.

In this passage from Stephen Crane's "The Bride Comes to Yellow Sky," the characters are confronting each other, but we get the impression that they aren't deadly serious, despite the fact that one is carrying a gun. Notice that the writer gets around the awkward repetition of "he said" by using descriptions of the character's movements to tell us who is speaking. A new paragraph is a sign that the speaker has changed. So is the accompaniment of an action with a line of dialogue, as in this next example:

"Henry," she asked, "could we have wine at dinner?"
"Sure we could. Say! That will be fine."

She was silent for a while; then she said, "Henry, at those prize fights do the men hurt each other very much?"

"Sometimes a little, not often. Why?"

"Well, I've read how they break noses, and blood runs down their chests. I've read how the fighting gloves get heavy and soggy with blood."

He looked around at her. "What's the matter, Elisa. I didn't know you read things like that." He brought the car to a stop, then turned to the right over the Salinas River bridge.

"Do any women ever go to the fights?" she asked.

"Oh, sure, some. What's the matter, Elisa? Do you want to go? I don't think you'd like it, but I'll take you if you really want to go."

She relaxed limply in the seat. "Oh, no. I don't want to go. I'm sure I don't." Her face was turned away from him. "It will be enough if we can have wine. It will be plenty."

When Elisa's husband looks around at her, in this passage from John Steinbeck's "The Chrysanthemums," we know that the next line of dialogue is his. This is a dialogue between a husband and wife whose relationship is not very deep. The husband's statements, contrasted with the questions from his wife (which even he recognizes as unusual) reveal her mood and the nature of the relationship between them.

Sometimes, the writer uses other methods to show us character, as in this next example:

"Did you say something, Sammy?"

"I said I quit." "I thought you did."

"You didn't have to embarrass them."

"It was they who were embarrassing us."

I started to say something that came out "Fiddle-de-do." It's a saying of my grandmother's, and I know she would have been pleased.

"I don't think you know what you're saying," Lengel said.

"I know you don't," I said. "But I do."

In "A & P," Updike has Sammy quitting his job in an effort to impress the girls who have just been asked to leave the store. The manager is direct and commanding in his speech, but Sammy is clearly confused because he can't admit his real reason for quitting. The "Fiddle-de-do" at the end of the example reaffirms that. Without having him say so directly, Updike shows us what kind of a person he is: a teenager whose raging hormones cause him to take an action he knows very soon he'll regret for a long time.

Dialogue is part of the story as a whole. Take note of things like the mood of the character speaking, the situation the character is in, and the character's relationship to others.

SYNTAX

Syntax refers to sentence structure, the arrangement of words within a sentence. It may be the single most important factor in the telling of a story, as in this excerpt from "Desiree's Baby":

> "Desiree had not changed the thin white garment nor the slippers which she wore. Her hair was uncovered and the sun's rays brought a golden gloss from ice brown meshes. She did not take the broad, beaten road which led to the far-off plantation of Valmonde. She walked across a deserted field, where the stubble bruised her tender feet, so delicately shod, and tore her thin gown to shreds.
>
> She disappeared among the reeds and willows that grew thick along the banks of the deep, sluggish bayou; and she did not come back again."

Each of the sentences in that passage begins with a basic subject-verb structure. This focuses the reader's attention on the action and conveys Desiree's single-mindedness and determination. It leads us to the final phrase "she did not come back again" in a way that underscores its finality and harshness.

In this next passage, from Arthur Clarke's "The Star," the author achieves a serious tone by first laying out the arguments that his colleagues will give (notice how they are equally structured) and then leads us to the solemn pronouncement "there is no God."

> "I know the answers that my colleagues will give when they get back to Earth. They will say that the universe has no purpose and no plan, that since a hundred suns exploded every year in our galaxy, at this very moment some race is dying in the depths of space. Whether that race has done good or evil during its lifetime will make no difference in the end: there is no divine justice, for there is no God."

The syntax underscores what's been happening with the character. The two balanced phrases "the universe has no purpose and no plan, that since a hundred suns exploded every year in our galaxy, at this very moment some race is dying in the depths of space" lead to the next statement, that it "will make no difference in the end," which is punctuated by the final two phrases.

The Periodic Sentence

A sentence that is not grammatically complete until the very end is called a periodic sentence. The writer creates suspense or prolongs our interest with such a sentence because the main idea (and our understanding of it) appears at the end. The closing sentence of "Desiree's Baby" follows this structure:

"But above all," she wrote, "night and day, I thank God for having so arranged our lives that our dear Armand will never know that his mother, who adores him, belongs to the race that is spread with the brand of slavery."

Only at the very end do we realize the irony of Armand's actions and the great injustice that Desiree has suffered. The ending startles us, partly as a result of the syntax of the final sentence. Arranged any other way, the ending might not have been as effective.

Reading Exercise:

See if you can determine the central idea in John Steinbeck's "The Chrysanthemums." After you've read the story, try writing a central idea statement. Then look at the metaphors and similes in the story and determine how they define the setting, or a character or conflict and how, in turn, those things support the central idea.

CHAPTER SEVEN

Tone

> *"When the letter reached Desiree she went with it to her husband's study, and laid it open upon the desk before which he sat. She was like a stone image: silent, white, motionless after she placed it there. In silence he ran his cold eyes over the written words. He said nothing. 'Shall I go, Armand?' she asked in tones sharp with agonized suspense.*
>
> *'Yes, go.'*
>
> *'Do you want me to go?'*
>
> *'Yes. I want you to go.'"*
>
> **from "Desiree's Baby," by Kate Chopin**

The tone of a story reveals the author's attitude toward the subject of the story. Sensitivity to a story's tone is crucial to identifying the central idea. In fact, the tone of a story often provides the only evidence to support an interpretation.

Tone is usually associated with sound, as in the quality of a spoken voice. It's the tone of voice that often reveals our feelings more than the words themselves. But how can a writer create tone without sound?

In speech, the pitch and volume of the speaker's voice, as well as facial expressions, tells us the intent. For example, if you say, "Be sure to return my textbook tomorrow," your tone and facial expression reveal:

You're tired of loaning things to people who never return them. (Your tone is angry or hostile and you are scowling.)

You're concerned because you need the book to study for a test. (Your tone suggests worry and anxiety and your brow is furrowed.)

You don't want the book back, and the person borrowing it knows you don't. (Your tone is humorous or ironic and you're smiling.)

DISCOVERING AND DESCRIBING THE TONE

Since we cannot hear an author's voice, tone must be expressed in other ways. Because there is a one-to-one correlation between tone and language, the tone is often created through the various techniques of language described in the previous chapter.

Similes and Metaphors

The choice of comparative elements provides a clue to the author's attitude toward the subject. Consider these similes from Arthur Clarke's "The Star":

> "I know how it must have blazed low in the east before sunrise, like a beacon in that oriental dawn."

> "Our ship fell toward this gigantic bull's-eye like an arrow into its target."

Clarke compares the star of the magi to a beacon, which is precisely the purpose it served to the wise men. As such, it is a solemn comparison. In the second instance, the ship's path to the planet is compared to the path of an arrow toward its target. The arrow has no choice; it is directed by the archer. The implication is that the spaceship, too, is being directed by something beyond its control. These similes help to set the serious tone of the story.

In the following examples from "The Bride Comes to Yellow Sky," notice how Stephen Crane's metaphors help to establish the story's tone:

> "Face to face with this girl in San Antonio, and spurred by his sharp impulse, he had gone headlong over all the social hedges. Save for the busy drummer and his companions in the saloon, Yellow Sky was dozing."

The first metaphor uses the image of someone diving over a hedge. Crane calls it "social hedge" to add some symbolism to the metaphor. The hedge separates the yards of social status. By saying the marshall went "headlong" over the hedge, he gives the marshall's action an air of recklessness. In the second metaphor, he establishes the town as a single entity. Rather than saying that the people in the town are quiet or sleeping, he says the town is dozing. (Notice that he also avoids the cliché of calling it a "sleepy village.") The diction here is important, too, since "dozing" implies a light nap, a sleep that is not deep.

Allusions

In his story "The Star," Clarke makes a couple of references to the founder of the main character's religious order:

"My colleagues have asked me that, and I have given what answers I can. Perhaps you could have done better, Father Loyola, but I have found nothing in the Exercitia Spiritualia that helps me here.

The Rubens engraving of Loyola seems to mock me as it hangs there above the spectrophoto-meter tracings. What would you, Father, have made of this knowledge that has come into my keeping, so far from the little world that was all the universe you knew? Would your faith have risen to the challenge, as mine has failed to do?"

Those references help to underscore the deep philosophical nature of the story's main conflict. Loyola was a writer who discussed the question of God's decisions. He established the principle of faith over matters that we cannot understand. This reference also establishes the serious, philosophically troublesome tone of the story.

Repetition

In James Thurber's story, "The Secret Life of Walter Mitty," the words "pocketa-pocketa" are repeated throughout the story. In Mitty's imagination, they represent an airplane's engine, then an anaesthetizer, and finally the sound of flamethrowers:

"The pounding of the cylinders increased; pocketa - pocketa - pocketa - pocketa - pocketa."

"A huge, complicated machine, connected to the operating table, with many tubes and wires, began at this moment to go pocketa-pocketa-pocketa."

"The pounding of the cannon increased; there was the rat-tat-tatting of machine guns, and from somewhere came the menacing pocketa-pocketa-pocketa of the new flamethrowers."

This repetition connects Mitty's daydreams and enhances the humorous tone of the story.

Diction

Edgar Allen Poe's choice of words and the phrasing of his stories established a tone for the horror story genre still popular today.

"In an instant he had reached the extremity of the niche, and finding his progress arrested by the rock, stood stupidly bewildered. A moment more and I had fettered him to the granite. In its surface were two iron staples, distant from each other about two feet, horizontally. From one of these depended a short chain, from the other a padlock. Throwing the links about his waist, it was but the work of a few seconds to secure it. He was too much astounded to resist. Withdrawing the key I stepped back from the recess."

Notice that Fortunato's progress was "arrested," that he stood "stupidly bewildered," and that Montresor "throws" the links about Fortunato's waist. Those words, combined with the precision with which the narrator describes the event, create a dispassionate and evil tone.

Symbolism

In "The Chrysanthemums," John Steinbeck creates a symbol from the boxing matches. In the beginning of the story, Henry good-naturedly teases Elisa about going to the fights:

"...I thought," he continued, "I thought how it's Saturday afternoon, and we might go into Salinas for dinner at a restaurant and then to a picture show to celebrate, you see."

"Good," she repeated. "Oh, yes. That will be good."

Henry put on his joking tone. "There's fights tonight. How'd you like to go to the fights?"

"Oh, no." she said breathlessly. "No, I wouldn't like fights."

But later, near the story's end, when Elisa asks Henry about the fights, Steinbeck is able to show us the intensity of her emotions:

She was silent for a while; then she said,
"Henry, at those prize fights do the men hurt each other very much?"

"Sometimes a little, not often. Why?"

"Well, I've read how they break noses, and blood runs down their chests. I've read how the fighting gloves get heavy and soggy with blood."

He looked around at her. "What's the matter, Elisa. I didn't know you read things like that." He brought the car to a stop, then turned to the right over the Salinas River bridge.

"Do any women ever go to the fights?" she asked.

"Oh, sure, some. What's the matter, Elisa? Do you want to go? I don't think you'd like it, but I'll take you if you really want to go."

She relaxed limply in the seat. "Oh, no. I don't want to go. I'm sure I don't."

The fights become a symbol of Elisa's anger and frustration. The discussion between Elisa and Henry is symbolic of the way Elisa feels.

Dialogue

As the exchange between Elisa and Henry demonstrates, the importance of dialogue in establishing tone is directly related to how the dialogue is used. John Updike's "A & P" relies completely upon the narrator's words. Sammy's choice of words tells us how he feels, but at the same time, they also tell us how Updike feels about the story:

> "You'll feel this for the rest of your life," Lengel says, and I know that's true, too, but remembering how he made that pretty girl blush makes me so scrunchy inside I punch the No Sale tab and the machine whirs "pee-pul" and the drawer splats out. One advantage to this scene taking place in summer, I can follow this up with a clean exit, there's no fumbling around getting your coat and galoshes, I just saunter into the electric eye in my white shirt that my mother ironed the night before, and the door heaves itself open, and outside the sunshine is skating around on the asphalt.
>
> I look around for my girls, but they're gone, of course."

Lengel is the one who tells Sammy (and the reader) in a very serious tone that he'll feel the repercussions of what he does for the rest of his life, but then Sammy adds that the girl blushing made him "scrunchy inside." He also includes the fact that his mother ironed his shirt the night before and describes the cash register sound as "pee-pul" (reminiscent of Walter Mitty's "pocketa-pocketa"). The frivolous tone of those words contrasts with Lengel's remarks. And when Sammy calls the girls "my girls" and adds "of course" to the end of his remarks, we can tell that the entire incident is not really a tragic event in the teenager's life. The tone tells us that the author sees this as something that all teenage boys must "live and learn" about.

Syntax

At the end of "I'm a Fool" by Sherwood Anderson, the first person narrator says:

> "I wish I had that fellow right here that had on a Windsor tie and carried a cane. I'd smash him for fair. Gosh darn his eyes. He's a big fool that's what he is.
>
> And if I'm not another you just go find me one and I'll quit working and be a bum and give him my job. I don't care nothing for working, and earning money, and saving it for no such boob as myself."

The first paragraph ends with the narrator calling the fellow with the Windsor tie a fool, but Anderson saves the narrator's conclusion, that he's the biggest "boob" of all, for the last (see the next section, "The Periodic Sentence"). Also notice how the second paragraph uses a trio of comments leading to the conclusion. This syntactical method of using threes (as in the 1-2-3 punch) is not uncommon, and Anderson uses it twice. First, the narrator says "[1] I'll quit working and [2] be a bum and [3] give him my job." Then he says he doesn't care for "[1] working, and [2] earning money, and [3] saving it...." The effect is an "aw shucks" tone of disappointment, much the same as that of Updike's narrator in "A & P."

The Periodic Sentence

Kate Chopin's "Desiree's Baby" concludes with a periodic sentence, saving the final revelation for the very last and leading up to it with information that underscores the story's irony:

> "'But above all,' she wrote, 'night and day, I thank God for having so arranged our lives that our dear Armand will never know that his mother, who adores him, belongs to the race that is spread with the brand of slavery.'"

"The race that is spread with the brand of slavery" tells us that Armand, not Desiree, is the source of the gene that made their baby mulatto. If the reader hasn't suspected that, the element of surprise gives the story its final melodramatic impact.

Irony

An author may also use irony to reveal the tone of the story and establish the preferred attitude toward the characters and events. Irony can transform an ordinary or humorous incident into one of great significance or tragedy. Such use of irony may even be the sole determinant of a story's central idea. In the previous example from "Desiree's Baby," irony plays a major role in the effect the story has on the reader. In Updike's "A & P," the irony in the fact that the girls Sammy wants so badly to impress miss his heroic gesture (his resignation), contributes significantly to the tone of the story.

DEFINING THE TONE

Discovering a story's tone is often as simple as answering questions like "What words describe my reaction to the story?" "How does this story make me feel?" The tone is usually responsible for the reader's emotional response. Therefore, in most cases, the words used to describe the emotional response to a story can also describe its tone.

Some Sample Passages

The tone of each of the following passages can be described with a few words. Notice how the words suggest the overall feel of the passage.

Comical/Humorous

"When Cass Edmonds and Uncle Buck ran back to the house they heard Uncle Buddy cursing and bellowing in the kitchen, then the fox and the dogs came out of the kitchen and crossed the hall into the dogs' room and they heard them run through the dogs' room into his and Uncle Buck's room, then they saw them cross the hall again into Uncle Buddy's room into the kitchen again and this time it sounded like the whole kitchen chimney had come down and Uncle Buddy bellowing like a steamboat blowing, and this time the fox and the dogs and five or six sticks of firewood all came out of the kitchen together with Uncle Buddy in the middle of them hitting at everything in sight with another stick. It was a good race."

This passage from William Faulkner's "Was" derives its humor from a chaotic chase sequence, much like those in slapstick comedies. The passage consists of only two sentences; that helps create the tone. The first sentence is very long and describes the wild confusion of the chase. Exaggerated imagery ("bellowing like a steamboat blowing") also contributes to the amusement. The second sentence adds to the comic tone because it's both brief and merely a comment on the action described in the first, providing a contrast also common to humor.

Sorrowful/Sad

"The dream was gone. Something had been taken from him. In a sort of panic he pushed the palms of his hands into his eyes and tried to bring up a picture of the waters lapping on Sherry Island and the moonlit veranda, and gingham on the golf-links and the dry sun and the gold color of her neck's soft down. And her mouth damp to his kisses and her eyes plaintive with melancholy and her freshness like new fine linen in the morning. Why, these things were no longer in the world! They had existed and they existed no longer.

For the first time in years the tears were streaming down his face. But they were for himself now."

This second selection, from F. Scott Fitzgerald's "Winter Dreams," suggests nostalgia, a longing for the past. This creates the sorrowful or sad tone that borders on sentimentality. It appeals to our emotions and sense of nostalgia by describing a man's reaction to his lost love. The romantic images ("the moonlit veranda," "her mouth damp to his kisses") are memories of an irrecoverable past. The tone of the passage makes it obvious that the author wants us to share the grief of a man who suddenly realizes that the dreams of his youth are lost forever.

Eerie/Fearful/Terrifying

"So far, I had not opened my eyes. I felt that I lay upon my back, unbound. I reached out my hand, and it fell heavily upon something damp and hard. There I suffered it to remain for many minutes, while I strove to imagine where and what I could be. I longed, yet dared not to employ my vision. I dreaded the first glance at objects around me. It was not that I feared to look upon things horrible, but that I grew aghast lest there should be nothing to see. At length, with a wild desperation at heart, I quickly unclosed my eyes. My worst thoughts, then, were confirmed. The blackness of eternal night encompassed me. I struggled for breath. The intensity of the darkness seemed to oppress and stifle me. The atmosphere was intolerably close."

The tone of this third passage, a selection from Edgar Allan Poe's "The Pit and the Pendulum," is typical of a horror story. The narrator is afraid to open his eyes for fear of what he may *not* see. Sure enough, when he finally opens his eyes, he finds a darkness so intense that he "struggled for breath." The author's use of fear of the unknown and imprisonment in total darkness creates the tone appropriate to a story of terror and suspense.

While these short passages satisfy the needs of our discussion, a single passage seldom reflects the tone of an entire story. Other words could have been chosen to describe any one of these passages, but the proper vocabulary is important in describing tone. A proper analysis, just like a well-written story, requires a good vocabulary.

TONE AND THE ELEMENTS OF FICTION

Another way the author creates tone is through the arrangement and manipulation of the elements of fiction. Some of these elements are dominant in the preceding examples, but all of these devices may not be of equal importance in any one story. If one element is the most significant in establishing tone, we refer to it as the dominant element.

For example, an author may use little or no figurative language and not specify the setting. Instead, the writer may rely almost exclusively on conflict and dialogue to produce the tone. (Read Ernest Hemingway's "The Killers" for a good example of that technique.) Or the point of view may be the most important factor in the tone of one story, while the personality of a central character may be most important in another. Every author chooses the element or elements that best convey the attitude most appropriate to the central idea.

Character

The personality of a central character may help establish the tone of a story. In the following passage, John Steinbeck reveals Elisa's personality to evoke a particular mood:

> She was kneeling on the ground looking up at him. Her breast swelled passionately.
>
> The man's eyes narrowed. He looked away self-consciously. "Maybe I know," he said. "Sometimes in the night in the wagon there." Elisa's voice grew husky. She broke in on him. "I've never lived as you do, but I know what you mean. When the night is dark why, the stars are sharp-pointed, and there's quiet. Why, you rise up and up! Every pointed star gets driven into your body. It's like that. Hot and sharp and lovely."
>
> Kneeling there, her hand went out toward his legs in the greasy black trousers. Her hesitant fingers almost touched the cloth. Then her hand dropped to the ground. She crouched low like a fawning dog.

Elisa is on the verge of surrendering to her repressed sexual desires. The phrase "Hot and sharp and lovely" describes not only the stars, but also her sensuous feelings and her awareness of them. Her "kneeling," her breathing "passionately," her crouching "like a fawning dog," all contribute to a sensual image. The tone of the passage helps reveal the author's attitude toward Elisa's situation: she is a sensitive person, craving love and affection; and we sympathize with her restricted life because the connotations of the words being used lead us to feel the tone of repression.

Conflict

The nature of the story's conflict can set the tone. For example, "The Star" by Arthur Clarke creates a philosophical and religious conflict. This conflict, between the new evidence the space traveler finds and his own faith in God is internal. Because the conflict deals with an issue that is extremely serious, the tone is serious as well.

Point of View

The point of view or narrative voice of a story may also be key to the tone. When making judgments about the accuracy and significance of information, we must consider the source. Therefore, the tone of a story may depend on whose voice we hear. Notice how the omniscient point of view, in this scene from Kate Chopin's "Desiree's Baby," establishes the tone:

> In silence he ran his cold eyes over the written words. He said nothing. "Shall I go, Armand?" she asked in tones sharp with agonized suspense. "Yes, go."
>
> "Do you want me to go?"
>
> "Yes, I want you to go."
>
> He thought Almighty God had dealt cruelly and unjustly with him; and felt, somehow, that he was paying Him back in kind when he stabbed thus into his wife's soul. Moreover he no longer loved her, because of the unconscious injury she had brought upon his home and his name. She turned away like one stunned by a blow, and walked slowly toward the door, "Good-bye, Armand," she moaned. He did not answer her. That was his last blow at Fate."

The revelation of each character's consciousness effectively conveys the author's bleak, mournful attitude toward the effects of racial fear and hatred.

Setting

The setting is often the dominant element for creating or reinforcing the tone. The description of conditions related to the setting (the time of day or year, the weather, the appearance of the location) can immediately set the tone. For example, the choice of the catacombs for the physical setting of Poe's "The Cask of Amontillado" establishes the somber and frightening tone of the story, especially when contrasted with the choice of season—the carnival.

Reading Exercise:

See if you can determine the central idea in Kate Chopin's "Desiree's Baby." After you've read the story, try writing a central idea statement. Then see if you can write a sentence stating the tone of the story. When you've done that, see if you can identify the relationship between the two.

CHAPTER EIGHT

The Creative Writing Process

> *"...this morning I want to issue a warning against certain tendencies in the writing of short stories. I had a story, Ralph, and on a day when I did not feel like writing I sat down to write it. Two days of work passed before I realized that I was doing it all wrong. And now it must be done again. Subconsciously I knew it was wrong from the beginning. But I blundered on, putting down words every one of which had an untrue ring. And so, Ralph, if you ever take up short stories as you no doubt will (everyone does) I implore you not to go on working when you have that feeling in your bones. I cannot describe it."*
>
> **(From the author's *Tortilla Flat* journal)**

To many, the process of creating a fictional work of literature—a short story, play, or novel—conjures up an image of an intense person writing furiously, creating great literature. The person is possessed, out of control, and at the mercy of some gut-wrenching emotion. But nothing could be further from the truth.

Most good writers are in complete control when it comes to their art. They know what they're doing. The fact that a few of them may not be able to explain their motives doesn't change the fact that their decisions are deliberate and that they are directed by a central idea. Perhaps it's because we still hear writers talk about their "vision" or "inspiration" that the image of the possessed artist persists.

JOHN STEINBECK'S CREATION OF "THE CHRYSANTHEMUMS"

John Steinbeck's writing is a model of conciseness. His style is direct and the syntax simple. The sentences flow so smoothly that the reader doesn't sense the author at work. But he's there, and what he has created is the result of much time and effort writing and rewriting until it's just right. In "The Chrysanthemums," Steinbeck tells the story of a woman who is unfulfilled. She is, all at once, strong and vulnerable, and these characteristics lead to her victimization by an itinerant worker, a tinker. Readers are unaware of what went into the development of the story, but records reveal that Steinbeck spent many hours shaping it.

The idea for the story appears to have germinated for a while before Steinbeck put pen to paper. It was written during the same period he was working on his novel *Tortilla Flat*. The central idea for the story was already clear, but how it ought to begin was not. The following excerpt is, as far as we know, "from his first attempt at writing this story," his first attempt at writing it. The excerpt appears in the same journal as the first version of *Tortilla Flat*. (If you notice any errors in punctuation or spelling in the excerpts in this chapter, that's because you're looking at the unedited, original text. This is exactly the way Steinbeck wrote it.)

"On a shelf over the kitchen sink, a little oblong mirror with fluted edges stood. In front of it lay four big hair pins, bent out of shape, shiny where the enamel was broken off at the U. Elisa, washing the noonday dishes, paused now and then to look at the mirror. Her face was now bloated now cadaverous as its reflection moved on the uneven glass. Her hands came out of the dishwater and rested palms down on the spongy wooden sink board. Each finger drained soapy water. She leaned forward, peered in the mirror and then she picked up one of the hair pins, deftly captured a loose strand of light brown hair and pinned it in back of her ear. In the living room, her husband coughed to make his presence felt. Elisa regarded her fingers puckered and unhealthily white from the hot water and strong soap."

At this point, the story stops and Steinbeck makes these remarks:

"Purple ink again. Apparently it doesn't make a difference in the writing. I'll give it a try. It looks pretty pale to me though. But it was a bargain not to be overlooked. How it will work on my post cards fine. Here is the sun. The good sun. This is to be a good story. Two personalities meet cross, flare, air and hate each other. Purple, if it were a little bit stronger, would be a good color for the story. It is coming stronger and stronger. There is a definite feeling of a change today, Wednesday the 31st of January. I feel that some change has taken place. Good or bad, I don't know. It will be interesting to see…"

Steinbeck now begins to ramble, expressing concerns about family and coming events. He states, "I can't make my mind get up on a barrel. It goes kiting off on petty affairs of its own…" Then he returns to his efforts at completing the story, writing two full pages, but finally gives it up, concluding, "This is the day's work. There's no sureness of touch in me today. I don't seem to be able to get at this story. I shouldn't be writing this story this way at all."

The next page of his journal, which may have been started at a later time, consists of a letter. In it, he talks about the creative writing process and provides us with some insight into the difficulties the writer encounters:

"My dear little hypothetical turnip. I have news for you and some advice. I think you will agree that my method is sound. We, all of us, probably even you, who don't exist at all have deep in the mass of our minds, a desire to give advice. We are not much interested in the outcome of our advice, the more because it usually turns out to be bad. The giving of it is the important thing. And no, Ralph, my child...having only friends who are convinced that they can manage their affairs better than I can, I am left with the necessity of creating you and advising you. I am naming you Ralph because Ralph is the kind of person who needs advice about nearly everything he does. The possibilities are endless. You need my help, the result of my mature judgment and, since you do not exist, there is little chance that my advice will bring disaster upon you...But this morning I want to issue a warning against certain tendencies in the writing of short stories. I had a story, Ralph, and on a day when I did not feel like writing I sat down to write it. Two days of work passed before I realized that I was doing it all wrong. And now it must be done again. Subconsciously I knew it was wrong from the beginning. But I blundered on, putting down words every one of which had an untrue ring. And so, Ralph, if you ever take up short stories as you no doubt will (everyone does) I implore you not to go on working when you have that feeling in your bones. I cannot describe it. You will know when you have it. My tendency, and no doubt yours, is to put more into a short story than belongs there. Keep out details that have no absolute bearing on your story. Keep out characterization which does not actually move the story on its way. I may and shall sometimes disobey the letter of this instruction, but don't you dare. I am inclined to be critical of you, hypercritical and that is natural enough. Remember what I say for I am sure my advice is sound. Don't bother to answer—"

Following this passage, "The Chrysanthemums" begins with the familiar description of the fog settling over the valley. Apparently, somehow, Steinbeck had finally found an approach that satisfied him.

THE REVISION PHASE

Writing the story was just the beginning. Many portions of "The Chrysanthemums" were revised many times. At least four versions of it exist; three have appeared in print. Though some of the changes were the result of the work of Steinbeck's editors (he was notoriously weak in his use of commas), many of the changes were his.

The remainder of this chapter presents comparisons between the author's manuscript version, which appears in his journal, and the Long Valley version, which is the most often published.

Character Revisions

Many of the changes in the story affect the character of Elisa. It's quite likely that as the story developed Elisa became more real to Steinbeck, and so her character became easier to shape. Consider these two descriptions of Elisa.

The Manuscript Version

"Elisa was thirty-five, but she looked older in her gardening costume, a man's black hat, pulled low down over her eyes, clodhopper shoes, and a big corduroy apron littered with pockets for snips, a little trowel and seeds. Elisa wore heavy leather gloves to protect her hands. She was thirty-five."

The Final Version

"Her face was lean and strong and her eyes were clear as water. Her figure looked blocked and heavy in her gardening costume, a man's black hat, pulled low down over her eyes, clodhopper shoes, a figured print dress almost completely covered by a big corduroy apron with four big pockets to hold the snips, the trowel and scratcher, the seeds and the knife she worked with. She wore heavy leather gloves to protect her hands while she worked."

Notice that her age, while still mentioned, becomes less of a factor than her physical appearance. That she looks older is dropped from the description; that she looks blocked and heavy is added.

Conflict Revisions

The conflict in "The Chrysanthemums" is subtle. The only external struggle is between Henry and Elisa. Steinbeck conveys its awkwardness through his descriptions of their behavior.

The Manuscript Version

"Henry looked down toward the tractor shed. When he looked back at her he was safe."

The Final Version

"Henry looked down toward the tractor shed, and when he brought his eyes back to her, they were his own again."

The external conflict between Henry and Elisa is also evident in the dialogue. In this next example, we can see how Steinbeck reworked Henry's words to clarify the character's confusion. That Henry cannot understand Elisa's dilemma is important to the development of her internal conflict.

The Manuscript Version

"Nice? You think I look nice? What do you mean by 'nice'?" Henry blundered on. "I mean you look strong, strong and happy." "I am strong? How strong? What do you mean 'strong'?" Henry was bewildered. "You're playing something" he said helplessly. "You look strong enough to break a calf over your knee, happy enough to eat it like a watermelon." For a second she lost her self...before how strong.

The Final Version

"Nice? You think I look nice? What do you mean by 'nice'?" Henry blundered on. "I don't know. I mean you look different strong and happy." "I am strong? Yes, strong. What do you mean 'strong'?" He looked bewildered. "You're playing some kind of a game," he said helplessly. "It's a kind of a play. You look strong enough to break a calf over your knee, happy enough to eat it like a watermelon." For a second she lost her rigidity...She grew complete again. "I am strong," she boasted. "I never knew before how strong."

Point of View Revisions

In the first example below, Steinbeck shifts the position of the narrator slightly in order to add the dropping of the coin more dramatic action.

The Manuscript Version

"She went into the house and brought him a fifty-cent piece."

The Final Version

"Elisa brought him a fifty-cent piece from the house and dropped it in his hand."

In this second example, Steinbeck maintains the point of view. Elisa still looks over her shoulder, but he alters the action. Instead of throwing back her shoulders, she throws out her chest. The result is the same, but there is a great deal of difference between the two.

The Manuscript Version

"She tightened her stomach, threw back her shoulders, she turned and looked over her shoulder at her back."

The Final Version

"She tightened her stomach and threw out her chest. She turned and looked over her shoulder at her back."

Setting Revisions

Following the tangential discussion with his little turnip, Steinbeck attempted to begin the story again. He probably thought it through and realized that a macro-vision of the setting would be more effective than the earlier version. The metaphor of the closed pot must have seemed especially apt. Here is how the second attempt began:

"The high gray flannel fog of winter closed off the Salinas valley from the sky and from the rest of the world. On all sides it sat like a lid on the mountains and made of the great valley a closed pot. On the broad level floor of the valley, the gang plows churned the dark rich and left the black earth shining like metal where the shares had cut."

But this is not the way the beginning ultimately appeared in print. The final, most frequently published version of the story begins this way:

"The high gray flannel fog of winter closed off the Salinas valley from the sky and from all the rest of the world. On every side it sat like a lid on the mountains and made of the great valley a closed pot. On the broad, level land floor the gang plows bit deep and left the black earth shining like metal where the shares had cut."

Notice these subtle changes to the description.

the addition of the word "all" to the first sentence, requiring the word's deletion from the second

the addition of the word "land" to the third sentence, emphasizing the earthy nature of the setting

the change in verbs, from "churned" to "bit deep," in the third sentence

Language Revisions

Imagery

Near the end of the story, Elisa and Henry talk about going to the fights. Steinbeck recognized the impact of the image of the boxing gloves soggy with blood and strengthened it by adding that they were "heavy" as well. Henry's response is modified too. In the final version he adds, "I don't think you'll like it," which is a further indication of Henry's lack of understanding and inability to relate to Elisa.

The Manuscript Version

"Well, I've read how they break noses, and blood runs down their chests, and the fighting gloves get soggy with blood." "Do you want to go? I'll take you if you really want to go."

The Final Version

"Well, I've read how they break noses, and blood runs down their chests. I've read how the fighting gloves get heavy and soggy with blood." "Do you want to go? I don't think you'd like it, but I'll take you if you really want to go."

Diction

Sometimes one word can make an important difference. For example, in the manuscript version of the story, Steinbeck used the word "quietly" to describe Elisa's voice:

> "Oh no," she said quietly. "I wouldn't like fights."

However, in the final version of the story the word has changed to "breathlessly," and the word "no" is repeated:

> "Oh no," she said breathlessly. "No, I wouldn't like fights."

To speak quietly is to be reticent, without feeling. But speaking breathlessly suggests a strong feeling. In the final version, Elisa nearly has her breath taken away at the thought of the fights. And twice she tells Henry no.

Syntax

The sequence of words is another feature that contributes to the effect. Notice how the placement of the description "lean and rangy mongrel" near the end of the sentence increases its impact.

The Manuscript Version

"A lean and rangy mongrel dog walked sedately underneath the wagon behind the wheels."

The Final Version

"Underneath the wagon, between the hind wheels, a lean and rangy mongrel dog walked sedately."

Syntax and Diction

Syntax and diction usually work together to create the sound of a phrase or a sentence. Steinbeck had an excellent ear for the English language. In many ways, the changes he made were aimed at improving the sound, to make the story read more smoothly. In the next two samples, he adds phrases to convey Elisa's feelings and he also simplifies the action to make it more dramatic.

The Manuscript Version

"She heard the gate being shut. In a few moments Henry's step sounded on the porch."

The Final Version

"She heard the gate bang shut and set herself for Henry's arrival. His step sounded on the porch."

Symbolism

The symbolic sexual interplay between Elisa and the tinker is a critical part of the story. The final version strengthens this interplay by cutting some words and making the sentences more direct.

The Manuscript Version

"Well, I can only tell you what it feels like to have them. It's when you're budding. Everything goes right down to your fingertips. You watch your fingers work. You can feel how it is. They pick and pick the buds...They may pick a bud off that looks biggest, but it isn't the best...Every pointed star gets driven into you, into your body...Hot and sharp and all lovely."

The Final Version

"Well, I can only tell you what it feels like. It's when you're picking off the buds you don't want. Everything goes right down to your fingertips. You watch your fingers work. They can do it themselves. You can feel how it is. They pick and pick the buds...They know. They never make a mistake. You can feel it...Every pointed star gets driven into your body...Hot and sharp and - lovely."

Irony

"The Chrysanthemums" makes its point through the use of irony, which is shown through Elisa's naivete and the tinker's exploitation of her situation. In this illustration, Steinbeck added the metaphor of the fawning dog to illustrate how Elisa relates to the tinker and to emphasize the ironic contrast of her strength with her weakness.

The Manuscript Version

"Kneeling there her hand went out toward his legs in the (greasy dirty) dirty black trousers, almost touched the cloth. Her hand dropped to the ground. She crouched low and cleared her throat on the rising sobs. She heard his voice coming from a distance. It's nice, just like you say.... Her lip curled back. How do you know? How can you tell? she said. He felt the contempt in her tone."

The Final Version

"Kneeling there, her hand went out toward his legs in the greasy black trousers. Her hesitant fingers almost touched the cloth. Then her hand dropped to the ground. She crouched low like a fawning dog. He said, 'It's nice, just like you say.'"

Tone Revisions

Many of the earlier changes presented here had an effect on the tone of the story. Changes in wording, syntax, and diction modify the overall tone, as do the following additional changes. In these two examples, the rewording of the passages sharpens the tone of sadness and loneliness mixed with frustration.

The Manuscript Version

"My mother had it too. She could stick anything in the ground and make it grow. She said it was planters' hands."

The Final Version

"My mother had it. She could stick anything in the ground and make it grow. She said it was having planters' hands that knew how to do it."

The Manuscript Version

"When you're like that you can't make a mistake. Do you see that! Can you understand that?" Her eyes were wet.

The Final Version

"When you're like that you can't do anything wrong. Do you see that? Can you understand that?"

Although many of Steinbeck's revisions might seem trivial, their impact is not. Much like sculptors who must painstakingly smooth some edges and sharpen others to make the work fit the concept, serious writers pay attention to the details of a story. They know that therein lies the difference between a good story and a great one.

CHAPTER NINE

Alternative Methods Of Analysis

The earlier chapters of this book focus on the analysis of short stories through a basic format involving three parts: a summary of the story, an interpretation of the central idea, and a discussion of the primary elements. While this approach serves the beginner well, alternative approaches to analysis can reveal more. In fact, an analysis through a dominant element, an analysis with an evaluation, or a comparison/contrast analysis is often better suited to many stories.

ANALYSIS THROUGH A DOMINANT ELEMENT

In many stories, one element serves as the author's primary means for conveying the central idea. When this happens, a single element will overshadow the others. They become subservient to it. Analyzing such a story requires that the central idea be defined through the dominant element. A subsequent discussion of the elements then focuses on the primary element, rather than on the central idea.

John Updike's "A & P" is a good example of a story where the element of character is central. The crux of the story depends on a change in Sammy's character. It is this change, one of the many steps toward maturation, that forms the central idea. An effective analysis of "A & P" would rely on the relationship of the other elements: setting, conflict, tone, language, and point of view to character. Such an analysis would explore the way the setting shapes the character, the way the first person point of view provides the insight into character that is necessary for a successful central idea, the fact that the real conflict in the story is internal and, therefore, directly tied to the character, and so on.

In the following example, written by a student, the dominant element of point of view unifies the analysis. All other elements result from its development, as is often true of a first person narrative. The first person is usually the main character and his or her perspective on the story dominates the central idea and directs the others. Notice how she uses quotes and details from the story to support statements about the character's personality.

Alice Munro's "How I Met My Husband" by Dana Ross

"How I Met My Husband" by Alice Munro is the story of a country girl's first encounter with luxury and sophistication. The first person narrative is the dominant element of the story as Edie's perspective is essential to revealing the author's theme. Munro's story illuminates the beauty of appreciating and making the most of what one has and shows how this wisdom may come more easily to simple, hard-working people than to those of different backgrounds and values.

Edie's character is a key ingredient to the story's theme and by choosing to tell it from her point of view, Munro creates a very effective story. Edie's narrative reveals her conscientious, principled, no-nonsense approach to life. Her sincere appreciation of simple things is appealing to the reader, and her honest and sensible nature make her a very likable character. Her simple observations, like realizing that taking a bath too often in a luxurious bathroom might make it less special, and that someone of simple background can probably imagine a life of luxury easier than someone of luxury could imagine an unadorned life, exemplify her wisdom. Her perceptiveness of human nature can be seen time and again as she sees past what people say. "Asking people to stay, just like that, is certainly a country thing . . . but not to Mrs. Peebles, from the way she said, 'oh yes, we have plenty of room,'" is a good example of this. Her frank opinions about people could make her appear smug and self-righteous, but because of the respect the reader feels for her, these are interpreted more as honest evaluations by a person with a strong sense of values.

Comparisons of Edie's homespun attitude with some of the other characters' attitudes are made through the author's use of point of view, and lead directly to the central idea. The contrast of Edie's wholesome simplicity with Mrs. Peeble's hollow sophistication humbles the reader and makes her examine her own values. The difference between Edie's honest, hard-working ways and Loretta Bird's gossiping, lazy ones increases the reader's admiration for Edie. The most potent effects of the first person point of view come from telling the story years after it has taken place, allowing the reader to see how Edie has matured. Edie has a good head on her shoulders even as a naive girl due, at least in part, to her upbringing in a strict, farming family that makes do with the bare necessities. The traits instilled in her childhood remain through the years and she becomes an honorable, upright, and kind woman. For years she allows her husband to believe that she went to the mailbox daily to see him, when she really was waiting for a letter from another man "because I like for people to think what pleases them and makes them happy."

Edie's conflict and the way she deals with it are revealed most effectively through the first person point of view. Her first job exposes Edie to many new things, luxuries, city people, and a worldly man, all things that would excite and interest a young girl, and quite possibly lead her astray. These things, the man in particular, do affect Edie but her good sense prevails. As Edie sees it, "If there are women all through life waiting, and women busy and not waiting, I knew which I had to be. Even though there might be things the second kind of woman has to pass up and never know about, it still is better." By accepting her place in life and knowing that a life of hard work would be one with less inner turmoil, she is able to resolve her conflict without much difficulty. The manner in which Edie handles her conflict establishes her as a heroine of ordinary circumstances, and this in conjunction with the unpretentious narrative makes the theme of the story universally appealing and easy to accept.

The traditional rural traits that Edie possesses are not necessarily shared by all people residing in the country. The story takes place at a time when city people are opting to live in the country, bringing different sets of values with them. The cultural conflicts this creates unfold vividly in the rural setting of the story, and they are made more apparent by telling the story through the eyes of a genuine country girl. The stark differences in the women of the story emphasize that where one lives is irrelevant. The values one adopts are what leads to a healthy state of mind. The veterinarian's character lends hope that Edie's wholesome attitude is not entirely a result of her country upbringing but possible for any person with the right approach to life.

All the elements of "How I Met My Husband" rest on Edie's down-to-earth narration. Munro's use of the first person narrative gives a simple story a powerful impact. Spending time wisely and productively offers more rewards than wasting time wishing for what might never be, and basic goodness and hard work can enable one to more fully appreciate what life has to offer.

ANALYSIS THROUGH EVALUATION

Our individual likes and dislikes often cause us to judge things on the basis of bias or prejudice rather than by objective means. We may declare that something is good or bad when all we really mean is that we like it or don't like it. But even though you may not like a story, it may be well-written. And a story you do like may not be well-written at all. In other words, the quality of a story is intrinsic; it's separate from our personal feelings. Quality is determined by applying the objective criteria like those detailed in this book.

An evaluation judges the level of a story's quality. Regardless of what we evaluate, we can't conduct a logical debate until we agree on a clear set of standards. Once the standards are agreed upon, a story provides the evidence for judging whether or not the story meets the standards.

Establishing Criteria for Evaluating Short Stories

Three major criteria are commonly used to evaluate short stories. These criteria, explained in the following sections, depend on the elements discussed in the earlier chapters of this text.

The elements must all work together

A story should be judged by how effectively all of the elements work together to achieve the central idea. Each element works with every other element to accomplish the story's goal. With that premise, you can review each element, its relation to the other elements, and its relation to the central idea. If this relationship is weak or lacking in some way, if a piece does not fit, then the story lacks the right combination of elements to be effective.

For example, a story in which the central idea is closely related to the personality of a particular character must use the other elements to support this. We must ask: Does the setting illuminate the character's personality? Does the language reinforce the character's traits? Does the tone tell us something about the character? Is the point of view supportive of the characterization?

The situation must be plausible

Even though we live in the real world rather than the fictional world of the story, the central idea must have "real world" significance. The story must speak to a human condition that is common to all of us, as well as to the specific characters of the story itself.

This is not to say that the story must be completely realistic or that it must mirror our reality. Instead, it should be true to itself. Whatever norms exist in the fictional world the author establishes must be plausible. The human (or even nonhuman) behavior, attitudes, and values should ring true.

Probability, not possibility, is the key factor. When Alice follows the white rabbit into Wonderland, we know that she has left our world and entered one with very different ways, but we quickly learn to accept them. They are plausible in the context of Lewis Carroll's story. Likewise, when Arthur C. Clarke's narrator says, in the beginning of "The Star" that "It is three thousand light-years to the Vatican," we are forewarned. We cannot apply our present ideas of the universe and space travel because the story is set in the future. Nonetheless, the story provides human emotions that are authentic and plausible, and the scientific basis of the story is probable enough to make us believe.

Could the story happen the way it happened? Do the words and actions of the characters seem authentic within the limits the author has set? These are the questions of plausibility we must ask when evaluating the story.

The story must stay fresh

A good story yields new insights through repeated readings. It remains fresh and provocative long after the first reading. Very often, it gnaws at one's mind. Rather than boring us, repeated readings should offer new ideas, even new and different interpretations. A story that yields everything on the first reading lacks this freshness.

Freshness, plausibility, and the effective relationship of all elements to the central idea are not the only standards for evaluation; other criteria may be equally valid. However, a judgment about quality is meaningless without such clearly stated criteria.

The following student essay evaluates a short story using specific criteria stated in the introductory paragraph and developed in the following paragraphs.

Charlotte Perkins Gillman's "The Yellow Wallpaper" by Sara Graham-Costain

"The Yellow Wallpaper," by Charlotte Perkins Gilman, is the story of a woman losing her sanity. Bedridden by mental illness and forbidden by her husband to work or socialize, she studies the wallpaper daily. Eventually, she begins to see things moving within it and goes crazy, tearing the wallpaper to shreds. It is a haunting story and an excellent work of short fiction, because it meets these criteria: the elements work well together, the situation is plausible, and the story bears repetition. Gilman manipulates these aspects of short fiction so well that she clearly and effectively evokes her theme that the constant rejection of one's ideas and feelings can alienate a person to the point that she becomes imprisoned in her own mind.

The point of view is the dominant element, providing insight into the woman's character. Using the first person, Gilman allows the reader to see the work through the eyes of her main character. The story is written as a private journal and all of the other elements are perceived through the main character's thought. "I would not say it to a living soul, of course," she writes, "but this is dead paper and a great relief to my mind." This clearly relates to the theme, as it shows her isolation from the rest of the world, even her husband, John. Because he forbids her to think about her condition, she focuses her attention on the house. In this way, the setting becomes an important element of the story. The peeling yellow wallpaper, with its confusing patterns, is a metaphor for her state of mind and she becomes lost in it. As her illness progresses, her perceptions about the wallpaper change. "Behind that outside pattern, the dim shapes get clearer everyday." It is at this point that she begins to see a woman caged within the wallpaper. Here again, the point of view is intertwined with the other elements. Finally, she becomes the woman within her fantasy, telling her husband, "I've got out at last, in spite of you. And I've pulled off most of the paper, so you can't put me back." She imagines that the wallpaper is a prison, in the same sense that she has become a prisoner, exemplifying the author's theme.

All of these story elements are dependent upon one another and Gilman's masterful use of language ties them together. It sets the tone for the story and helps reveal the character's state of mind. After she begins to retreat into her fantasy world, she writes in her diary a description of the wallpaper that is becoming the focus of her attention, "Nobody could climb through that pattern—it strangles so; I think that is why it has so many heads. They get through and then the pattern strangles them off and makes their eyes white." This creates a disturbing tone, revealing to the reader that the main character's thinking is unsound, while at the same time creating a vivid picture of her encroaching madness. The repeated use of the connotative word, "strangle," emphasizes the theme by reflecting her feelings of oppression. It is her husband who oppresses her and this conflict between husband and wife is another element which the author successfully integrates into the story. John is a doctor who trivializes his wife's illness and rejects any ideas that she has regarding her needs. Although she believes that "congenial work, with excitement and change," would do her good, he forbids it. The more that John rejects her, the deeper she withdraws into herself. Since she must say what she thinks and feels in some way, she writes in her journal and gets pulled deeper into the fantasy prison of the yellow wallpaper. All of the elements of the story work together in this way to emphasize the theme.

Even though the world that the woman creates within the yellow wallpaper is insane and unbelievable, the story is painfully plausible. The characters, the conflict, and even the imagery are so clearly illustrated that the reader is drawn into the story. It is clear that she believes what she sees and the descriptions of what she sees are so vivid and precise that the reader can see them as well. The conflict and theme are universal and could affect anyone. The lack of communication, the lack of understanding, the domineering male who takes control of his wife's life, these are things any reader can empathize with. It happens to many married couples. The reader, understanding her feelings of imprisonment and her need to create a fantasy world, is therefore able to accept and even feel her distorted reality. This makes the action of the story even more moving. The insanity which grows out of the conflict is believable because the conflict is believable.

The author's use of language also helps to create a plausible story. The reader becomes so involved in her thought process, gets so involved in the story because of the detail used to describe it. For example, in describing the oppressive smell of the wallpaper, she writes, "...the smell is here. It creeps all over the house. I find it hovering in the dining room, skulking in the parlor, hiding in the hall, lying in wait for me on the stairs." Through her use of language and her detailed description of the steady progression of the woman's illness, Gilman makes the madness so believable that it has the ring of universal truth.

Even though the story was written in 1892, it reads and feels as if it could've been written yesterday. Based on experiences from Gilman's own life (after giving birth to a daughter, she suffered a similar mental breakdown), the story gnaws at the reader. It has the immediacy of a real experience, even though it takes us into an unreal world. On first reading, one senses something strange about the house; perhaps it's haunted. The wallpaper is shredded and there's only one piece of furniture, a bed with legs that look like they've been chewed on. A foul odor permeates the bedroom. It makes the reader think there's something wrong with the house, "...else why should it be let so cheaply?" This feeling of suspense, of waiting for something to happen, makes the story exciting and engaging on a dramatic level. But the story becomes more complicated. On further analysis, it is the extent of detail she uses in describing the progression of her illness, where layers of meaning can be deciphered through repeated readings.

Gilman's theme, that the constant rejection of one's ideas and feelings can alienate a person to the point that she becomes imprisoned in her own mind, unfolds beautifully due to her masterful integration of these various aspects. All of the elements work well together, the story is believable, and new insight may be gained through repeated reading. These aspects combined, serve to create a throught provoking and haunting story of the highest caliber.

ANALYSIS THROUGH COMPARISON/CONTRAST

Another approach to analysis is through comparison and contrast. To compare is to identify similarities, to discuss the aspects of two or more things as they are like one another. To contrast is to identify the differences, to discuss those aspects that are unlike one another. In addition, the reasons for the similarities and differences should be addressed.

Although two stories may have the same central idea, the reader should be able to identify the causes behind the authors' choices. These choices—the arrangement and emphasis of elements in a story—are related to the central idea, but it is a mistake to assume that the elements of two stories with the same central idea would be the same. Every author is unique, and each chooses to reach the same point or achieve the same purpose through different means.

Much of the pleasure of reading comes from understanding how an author constructs the story so that the central idea is achieved. An even greater pleasure and deeper understanding is possible when we become aware of the ways in which different authors achieve the same purpose, but in different ways. Comparison/contrast focuses our attention on such similarities and differences, making us aware of the variety in literature.

In the following example, a student looks at the similarities and differences between two stories with a common central idea: how people escape from the harsh reality of their lives. The student analyzes each of the elements and discusses how the authors have used them to support their approach to the idea. The student compares the main characters; explains how the conflicts, while similar, are resolved differently; explains how the point of view in each story is the same (first person); and notes the differences in language and tone. The final paragraph sums up the different approaches by emphasizing their primary difference, a serious as opposed to a humorous tone.

A Comparative Analysis of Katherine Mansfield's "Miss Brill" and James Thurber's "The Secret Life of Walter Mitty"

Katherine Mansfield draws a sad picture of escapism in her short story "Miss Brill." It is the story of how a single woman fills her lonely Sunday afternoons by attending band concerts in a nearby park. Miss Brill loses herself completely in her surroundings and feels much at home, as if this park is her only niche in life. This illusion is rudely shattered by a young couple sitting beside her on the bench. A few harsh words, closely followed by a few vulgar ones, burst Miss Brill's bubble.

Another form of escapism is found in James Thurber's "The Secret Life of Walter Mitty." Mr. Mitty is the henpecked husband of a seemingly overbearing, domineering woman. Mitty escapes his insufferable life by imagining himself in a variety of adventurous episodes. Mansfield's purpose seems to be to point out the futility of escapism, while Thurber's seems to be that escapism is not only necessary, but also an entertaining, beneficial pastime. The apathy and sadness Miss Brill exhibits at the end of the story suggests her inability to meet life head-on. Perhaps she will find another form of pleasurable escape, but the reader is left thinking this will probably not happen. Mitty is a very similar character, with the key difference being his elasticity. He has the ability to snap back each time the world destroys his illusions. Mitty, therefore, is a very static character, but Miss Brill's experience produces a dynamic change. Miss Brill's conflict is brought to the reader's attention when the young couple on her bench are rudely inconsiderate of her presence. She imagines herself to be a key character in her mocked-up play of life, but the young man makes her aware of her unimportance. Walter Mitty has his bubble burst every day, however, and finds it an easy thing to deal with life's little obstacles. In both stories the characters' escapes are rudely shattered, but Mitty simply throws himself into a new adventure, whereas Miss Brill has a very important part of her life permanently destroyed.

Mansfield uses the limited omniscient point of view to focus the reader's attention strictly on Miss Brill's perception of those around her. The reader becomes intimately aware of Miss Brill and feels the pain so thoughtlessly inflicted by the coarse young man. Thurber also uses the limited omniscient point of view to familiarize the reader with Walter Mitty. The shift in Mitty's thinking from reality to fantasy is deceptive, but the point of view is consistent throughout. Both authors are very effective in their use of the omniscient narrative voice.

While the physical settings are very different, the psychological settings in both stories are very similar. Both characters are unable to deal with life, and both seek escape as an adjustive reaction. This defense mechanism acts as an emotional insulator for both Miss Brill and Walter Mitty. The actual time and geographical location do not seem to have much bearing on either author's story. The total setting (emotional, psychological, physical) brings each author's theme into clearer focus.

Mansfield's language differs significantly from that used by Thurber. Eloquence and gracefulness are typical of Mansfield's style, while Thurber writes with a very tongue-in-cheek manner. Mansfield uses personification and imagery in her very literary approach, and it is highly effective because it seems to be appropriate to Miss Brill's way of thinking. Thurber's narrative is more direct and seems very appropriate to his main character. He uses a recurring phrase (pocketa-pocketa) in most of Mitty's daydreams; this helps unify the story even though Mitty's mind flashes from one fantasy to the next.

Even for the reader who approaches Mansfield's story for the first time, the tone is quickly evident as one of forced (and false) gaiety. Miss Brill seems to try to trill her way through life, totally rejecting any negative thoughts or happenings. This use of tone is the most effective part of the story. Miss Brill is obviously being set up for a harsh fall, and the reader is prepared for this because of the tone. On the other hand, Thurber's story is ironic and humorous. Mitty continually imagines himself in fantastic situations, only to be yanked from his reveries by the real world.

Because of Thurber's special brand of humor, the reader looking purely for entertainment will find "The Secret Life of Walter Mitty" to be the more enjoyable story. Thurber's story does not require the reader to ponder too deeply the merits of Mitty's lifestyle, simply because his fantasies are so blatant. Mansfield's story would be more appreciated by the reader looking for intricacy. Miss Brill is a sad and lonely character, a good candidate for psychoanalysis. Mitty, however, is a charming blunderer with whom most readers can easily identify.

The next example compares two different authors' treatment of the "battle of the sexes." Notice how the student focuses on the use of irony in both stories.

A Comparative Analysis of Roald Dahl's "The Way Up to Heaven" and James Thurber's "The Catbird Seat" by Lee Anne Aspra

Roald Dahl's "The Way Up to Heaven," a scathing portrayal of the relationship of a long-married couple, illustrates the universal themes of victory versus oppression and the triumph of good over evil. The backdrop for this central idea is the account of Mrs. Foster's struggle to catch a plane for a greatly anticipated trip to Paris, juxtaposed with her husband's not-so-subtle attempts to thwart her plans. Their departure for the airport has again been delayed by Mr. Foster who conveniently "forgets" something in the house just as they are preparing to drive off. When he returns to retrieve the missing item, Mrs. Foster hurries behind, but stops abruptly at the unmistakable sound of the elevator jamming inside. Instead of continuing into the house, she runs back to the car and races to the airport, leaving her husband trapped behind in the elevator.

James Thurber, too, has designed a very amusing tale around the theme of justice prevailing in "The Catbird Seat." In this case, the story centers around a Mr. Erwin Martin, file room manager of the esteemed firm, F & S, and the newly appointed special advisor to the president, Mrs. Ulgine Barrows. It seems that Mrs. Barrows proposes a complete revision of the existing organization of F & S, which includes ridding the firm of Mr. Martin, whose loyal, flawless tenure exceeds 22 years. What transpires is Mr. Martin's scheme to "rub out" Mrs. Barrows, whose hiring he considers a simple error in judgment by the company president. Capitalizing on his pristine reputation as a non-smoking teetotaler, he pays a visit to the home of Mrs. Barrows, intent on killing her, and winds up falling into the perfect method for doing her in. That is to say, he helps her do herself in. As in "The Way Up to Heaven," justice finds a way.

In both stories, the chief protagonists are of sterling character. Mrs. Foster has served her husband loyally and without question throughout their marriage and Mr. Foster has taken advantage of her deferential nature. He is hostile and manipulative, choosing to exploit her weaknesses, which actually amount only to having a compulsive need to be on time for every occasion. Thurber's characters have a similar dichotomy. But this time it's Mr. Martin who is a bit of a compulsive, needing to fastidiously maintain his filing system without interference. Mrs. Barrow blasts herself onto the scene like a tornado, a vulgar, bombastic assault on Mr. Martin's orderly world and he sees eliminating her as the only possible solution to his torment. The protagonists in these stories find revenge and freedom in the end, and in both cases their adversaries cut their own throats.

The conflicts are similar as well and both internal and external issues are represented. Mrs. Foster and Mr. Martin have rather modest wants. They don't ask for much out of this world, and both of them have a person in their life who systematically seeks to oppress and crush them. In addition, the conflict of righteousness against unrighteousness touches on the central theme. But the lead characters are vindicated. Perhaps not in a way one could recommend as the proper course of action, but they are freed none the less.

Both stories are set in New York City in what appears to be the same time period, the 1940s. Mr. and Mrs. Foster share an affluent life, living in a six-story house with four servants and a chauffeur. But it is not money and comfort that Mrs. Foster lacks; it is quite clearly love and respect. The ugliness that her husband displays know no social bounds. In contrast, Mr. Martin leads a completely unassuming life, living alone and not bothering a soul. His domain is his office and his precious files. Both settings add richness and definition to these stories. Obviously the elevator, as the setting of Mr. Foster's demise, is an essential detail in Dahl's sketch while it is entirely appropriate for Thurber to use New York City as the main prop for his satire on the murder story.

Roald Dahl and James Thurber have used similar aspects of language to tell their stories. The most distinctive is that of irony, the unifying feature of both. Another is the use of description which in the case of "The Catbird Seat" creates a hilarious picture of Mrs. Barrows. One visualizes a large, domineering woman who yells instead of speaks and borrows all sorts of silly baseball chants and epithets such as "Don't scrape the bottom of the pickle barrel" and "Are you sitting in the catbird seat?" The narrator has a marvelous time telling of her "quacking voice" and "braying laugh," and before it's over the reader is convinced of Mr. Martin's need to remove her from the picture. Dahl gives a darkly ironic twist to his story. Mrs. Foster overcomes her oppression by leaving a trapped Mr. Foster in the elevator and dashing off to Paris for weeks. His death will naturally be seen as an accident, although Mr. Foster himself will know that his wife finally defended herself and delivered the last word. It is the same for Mrs. Barrows. She knows that the normally composed Mr. Martin visited her apartment and behaved outrageously, and that this was his way of getting back at her. He barely had to swing a punch, instead relying on her character and behavior to do the work of getting rid of her.

In the final analysis, both Dahl and Thurber write entertaining stories of revenge. The reader is riveted by suspense, sensing an astonishing finale that is richly rewarded. "The Way Up to Heaven" is not nearly as comical as "The Catbird Seat," but it is equally engaging, leaving the reader feeling superbly satisfied with the outcome. One is called to perhaps cheer a little louder for Mrs. Foster than for Mr. Martin, since she is truly being victimized by a mean little man to the point of acute mental torment; however, Mrs. Barrows is sufficiently portrayed as a detriment to Mr. Martin's sanity to warrant the reader's sympathy.

READING FOR COMPARISON/CONTRAST

The turmoil coming of age is a popular theme, but the experience varies with the background, environment, and circumstances of the character. "A & P" by John Updike chronicles the experience of a middle-class adolescent boy to depict a universal weakness. The main character in Sherwood Anderson's "I'm a Fool" has much in common with Updike's Sammy, but there are critical differences. After you read both stories, consider these questions:

- What are the differences between the main characters in each story and what creates those differences?
- What is the statement in each story that defines the main character's understanding of the events that have taken place?
- What role do Mr. Lengel and the black man play in the stories?
- How is the point of view different in each story and what effect does it have?

CHAPTER TEN

Sample Essays

The following examples were written by students enrolled over the years in our classes at Austin Community College. They have kindly allowed us to include them to illustrate the various techniques we've outlined in this book. While certainly not perfect, they do represent the wide variety of writing styles and the range of skills and critical abilities students bring to the subject. As such, they stand as reasonable models of what a good student can be expected to achieve.

A STANDARD APPROACH TO ANALYSIS

Here are three examples of the basic approach to analysis. In the first example, the student uses character, conflict, point of view, setting, and language to support the central idea. Notice how the conflict is clearly identified and the role of the setting is tied directly to the central idea. Also, note the use of quotes in the paragraph on language. The final paragraph, summarizing the paper, strengthens the student's case.

The author of the second paper does an excellent job with the classic story of Walter Mitty, the little man who dreams of being bigger. As each element is discussed, it is tied to the central idea. And for each element, evidence from the story is provided as support for the student's interpretation.

The third paper also follows the basic structure of an analytical essay. The first paragraph summarizes the story and concludes with an interpretation, but notice how the first sentence neatly sums up the force that lies at the heart of the story. The second paragraph discusses the characters, the third the conflict, and so on. Each paragraph concludes with a statement relating the element discussed to the central idea of the story. (If you haven't read this story, you should do so before reading this paper.)

An Analysis of Guy de Maupassant's "The Necklace" by Karen Gray

Guy de Maupassant's "The Necklace" is the story of Mathilde Loisel, who resents her "station" in life. When Monsieur Loisel presents his wife with an invitation to a formal ball, she bursts into tears because she has nothing to wear. Mathilde's husband agrees to let her buy a gown, and, following his suggestion, she borrows a beautiful necklace from a friend. Consequently, she has a wonderful time at the ball. Upon returning home, she realizes that she has lost the necklace. The Loisels replace it with a similar one, for which they enter into debt for ten years. One day, Mathilde sees her old friend and decides to tell her the truth, only to discover that the original necklace had been a cheap imitation. The central idea of the story is that, in the pursuit of material wealth and superficial things, people may inadvertently make their situations change for the worse.

Mathilde Loisel is shown to be a vain and ungrateful person who believes that she was born to have a better life. She feels that she has married beneath her, in spite of the fact that her husband is a hard working and dependable man. Sadly, Mathilde is unable to recognize and appreciate the good things in her life. "She had no fine clothes, no jewels, nothing; these were the only things she loved; she felt that she was made for them." In her vain attempt to appear wealthy, Mathilde actually dooms herself and her husband to years of poverty. In spite of her shortcomings, Madame Loisel is a woman of integrity; she replaces the necklace instead of disappointing her friend. Mathilde Loisel is the ideal type of character to convey the author's warning that vanity and greed can lead to a life of hardship and misery.

The central conflict in this story is between Mathilde's desire for a life of luxury and the reality of her humble lifestyle. "She suffered endlessly, feeling herself born for every delicacy and luxury." She has even given up the friendship of an old schoolmate who happens to be wealthy. Monsieur Loisel expects his wife to be thrilled about being invited to such a formal affair, but she agrees to go only after he promises to buy her a dress. The conflict comes to a head when, after a glorious evening of dancing and socializing, Mathilde realizes with horror that she has lost the borrowed necklace. Mathilde's internal conflict, between fantasy and reality, leads her into a life of abject poverty.

The author uses the omniscient point of view to offer insight which helps the reader to better understand the reasons for Mathilde Loisel's actions. The dramatic point of view would have merely shown readers a moody and vain woman, without giving any clues as to why she is so unhappy with her life. Similarly, the first person narrator would have been inappropriate. It is unlikely that Mathilde could explain that she was born for luxury and fine things without appearing insufferably arrogant. Guy de Maupassant effectively uses the omniscient point of view to show the complex personality of the central character.

The story is set in the Rue des Martyrs in Paris, France. The setting is closely tied to Mathilde's fate; she is a "martyr" to false values and pride. The period of time is unclear, but one's social standing is obviously very important. The Loisel's home is a modest one; the chairs are worn and the curtains are ugly, in stark contrast with the luxurious home Mathilde dreams of. It is ironic that Mathilde must give up the apartment she hates to move into a much smaller and less comfortable place. Additionally, as a result of the expense of replacing the necklace, Mathilde must let her maid go and do her own household chores. Her former life no longer seems so oppressive.

The author uses irony to convey the central idea. The very same item that wins for Mathilde "a victory so dear to her feminine heart" actually brings her to a lower station in life. Her vanity is the cause of her downfall and the necklace is a symbol of her vanity and her skewed sense of priorities. The author also makes use of metaphor in the story. "She suffered from the poorness of her house, from its mean walls, worn chairs, and ugly curtains." Repetition is used throughout the story; the reader learns that Mathilde is always sad, or "utterly miserable." It follows that Mathilde, in her vain attempt to glorify herself, has created a sort of prison for herself and her husband.

The author defines the tone of the story through the central character. As Mathilde creates a less favorable situation for herself, the reader may feel pity for her. The story's tone suggests that the author may have a less than favorable opinion of women. "Her tastes were simple because she had never been able to afford otherwise, but she was as unhappy as though she had married beneath her; for women have neither caste nor class—their beauty grace and charm serving them for birth or family." The false pursuit of beauty, grace and charm causes Mathilde to age beyond her years and to endure more hardship than she has ever known.

An Analysis of James Thurber's "The Secret Life of Walter Mitty"
by Roy Burgess

"The Secret Life of Walter Mitty" is the story of a man living in a fantasy world. The story begins with the Commander of a Navy hydroplane preparing to lead the plane through a hurricane. Suddenly, it becomes obvious that this is actually a fantasy in the mind of Walter Mitty. He is driving his wife to the hairdresser's. His wife expresses concern over him and his erratic driving. He drops her off and proceeds to run his errands and to fantasize again. This time he is a world-renowned surgeon who is about to perform a complicated operation. The operation runs into trouble, but Mitty manages to hold things together. The fantasy distracts Mitty from his driving; he nearly wrecks the car, and an attendant has to park it for him. Mitty's fantasies distract him to the point that he barely manages to remember his errands. He picks up his wife, who is now even more concerned with his lack of attention. The story ends with Mitty, in a fantasy again, bravely preparing to face a firing squad. The central idea of the story is that people who have difficulty dealing with reality will sometimes escape into fantasy worlds which they have created.

As the main character, Mitty is depicted as a henpecked and timid old man. He lacks aggression and is physically and emotionally weak. He is unable to stand up to his domineering, overprotective wife, who has taken charge of his life. His weak personality causes him to create fantasy personalities. In these fantasies he is a strong, bold, commanding figure who is always in control, extremely competent, and admired by beautiful women. It is this fantastic self into which he retreats when everyday life overwhelms him.

The conflict of this story is internal, between reality and fantasy. Although Mitty desires to be strong and aggressive, he lacks the will. He is intimidated by everyone and everything. His wife makes him feel weak. People accomplish things which he is unable to do. Because he is so overwhelmed by real life, he creates a world where he is respected and is in control. Unfortunately, his fantasy world makes life even more difficult for him.

The author uses the limited omniscient point of view, focusing only on Mitty's thoughts. This point of view is crucial to the success of the theme because it allows the reader to see Mitty's perception of the world around him. The reader is able to see and feel Mitty's frustration and anger at himself and the people he has contact with. This point of view also reveals Mitty's solution to his dilemma. His fantasies give the reader a good look at the man Mitty wants to be. A first person point of view would have been biased, and the dramatic point of view could not have revealed his thoughts.

The story is set in the city and also in Mitty's mind. Because of this, two different worlds are created. In the real world, the atmosphere is one of suffocation as the city seems to be closing in on Mitty. People and inanimate objects seem to ridicule him; however, in his mind, Mitty is in complete control. The situations Mitty fantasizes are situations which would easily put a person under stress. Mitty creates this environment to compensate for the dull reality of his actual life.

The language in this story is very effective. The dialogue between Mitty and his wife reveals their roles in their relationship. His wife is constantly telling him what to do and Mitty's weak responses reveal his submissive character. Mitty's dialogues in his fantasies contrast with those in his real life. He speaks more directly and more often, and he talks as if he knows what he is talking about. In Mitty's real world, the people around him are insolent. Doors make derisive sounds; buildings rise up and surround him; things close in. In his fantasy world he has a low, cool voice. He is undefeated and inscrutable. It is ironic that the fantasies which he looks to for comfort from his difficult life make life even more difficult for him. Mitty's final fantasy—facing a firing squad—is symbolic of his feelings of persecution by the world.

The tone of the story is a blend of humor and sympathy. A chaotic atmosphere is created by the rapid movement between Mitty's fantasies and reality. The reader senses the confusion in Mitty's life and the overpowering reality which causes him to retreat into a fantasy world. But the comical manner in which the bumbling Mitty repeatedly becomes a hero leaves us laughing.

An Analysis of John Steinbeck's "The Chrysanthemums" by R. C. Dumas

"The Chrysanthemums" by John Steinbeck is the story of a woman's repressed sexuality. Elisa lives with her husband on a ranch in California. They have no children and her husband has little interest in her, other than as a working partner, so Elisa lavishes all the love she has on the chrysanthemums she raises. One day, a tinker stops by. He is looking for work, but Elisa turns him down. He then compliments her on her flowers and she responds to the flattery. They talk about the flowers and as they do Elisa becomes infatuated and aroused. She quickly regains her composure and gives him pots to mend. She even gives him a pot of her precious chrysanthemums.

After the tinker leaves, Elisa prepares for her date with her husband. On their way to town, Elisa sees that the tinker has discarded the flowers she gave him. She starts to cry because of her disappointment and unfulfilled desires. The central idea of this story is that a person's feelings can be repressed only so long before exploding into expression.

The central character of this story is Elisa. The author's description of her elicits the picture of the type of sturdy woman who pioneered the American West. Her thoughts and feelings can only be inferred from her words and actions. The author does not choose to round out her character beyond the strong, attractive exterior which hides her repressed sexual desires. This is shown through the dynamic change which occurs in her from her start as the sturdy wife to the woman who cries weakly at the end. Her feelings, repressed for so long, explode into expression.

The conflict in this story is an inner conflict within the main character as she struggles to contain her emotions. The conflict develops while she and the tinker are talking; it climaxes when she is on her knees in front of him in a spasm of desire, and it is resolved as she regains her composure when the tinker does not react to her. Her weak crying at the end of the story is an apparent result of this sudden flood of emotions, contrasted with her unmet needs. She has relapsed into her ordinary life without hope of fulfillment. Without this conflict, there would be no story, no repressed feelings, no explosion of expression.

The point of view of the story is in the dramatic mode. In this mode, the reader can sense the central character's thoughts and emotions, as well as those of the more minor characters. The climax of the story is expressed in Elisa's words and actions as she becomes aroused by the tinker, and these relate to the central idea. Each reader is allowed to use his or her own emotional make-up to draw conclusions about the characters' thoughts and feelings.

The setting of this story is the Salinas Valley in rural California, and it is winter. The remoteness of the setting reflects the main character's personality and contributes to her loneliness; however, the events that occur could take place in almost any setting at any time. This universality is what makes the story a true-sounding tale of human emotion. The drabness of this setting is symbolically related to Elisa's mood and to the central idea since the remoteness contributes to her conflict.

The use of language of the story is rich in its variations. The setting is described through imagery, similes and metaphors: the image of the valley, "a pot," the metaphor of the fog, "a lid", and the simile of the plows and the earth, fertility and nature. Elisa's description of the stars educes a phallic symbol, and the chrysanthemums are symbols of the children she does not have. It is ironic that Elisa's sexual desires are aroused by this odd stranger. And it is just as ironic that he does not respond to her. The almost explicit sexual nature of Elisa's words during her flurry of emotion directly relates to the central idea by showing how feelings, repressed so long, explode into expression.

The tone of this story is one of sadness. Elisa is clearly unhappier at the end than she was in the beginning. She all but bares her soul to the tinker, but she is ignored. Through the tone, the author displays empathy for the pathos in Elisa's life. The sad tone is sympathetic to her and to the conflict she experiences. In the end, she must resign herself to continue living her drab lonely life, and nothing is gained by her attempt to achieve release from her tensions. Perhaps the greatest tragedy is her husband's almost total lack of help and understanding. At the end of the story, the sad tone is underscored by the discovery that the tinker has thrown away the chrysanthemum plant Elisa had given him, symbolic of further rejection and serving as the trigger for the explosion of repressed feelings.

ANALYSIS THROUGH A DOMINANT ELEMENT

Authors sometimes reveal their theme through a particular element. By organizing the story around a character, setting, or point of view, the reader is forced to focus on that element that is critical to the story's meaning. In the paper below, the student uses specific examples to illustrate and support the interpretation. (Compare this essay with the approach taken in our first example, which analyses the same story.)

An Analysis of Character in Guy de Maupassant's "The Necklace" by Rachel Back

"The Necklace" by Guy de Maupassant is the story of a woman of modest upbringing who dreams of being wealthy. In the story, Mathlide's pride and vanity cause her downfall. This collapse forces her to become everything she despises in order to understand the narrowness of her idea that she needs money to be happy. In understanding the symbolism of the necklace and the metamorphosis of the character's personality, Mathlide plays an essential role. Therefore, the central character is the critical element of the story. The roundness of Mathlide's personality and the dynamic change she undergoes make it possible for the reader to understand these two substantial elements.

The symbolism of the necklace would not be as profound without the awareness of Mathlide's personality. She is bewitched by the diamonds' sparkle and beauty, but does not realize that it is a mere imitation. Her ignorance regarding the quality of the jewelry proves two important things. The first is that Mathlide is the not the refined, elegant person she believes herself to be. She cannot tell a genuine diamond from a fake, which proves that despite having the necessary apparel to appear regal and wealthy, she does not have the knowledge or the discriminating taste of the truly elite. The second and more important matter that the phony necklace reveals is Mathlide's "fake" persona. She is insincere, unkind, and delights herself by believing that she is better than everyone. She endures the life of a middle-class housewife unhappily and fails to realize how fortunate she is. The omniscient narrator reveals that she feels that she married beneath her. The fact is that she married a caring man who gave up his indulgences so that she could buy a dress for the ball.

Mathlide's need to feel superior contributes to her rude and petulant attitude. An example of this is when she throws the invitation to the grand ball across the room in anger because she does not have anything proper to wear. She is angry because the invitation is a reminder of the fact that she is not an actual member of the upper echelon. Also, when Mathlide has a lovely dress, she again becomes irritated because she does not have any jewelry to wear. She says, "...there's nothing so humiliating as looking poor in the company of rich women." She chooses to blame others for her lack of self-esteem and contentment with who she is. She is constantly reminded of her lack of social standing, and reacts with anger to cover her shame.

The glittering diamond necklace is a symbol of Mathlide's dreams. She spends so much time thinking about the things that she wants that she does not take the time to appreciate what is right before her. The author devotes two paragraphs to Mathlide's daydreams of her imaginary home, which is richly decorated, filled with servants, exquisite pieces of furniture, gleaming silver, and gourmet meals. Mathlide is a dreamer, but she's lazy. She will never achieve the status that the necklace represents because she does not feel that she should work for it. The author states, "She was one of those pretty and charming women born, as though fate had blundered, into a family of junior clerks." Mathlide believes that she was meant to be a wealthy woman, but was cheated. When Mathlide sees the diamond necklace for the first time, the reader almost feels that Mathlide is familiar with it. Mathlide immediately wants the necklace because she identifies herself with the beauty and distinction of it. At this point in the story, Mathlide considers herself worthy of the necklace, not knowing that it is a cheap imitation, just as she is.

The sharpness of the central character is significant in appreciating the metamorphosis of Mathlide's personality. After losing the necklace, the change in Mathlide's life is dramatic. She becomes the kind of woman she always believed that she loathed. She does heavy housework, haggles over prices with the grocer, and dresses like a poor woman. After ten years of this toil, the debts are paid; however, Mathlide does not return to being the snobby, fretful woman she once was. She is old and hardened, but the change is more than physical. The author subtly reveals to the reader that Mathlide has a confidence that beauty or money cannot provide. She is proud of her life, of what she has accomplished, and who she is. This strength of character is so great that Mathlide is not intimidated as she approaches a still young and beautiful Madame Forestier. No longer consumed with what people will think of her clothes or status, she has the ability to regard herself equal to others, without needing to be superior. She has discovered what has eluded her for so long, that confidence and respect do not come with money. She has learned about the two types of pride, false and merited. False pride caused her downfall and merited pride brought her up out of the ashes to a place where she could assuredly hold her head high.

These elements of "The Necklace" are revealed through Maupassant's skillful development of the central character. The symbolism of the diamond necklace would be lost without the roundness of Mathlide's disposition, and the evolution of her personality would go unnoticed without the dynamic nature of her change.

ANALYSIS WITH AN EVALUATION

Judging the quality of a story requires the use of criteria that are either stated "up front" or implied in the writing. The paper below evaluates a story by measuring it against clearly stated criteria. The student says that for a story to be judged well-written it must be plausible and cohesive, and it must produce fresh insights with additional readings. Notice how the sections of the paper are divided along these lines rather than those of the elements as used with the basic approach.

An Evaluative Analysis of D.H. Lawrence's "The Rocking Horse Winner" by Gail Davis

"The Rocking Horse Winner" by D.H. Lawrence captivates the reader with its tragic story of a young boy trying to alleviate the family financial woes that have been tormenting his selfish, self-centered mother. The child eventually succumbs to death under the weight of providing sustenance to the unsustainable, a burden far too great for his young psyche. By carefully analyzing "The Rocking Horse Winner" using the criteria of plausibility, the cohesiveness of the elements, and the ability of the story to produce fresh insights with additional readings, one can declare the story exceptionally well-written.

For this story to be readily accepted by the reader, Mr. Lawrence had to allow us insight into a dysfunctional turn-of-the-century family. The characters' timeless trait of self-absorption and the belief that money will solve all of their problems give the story the needed plausibility. At the clap of hands, children are expected to appear, to perform some arbitrary function and then disappear as quickly into whatever world they can manage to create for themselves within the confines of their environment. The adults then, as now, seldom take the time to inspect that world for the dangerous signs of a loss of balance, or a child going over the edge into fantasy. In the story one can sense the young boy's desperation to appease his mother's gargantuan appetite for money. He desperately hopes that having her hunger satiated, she will perhaps find room in her heart and time in her life for her children. Alas, the gifts of both time and money seldom come hand in hand; when one has plenty of the one thing, there is seldom enough left of the other. When her maternal instinct appears to be awakening and she begins to feel at least some concern for her son, it is too late. He has sacrificed his life for her obsession with money.

Mr. Lawrence has written a story with all elements tightly woven and interdependent. The preoccupied and disengaged mother remains true to character throughout the story. She never takes a moment, until it is too late, to really pay attention to her pitifully distressed young son. The child's conceptions of the reasons for the deterioration of the family are within the simplistic reasoning of a young child. He desperately wants to "fix" things and naturally targets what would appear to a child as the most obvious solution—to acquire more money. The setting puts the family in the unenviable position of living outside their means. They are living in an upper-class neighborhood where they feel they belong, but are at a loss as to what to do to maintain their status. The conflict in the story between the material and superficial money-lust of the mother and the inability of anyone to find gainful employment to meet her demands is set with an ominous tone. The author's use of omniscient narration provides rich, probing details of the state of affairs affecting each family member.

"The Rocking Horse Winner" is a complex and deeply disturbing story that the reader is able to enjoy more with each additional reading. With more careful study, one finds nuances and subtleties that give added insight. One comes to understand the child's descent into madness and eventual collapse as the culminating inescapable trap from which no one seems capable of saving him. Initially, the mother appears to be the cause of his victimization, but one comes to understand that all of the adults are incapable, being too wrapped up in their own greedy excesses to save the boy from death. The uncle, who at first appears to have the young boy's best interest at heart, eventually ignores Paul's growing desperation as cruelly as does the mother. Even Basset, the young gardener, seemingly protective of Paul's best interest at first, becomes just one more adult dependent upon Paul to make him wealthy. Each time the story is read one can better feel the weight of everyone's happiness resting on Paul's young shoulders.

Mr. Lawrence has written a story that is as relevant and haunting today as it was when it was written over fifty years ago. It is a story that requires every reader to question what unspoken messages are being whispered about in their own homes. Mr. Lawrence's message is not only riveting, but his writing skills, which allow all elements to work together, keep the story fresh and enlightening with each successive reading.

ANALYSIS THROUGH COMPARISON AND CONTRAST

The comparison and contrast approach discusses the similarities and differences between two stories that are chosen because they have something in common—usually a central idea or an element. In this next sample, the student/author compares two stories that examine love relationships. She concludes with an evaluation, explaining why, in her opinion, one story is better than the other. Notice how she repeatedly points out the similarities and differences between the two stories and explains the reasons each author made a different choice.

A Comparative Analysis of Irwin Shaw's "The Girls in Their Summer Dresses" and Ernest Hemingway's "Hills Like White Elephants"

"The Girls in Their Summer Dresses" by Irwin Shaw is the story of a deteriorating relationship between a couple, Michael, and his wife, Frances. Frances requests that they spend the day alone, without interference from the Stevensons or other friends. As they stroll the streets of New York City, Frances notices that Michael is very busy admiring the women. Frances questions Michael concerning his preoccupation, and she seeks reassurance of his love for her. Michael reveals that he loves the way women look and when Frances asserts that one day he will be unfaithful, Michael agrees with her. Frances feels that the day is now ruined and resorts to calling the Stevensons. As Frances leaves the table, Michael admires her beauty, showing us that he thinks of his wife as just another pretty girl. Shaw's central idea is that relationships may stagnate due to a lack of communication and become relationships based solely on convenience.

"Hills Like White Elephants" by Ernest Hemingway is the story of a couple's conversation in a bar at a railroad station in Spain. As the couple consume their drinks, they speak of the girl's forthcoming operation. (Though never stated specifically, we can infer that it's an abortion.) The man repeatedly claims that the operation is solely her decision, but he states that he wants only her and that if she proceeds with the operation their relationship will revert to its former status. The man is very concerned that the girl will not go through with the operation, thus altering his present lifestyle. Hemingway's story, like Shaw's, demonstrates that honest communication is crucial to a loving relationship between people.

In both stories the characters are presented indirectly through dialogue and actions. Shaw and Hemingway create male characters who are insensitive to or inconsiderate of the feelings of the women in their lives. Michael blithely dismisses Frances' pleas for reassurance, while the American in "Hills Like White Elephants" attempts to coerce the woman to do what he wants her to do without blaming him for the consequences. Both women are insecure and concerned about their relationships, but neither is able to communicate with their partners; therefore, their futures are bleak.

The conflict in each story is between two people in a deteriorating relationships who fail to acknowledge that deterioration. Neither couple attempts to resolve their problems by further discussions; instead, they choose to ignore them.

Both stories have a dramatic point of view that requires the reader to interpret the main characters' feelings and attitudes, thereby creating a sense of intimacy between the characters and the reader. The point of view in Shaw's story shifts to the limited omniscient in the final paragraph in order to provide the important (and necessary) insight into Michael's attitude and values.

The settings of the stories are similar in that they are vague and not entirely necessary to portray the deteriorating relationships of couples. Shaw uses a clear sunny day in New York City for his setting, but as the story progresses the setting shifts to a crowded area filled with stunted trees, and the story ends in a bar. The setting in Hemingway's story remains the same: the bar in a railroad station where the land is barren and desolate. Across the tracks are a river, trees, and fertile fields, indicating the full and rich relationship the girl would like to have.

Both authors use dialogue as the primary language device to influence the reader's attitude toward the characters and show the strain in the characters' relationships. Both Shaw and Hemingway use irony and symbolism; however, Hemingway uses short sentences and phrases, whereas the sentence structure in Shaw's story is more complex. The language in both stories is tense and often sarcastic.

The tone in Shaw's story is serious and tense. Frances pleads with her husband, only to be hurt and angered by his unemotional and carefree attitude. The tone in "Hills Like White Elephants" is detached and impersonal, which parallels the failing relationship. Both stories leave the reader depressed, not only because the relationships are deteriorating, but also because none of the characters in either story makes an attempt to correct the situation.

"Hills Like White Elephants" and "The Girls in Their Summer Dresses" remind us that open communication between people is important to a relationship in order to keep the relationship from deteriorating. Both stories are well unified, but Hemingway's decision not to name the operation in "Hills Like White Elephants" and his extensive use of symbolism make this a better story because the reader is more involved with an intensive examination of the story. "Hills Like White Elephants" initially leaves the reader puzzled, but after analyzing the symbolism, we become aware of Hemingway's creativity and theme.

Selected Stories for Analysis

A & P
by John Updike

In walks these three girls in nothing but bathing suits. I'm in the third checkout slot, with my back to the door, so I don't see them until they're over by the bread. The one that caught my eye first was the one in the plaid green two-piece. She was a chunky kid, with a good tan and a sweet broad soft-looking can with these two crescents of white just under it, where the sun never seems to hit, at the top of the backs of her legs. I stood there with hand on a box of Hi Ho crackers trying to remember if I rang it up or not. I ring it up again and the customer starts giving me hell. She's one of those cash register-watchers, a witch about fifty with rouge on her cheekbones and no eye makeup. She'd been watching cash registers for fifty years and probably never seen a mistake before.

By the time I get her feathers smoothed and her goodies into a bag—she gives me a little snort in passing, if she'd been born at the right time they would have burned her over in Salem—by the time I get her on her way the girls had circled around the bread and were coming back, without a pushcart, back my way along the counters, in the aisle between the checkouts and the Special bins. They didn't even have shoes on. There was this chunky one, with the two piece—it was bright green and the seams on the bra were still sharp and her belly was still pretty pale so I guessed she just got it (the suit)—there was this one, with one of those chubby berry-faces, the lips all bunched together under her nose, this one, and a tall one, with black hair that hadn't quite frizzed right, and one of these sunburns right across under the eyes, and a chin that was too long—you know, the kind of girl the other girls think is very "striking" and "attractive" but never quite makes it, as they very well know, which is why they like her so much—and then the third one, that wasn't quite so tall. She was the queen. She kind of led them, the other two peeking around and making their shoulders round. She didn't look around, not this queen, she just walked straight on slowly, on these long white primadonna legs. She came down a little hard on her heels, as if she didn't walk in bare feet that much, putting down her heels and then letting the weight move along to her toes as if she was testing the floor with every step, putting a little deliberate extra action into it. You never know for sure how girls' minds work (do you really think it's a mind in there or just a little buzz like a bee in a glass jar?) but you got the idea she had talked the other two into coming in here with her, and now she was showing them how to do it, walk slow and hold yourself straight.

She had on a kind of dirty-pink—beige maybe, I don't know—bathing suit with a little nubble all over it and what got me, the straps were down. They were off her shoulders looped loose around the cool tops of her arms, and I guess as a result the suit had slipped a little on her, so all around the top of the cloth there was this shining rim. If it hadn't been there you wouldn't have known there could have been anything whiter than those shoulders. With the straps pushed off, there was nothing between the top of the suit and the top of her head except just her, this clean bare plane of the top of her chest down from the shoulder bones like a dented sheet of metal tilted in the light. I mean, it was more than pretty.

She had a sort of okay hair that the sun and salt had bleached, done up in a bun that was unravelling, and a kind of prim face. Walking into the A & P with the straps down, I suppose it's the only kind of face you can have. She held her head so high her neck, coming up out of those white shoulders, looked kind of stretched, but I didn't mind. The longer her neck was, the more of her there was.

She must have felt in the corner of her eye me and over my shoulder Stoksie in the second slot watching, but she didn't tip. Not this queen. She kept her eyes moving across the racks, and stopped, and turned so slow it made my stomach rub the inside of my apron, and buzzed to the other two, who kind of huddled against her for relief, and they all three of them went up the cat-and-dog-food-breakfast-cereal-macaroni-rice-raisins-seasonings-spreads-spaghetti-soft-drinks-crackers-and-cookies aisle. From the third slot I looked straight up this aisle to the meat counter, and I watched them all the way. The fat one with the tan sort of fumbled with the cookies, but on second thought she put the package back. The sheep pushing their carts down the aisle—the girls were walking against the usual traffic (not that we have one-way signs or anything)—were pretty hilarious. You could see them, when Queenie's white shoulders dawned on them, kind of jerk, or hop, or hiccup, but their eyes snapped back to their own baskets and on they pushed. I bet you could set off dynamite in an A & P and the people would by and large keep reaching and checking oatmeal off their lists and muttering "Let me see, there was a third thing, began with A, asparagus, no, ah, yes, applesauce!" or whatever it is they do mutter. But there was no doubt, this jiggled them. A few housewives in pin curlers even looked around after pushing their carts past to make sure what they had seen was correct.

You know, it's one thing to have a girl in a bathing suit down on the beach, where what with the glare nobody can look at each other much anyway, and another thing in the cool of the A & P, under the fluorescent lights, against all those stacked packages, with her feet paddling along naked over our checkerboard green-and-cream rubber floor.

"Oh Daddy," Stoksie said beside me. "I feel so faint."

"Darling," I said. "Hold me tight." Stoksie's married, with two babies chalked up on his fuselage already, but as far as I can tell that's the only difference. He's twenty-two, and I was nineteen this April.

"Is it done?" he asks, the responsible married man finding his voice. I forgot to say he thinks he's going to be manager some sunny day, maybe in 1990 when it's called the Great Alexandrov and Petrooshki Tea Company or something.

What he meant was, our town is five miles from a beach, with a big summer colony out on the Point, but we're right in the middle of town, and the women generally put on a shirt or shorts or something before they get out of the car into the street. And anyway, these are usually women with six children and varicose veins mapping their legs and nobody, including them, could care less. As I say, we're right in the middle of town and if you stand at our front doors you can see two banks and the Congregational church and the newspaper store and three real-estate offices and about twenty-seven old freeloaders tearing up Central Street because the sewer broke again. It's not as if we're on the Cape, we're north of Boston and there's people in this town haven't seen the ocean for twenty years.

The girls had reached the meat counter and were asking McMahon something. He pointed, they pointed, and they shuffled out of sight behind a pyramid of Diet Delight peaches. All that was left for us to see was old McMahon patting his mouth and looking after them sizing up their joints. Poor kids, I began to feel sorry for them, they couldn't help it.

Now here comes the sad part of the story, at least my family says it's sad, but I don't think it's so sad myself. The store's pretty empty, it being Thursday afternoon, so there was nothing much to do except lean on the register and wait for the girls to show up again. The whole store was like a pinball machine and I didn't know which tunnel they'd come out of. After a while they came around out of the far aisle, around the light bulbs, records at discount of the Caribbean Six or Tony Martin Sings or some such gunk you wonder they waste the wax on, six packs of candy bars, and plastic toys done up in cellophane that fall apart when a kid looks at them anyway. Around they come, Queenie still leading the way, and holding a little gray jar in her hand. Slots Three through Seven are unmanned and I could see her wondering between Stoksie and me, but Stoksie with his usual luck draws an old party in baggy gray pants who stumbles up with four giant cans of pineapple juice (what do these bums do with all that pineapple juice? I've often asked myself) so the girls come to me. Queenie puts down the jar and I take it into my fingers icy cold. Kingfish Fancy Herring Snacks in Pure Sour Cream: 49 cents. Now her hands are empty, not a ring or a bracelet, bare as God made them, and I wonder where the money's coming from. Still with that prim look she lifts a folded dollar bill out of the hollow at the center of her nubbled pink top. The jar went heavy in my hand. Really, I thought that was so cute.

Then everybody's luck begins to run out. Lengel comes in from haggling with a truck full of cabbages on the lot and is about to scuttle into that door marked MANAGER behind which he hides all day when the girls touch his eye. Lengel's pretty dreary, teaches Sunday school and the rest, but he doesn't miss that much. He comes over and says, "Girls, this isn't the beach."

Queenie blushes, though maybe it's just a brush of sunburn I was noticing for the first time, now that she was so close. "My mother asked me to pick up a jar of herring snacks." Her voice kind of startled me, the way voices do when you see the people first, coming out so flat and dumb yet kind of tony, too, the way it ticked over "pick up" and "snacks." All of a sudden I slid right down her voice into her living room. Her father and the other men were standing around in ice-cream coats and bow ties and the women were in sandals picking up herring snacks on toothpicks off a big glass plate and they were all holding drinks the color of water with olives and sprigs of mint in them. When my parents have somebody over they get lemonade and if it's a real racy affair Schlitz in tall glasses with "They'll Do It Every Time" cartoons stencilled on.

"That's all right," Lengel said. "But this isn't the beach." His repeating this struck me as funny, as if it had just occurred to him, and he had been thinking all these years the A & P was a great big dune and he was the head lifeguard. He didn't like my smiling—as I say he doesn't miss much—but he concentrates on giving the girls that sad Sunday-school-superintendent stare.

Queenie's blush is no sunburn now, and the plump one in plaid, that I liked better from the back—a really sweet can—pipes up, "We weren't doing any shopping. We just came in for one thing."

"That makes no difference," Lengel tells her, and I could see from the way his eyes went that he hadn't noticed she was wearing a two-piece before. "We want you decently dressed when you come in here."

"We are decent," Queenie says suddenly, her lower lip pushing, getting sore now that she remembers her place, a place from which the crowd that runs the A & P must look pretty crummy. Fancy Herring Snacks flashed in her very blue eyes.

"Girls, I don't want to argue with you. After this come in here with your shoulders covered. It's our policy." He turns his back. That's policy for you. Policy is what the kingpins want. What the others want is juvenile delinquency.

All this while, the customers had been showing up with their carts but, you know, sheep, seeing a scene, they had all bunched up on Stoksie, who shook open a paper bag as gently as peeling a peach, not wanting to miss a word. I could feel in the silence everybody getting nervous, most of all Lengel, who asks me, "Sammy, have you rung up their purchase?"

I thought and said "No" but it wasn't about that I was thinking. I go through the punches, 4, 9, GROC, TOT it's more complicated than you think, and after you do it often enough it begins to make a little song, that you hear words to, in my case "Hello (bing) there, you (gung) hap-py pee-pul (splat)!"—the splat being the drawer flying out. I uncrease the bill, tenderly as you may imagine, it just having come from between the two smoothest scoops of vanilla I had ever known there were, and pass a half and a penny into her narrow pink palm, and nestle the herrings in a bag and twist the neck and hand it over, all the time thinking.

The girls, and who'd blame them, are in a hurry to get out, so I say "I quit" to Lengel quick enough for them to hear, hoping they'll stop and watch me, their unsuspected hero. They keep right on going, into the electric eye; the door flies open and they flicker across the lot to their car. Queenie and Plaid and Big Tall Goony-Goony (not that as raw material she was so bad), leaving me with Lengel and a kink in his eyebrow.

"Did you say something, Sammy?"

"I said I quit."

"I thought you did."

"You didn't have to embarrass them."

"It was they who were embarrassing us."

I started to say something that came out "Fiddle-de-do." It's a saying of my grandmother's, and I know she would have been pleased.

"I don't think you know what you're saying," Lengel said.

"I know you don't," I said. "But I do." I pull the bow at the back of my apron and start shrugging it off my shoulders. A couple of customers that had been heading for my slot begin to knock against each other, like scared pigs in a chute.

Lengel sighs and begins to look very patient and old and gray. He's been a friend of my parents for years. "Sammy, you don't want to do this to your Mom and Dad," he tells me. It's true. I don't. But it seems to me that once you begin a gesture it's fatal not to go through with it. I fold the apron, "Sammy" stitched in red on the pocket, and put it on the counter, and drop the bow tie on top of it. The bow tie is theirs, if you've ever wondered. "You'll feel this for the rest of your life," Lengel says, and I know that's true, too, but remembering how he made that pretty girl blush makes me so scrunchy inside I punch the No Sale tab and the machine whirs "pee-pul" and the drawer splats out. One advantage to this scene taking place in summer, I can follow this up with a clean exit, there's no fumbling around getting your coat and galoshes, I just saunter into the electric eye in my white shirt that my mother ironed the night before, and the door heaves itself open, and outside the sunshine is skating around on the asphalt.

I look around for my girls, but they're gone, of course. There wasn't anybody but some young married screaming with her children about some candy they didn't get by the door of a powder-blue Falcon station wagon. Looking back in the big windows, over the bags of peat moss and aluminum lawn furniture stacked on the pavement, I could see Lengel in my place in the slot, checking the sheep through. His face was dark gray and his back stiff, as if he's just had an injection of iron, and my stomach kind of fell as I felt how hard the world was going to be to me hereafter.

ARRANGEMENT IN BLACK AND WHITE
by Dorothy Parker

The woman with the pink velvet poppies twined round the assisted gold of her hair traversed the crowded room at an interesting gait combining a skip with a sidle, and clutched the lean arm of her host.

"Now I got you!" she said. "Now you can't get away!"

"Why, hello," said her host. "Well. How are you?"

"Oh, I'm finely," she said. "Just simply finely. Listen. I want you to do me the most terrible favor. Will you? Will you please? Pretty please?"

"What is it?" said her host.

"Listen," she said. "I want to meet Walter Williams. Honestly, I'm just simply crazy about that man. Oh, when he sings! When he sings those spirituals! Well, I said to Burton, 'It's a good thing for you Walter Williams is colored,' I said, 'or you'd have lots of reason to be jealous.' I'd really love to meet him. I'd like to tell him I've heard him sing. Will you be an angel and introduce me to him?"

"Why, certainly," said her host. "I thought you'd met him. The party's for him. Where is he, anyway?"

"He's over there by the bookcase," she said. "Let's wait till those people get through talking to him. Well, I think you're simply marvelous, giving this perfectly marvelous party for him, and having him meet all these white people, and all. Isn't he terribly grateful?"

"I hope not," said her host.

"I think it's really terribly nice," she said. "I do. I don't see why on earth it isn't perfectly all right to meet colored people. I haven't any feeling at all about it not one single bit. Burton oh, he's just the other way. Well, you know, he comes from Virginia, and you know how they are."

"Did he come tonight?" said her host.

"No, he couldn't," she said. "I'm a regular grass widow tonight. I told him when I left, 'There's no telling what I'll do,' I said. He was just so tired out, he couldn't move. Isn't it a shame?"

"Ah," said her host.

"Wait till I tell him I met Walter Williams!" she said. "He'll just about die. Oh, we have more arguments about colored people. I talk to him like I don't know what, I get so excited. 'Oh, don't be so silly,' I say. But I must say for Burton, he's a heap broader-minded than lots of these Southerners. He's really awfully fond of colored people. Well, he says himself, he wouldn't have white servants. And you know, he had this old colored nurse, this regular old nigger mammy, and he just simply loves her. Why, every time he goes home, he goes out in the kitchen to see her. He does, really, to this day. All he says is, he says he hasn't got a word to say against colored people as long as they keep their place. He's always doing things for them, giving them clothes and I don't know what all. The only thing he says, he says he wouldn't sit down at the table with one for a million dollars. 'Oh,' I say to him, 'you make me sick, talking like that.' I'm just terrible to him. Aren't I terrible?"

"Oh, no, no, no," said her host. "No, no."

"I am," she said. "I know I am. Poor Burton! Now, me, I don't feel that way at all. I haven't the slightest feeling about colored people. Why, I'm just crazy about some of them. They're just like children, just as easy-going, and always singing and laughing and everything. Aren't they the happiest things you ever saw in your life? Honestly, it makes me laugh just to hear them. Oh, I like them. I really do. Well, now, listen, I have this colored laundress, I've had her for years, and I'm devoted to her. She's really a character. And I want to tell you, I think of her as my friend. That's the way I think of her. As I say to Burton, 'Well, for Heaven's sakes, we're all human beings!' Aren't we?"

"Yes," said her host. "Yes, indeed."

"Now this Walter Williams," she said. "I think a man like that's a real artist. I do. I think he deserves an awful lot of credit. Goodness, I'm so crazy about music or anything, I don't care what color he is. I honestly think if a person's an artist, nobody ought to have any feeling at all about meeting them. That's absolutely what I say to Burton. Don't you think I'm right?"

"Yes," said her host, "Oh, yes."

"That's the way I feel," she said. "I just can't understand people being narrow-minded. Why, I absolutely think it's a privilege to meet a man like Walter Williams. Yes, I do. I haven't any feeling at all. Well, my goodness, the good Lord made him, just the same as He did any of us. Didn't He?"

"Surely," said her host. "Yes, indeed."

"That's what I say," she said. "Oh, I get so furious when people are narrow-minded about colored people. It's just all I can do not to say something. Of course, I do admit when you get a bad colored man, they're simply terrible. But as I say to Burton, there are some bad white people, too, in this world. Aren't there?"

"I guess there are," said her host.

"Why, I'd really be glad to have a man like Walter Williams come to my house and sing for us, some time," she said. "Of course, I couldn't ask him on account of Burton, but I wouldn't have any feeling about it at all. Oh, can't he sing! Isn't it marvelous, the way they all have music in them? It just seems to be right in them. Come on, let's us go on over and talk to him. Listen, what shall I do when I'm introduced? Ought I to shake hands? Or what?"

"Why, do whatever you want," said her host.

"I guess maybe I'd better," she said. "I wouldn't for the world have him think I had any feeling. I think I'd better shake hands, just the way I would with anybody else. That's just exactly what I'll do."

They reached the tall young Negro, standing by the bookcase. The host performed introductions; the Negro bowed.

"How do you do?" he said.

The woman with the pink velvet poppies extended her hand at the length of her arm and held it so for all the world to see, until the Negro took it, shook it, and gave it back to her.

"Oh, how do you do, Mr. Williams," she said. "Well how do you do. I've just been saying, I've enjoyed your singing so awfully much. I've been to your concerts, and we have you on the phonograph and everything. Oh, I just enjoy it!"

She spoke with great distinctness, moving her lips meticulously, as if in parlance with the deaf.

"I'm so glad," he said.

"I'm just simply crazy about that 'Water Boy' thing you sing," she said. "Honestly, I can't get it out of my head. I have my husband nearly crazy, the way I go around humming it all the time. Oh, he looks just as black as the ace of… Well. Tell me, where on earth do you ever get all those songs of yours? How do you ever get hold of them?"

"Why," he said, "there are so many different…"

"I should think you'd love singing them," she said. "It must be more fun. All those darling old spirituals oh, I just love them! Well, what are you doing, now? Are you still keeping up your singing? Why don't you have another concert, some time?"

"I'm having one the sixteenth of this month," he said.

"Well, I'll be there," she said. "I'll be there, if I possibly can. You can count on me. Goodness, here comes a whole raft of people to talk to you. You're just a regular guest of honor! Oh, who's that girl in white? I've seen her some place."

"That's Katherine Burke," said her host.

"Good Heavens," she said. "Is that Katherine Burke? Why, she looks entirely different off the stage. I thought she was much better-looking. I had no idea she was so terribly dark. Why, she looks almost like… Oh, I think she's a wonderful actress! Don't you think she's a wonderful actress, Mr. Williams? Oh, I think she's marvelous. Don't you?"

"Yes, I do," he said.

"Oh, I do, too," she said. "Just wonderful. Well, goodness, we must give someone else a chance to talk to the guest of honor. Now, don't forget, Mr. Williams, I'm going to be at that concert if I possibly can. I'll be there applauding like everything. And if I can't come, I'm going to tell everybody I know to go, anyway. Don't you forget!"

"I won't," he said. "Thank you so much."

"Oh, my dear," she said. "I nearly died! Honestly, I give you my word, I nearly passed away. Did you hear that terrible break I made? I was just going to say Katherine Burke looked almost like a nigger. I just caught myself in time. Oh, do you think he noticed?"

"I don't believe so," said her host.

"Well, thank goodness," she said, "because I wouldn't have embarrassed him for anything. Why, he's awfully nice. Just as nice as he can be. Nice manners, and everything. You know, so many colored people, you give them an inch, and they walk all over you. But he doesn't try any of that. Well, he's got more sense, I suppose. He's really nice. Don't you think so?"

"Yes," said her host.

"I liked him," she said. "I haven't any feeling at all because he's a colored man. I felt just as natural as I would with anybody. Talked to him just as naturally, and everything. But honestly, I could hardly keep a straight face. I kept thinking of Burton. Oh, wait till I tell Burton I called him 'Mister'!"

THE BRIDE COMES TO YELLOW SKY
by Stephen Crane

Stephen Crane created the classic conflict-based western tale in this story of a small town and a gunfight that never materializes. There is an external conflict (the on-again/off-again feud between two men) and an internal conflict (the main character's anxiety about breaking the news of his marriage to his friends).

These conflicts are simple, but effective. The author sustains tension and suspense to the end, but the tone of the story suggests a second level of interpretation. Something more than a bride is coming to Yellow Sky. The bride can be interpreted as the symbol of a new age, as civilization coming to the American West.

As you read this story, look particularly at these features:

- *The conflicting forces, but not just the two men (the marshall and Scratchy), but other conflicts as well.*
- *Notice the effect the marshall's personal conflict has upon his character.*
- *The resolution of the conflict (or lack of one) has a special impact on the central idea; what is it?*
- *Note how the external conflict between the marshall and Scratchy (and the marshall's response to it) reinforces the central idea.*

I

The great Pullman was whirling onward with such dignity of motion that a glance from the window seemed simply to prove that the plains of Texas were pouring eastward. Vast flats of green grass, dull-hued spaces of mesquite and cactus, little groups of frame houses, woods of light and tender trees, all were sweeping into the east, sweeping over the horizon, a precipice.

A newly married pair had boarded this coach at San Antonio. The mans face was reddened from many days in the wind and sun, and a direct result of his new black clothes was that his brick-colored hands were constantly performing in a most conscious fashion. From time to time he looked down respectfully at his attire. He sat with a hand on each knee, like a man waiting in a barber's shop. The glances he devoted to other passengers were furtive and shy.

The bride was not pretty, nor was she very young. She wore a dress of blue cashmere, with small reservations of velvet here and there, and with steel buttons abounding. She continually twisted her head to regard her puff sleeves, very stiff, straight, and high. They embarrassed her. It was quite apparent that she had cooked, and that she expected to cook, dutifully. The blushes caused by the careless scrutiny of some passengers as she had entered the car were strange to see upon this plain, underclass countenance, which was drawn in placid, almost emotionless lines.

They were evidently very happy. "Ever been in a parlor-car before?" he asked, smiling with delight.

"No," she answered; "I never was. It's fine, ain't it?"

"Great! And then after a while we'll go forward to the diner, and get a big lay-out. Finest meal in the world. Charge a dollar."

"Oh, do they?" cried the bride. "Charge a dollar? Why, that's too much—for us—ain't it, Jack?"

"Not this trip, anyhow," he answered bravely. "We're going to go the whole thing."

Later he explained to her about the trains. "You see, it's a thousand miles from one end of Texas to the other; and this train runs right across it, and never stops but four times." He had the pride of an owner. He pointed out to her the dazzling fittings of the coach; and in truth her eyes opened wider as she contemplated the sea-green figured velvet, the shining brass, silver, and glass, the wood that gleamed as darkly brilliant as the surface of a pool of oil. At one end a bronze figure sturdily held a support for a separated chamber, and at convenient places on the ceiling were frescos in olive and silver.

To the minds of the pair, their surroundings reflected the glory of their marriage that morning in San Antonio; this was the environment of their new estate; and the mans face in particular beamed with an elation that made him appear ridiculous to the negro porter. This individual at times surveyed them from afar with an amused and superior grin. On other occasions he bullied them with skill in ways that did not make it exactly plain to them that they were being bullied. He subtly used all the manners of the most unconquerable kind of snobbery. He oppressed them; but of this oppression they had small knowledge, and they speedily forgot that infrequently a number of travelers covered them with stares of derisive enjoyment. Historically there was supposed to be something infinitely humorous in their situation.

"We are due in Yellow Sky at 3:42," he said, looking tenderly into her eyes.

"Oh, are we?" she said, as if she had not been aware of it. To evince surprise at her husbands statement was part of her wifely amiability. She took from a pocket a little silver watch; and as she held it before her, and stared at it with a frown of attention, the new husband's face shone.

"I bought it in San Anton from a friend of mine," he told her gleefully.

"It's seventeen minutes past twelve," she said, looking up at him with a kind of shy and clumsy coquetry. A passenger, noting this play, grew excessively sardonic, and winked at himself in one of the numerous mirrors.

At last they went to the dining-car. Two rows of negro waiters, in glowing white suits, surveyed their entrance with the interest, and also the equanimity, of men who had been forewarned. The pair fell to the lot of a waiter who happened to feel pleasure in steering them through their meal. He viewed them with the manner of a fatherly pilot, his countenance radiant with benevolence. The patronage, entwined with the ordinary deference, was not plain to them. And yet, as they returned to their coach, they showed in their faces a sense of escape.

To the left, miles down a long purple slope, was a little ribbon of mist where moved the keening Rio Grande. The train was approaching it at an angle, and the apex was Yellow Sky. Presently it was apparent that, as the distance from Yellow Sky grew shorter, the husband became commensurately restless. His brick-red hands were more insistent in their prominence. Occasionally he was even rather absent-minded and far-away when the bride leaned forward and addressed him.

As a matter of truth, Jack Potter was beginning to find the shadow of a deed weigh upon him like a leaden slab. He, the town marshal of Yellow Sky, a man known, liked, and feared in his corner, a prominent person, had gone to San Antonio to meet a girl he believed he loved, and there, after the usual prayers, had actually induced her to marry him, without consulting Yellow Sky for any part of the transaction. He was now bringing his bride before an innocent and unsuspecting community.

Of course people in Yellow Sky married as it pleased them, in accordance with a general custom; but such was Potter's thought of his duty to his friends, or of their idea of his duty, or of an unspoken form which does not control men in these matters, that he felt he was heinous. He had committed an extraordinary crime. Face to face with this girl in San Antonio, and spurred by his sharp impulse, he had gone headlong over all the social hedges. At San Antonio he was like a man hidden in the dark. A knife to sever any friendly duty, any form, was easy to his hand in that remote city. But the hour of Yellow Sky—the hour of daylight—was approaching.

He knew full well that his marriage was an important thing to his town. It could only be exceeded by the burning of the new hotel. His friends could not forgive him. Frequently he had reflected on the advisability of telling them by telegraph, but a new cowardice had been upon him. He feared to do it. And now the train was hurrying him toward a scene of amazement, glee, and reproach. He glanced out of the window at the line of haze swinging slowly in toward the train.

Yellow Sky had a kind of brass band, which played painfully, to the delight of the populace. He laughed without heart as he thought of it. If the citizens could dream of his prospective arrival with his bride, they would parade the band at the station and escort them, amid cheers and laughing congratulations, to his adobe home.

He resolved that he would use all the devices of speed and plainscraft in making the journey from the station to his house. Once within that safe citadel, he could issue some sort of vocal bulletin, and then not go among the citizens until they had time to wear off a little of their enthusiasm.

The bride looked anxiously at him. "What's worrying you, Jack?"

He laughed again. "I'm not worrying, girl; I'm only thinking of Yellow Sky."

She flushed in comprehension.

A sense of mutual guilt invaded their minds and developed a finer tenderness. They looked at each other with eyes softly aglow. But Potter often laughed the same nervous laugh; the flush upon the bride's face seemed quite permanent.

The traitor to the feelings of Yellow Sky narrowly watched the speeding landscape. "We're nearly there," he said.

Presently the porter came and announced the proximity of Potter's home. He held a brush in his hand, and, with all his airy superiority gone, he brushed Potter's new clothes as the latter slowly turned this way and that way. Potter fumbled out a coin and gave it to the porter, as he had seen others do. It was a heavy and muscle-bound business, as that of a man shoeing his first horse.

The porter took their bag, and as the train began to slow they moved forward to the hooded platform of the car. Presently the two engines and their long string of coaches rushed into the station of Yellow Sky.

"They have to take water here," said Potter, from a constricted throat and in mournful cadence, as one announcing death. Before the train stopped his eye had swept the length of the platform, and he was glad and astonished to see there was none upon it but the station-agent, who, with a slightly hurried and anxious air, was walking toward the water-tanks. When the train had halted, the porter alighted first, and placed in position a little temporary step.

"Come on, girl," said Potter, hoarsely. As he helped her down they each laughed on a false note. He took the bag from the negro, and bade his wife cling to his arm. As they slunk rapidly away, his hang-dog glance perceived that they were unloading the two trunks, and also that the station-agent, far ahead near the baggage-car, had turned and was running toward him, making gestures. He laughed, and groaned as he laughed, when he noted the first effect of his marital bliss upon Yellow Sky. He gripped his wife's arm firmly to his side, and they fled. Behind them the porter stood, chuckling fatuously.

II

The California express on the Southern Railway was due at Yellow Sky in twenty-one minutes. There were six men at the bar of the Weary Gentleman Saloon. One was a drummer, who talked a great deal and rapidly; three were Texans, who did not care to talk at that time; and two were Mexican sheep-herders, who did not talk as a general practice in the Weary Gentleman Saloon. The barkeeper's dog lay on the board walk that crossed in front of the door. His head was on his paws, and he glanced drowsily here and there with the constant vigilance of a dog that is kicked on occasion. Across the sandy street were some vivid green grass-plots, so wonderful in appearance, amid the sands that burned near them in a blazing sun, that they caused a doubt in the mind. They exactly resembled the grass mats used to represent lawns on the stage. At the cooler end of the railway station, a man without a coat sat in a tilted chair and smoked his pipe. The fresh-cut bank of the Rio Grande circled near the town, and there could be seen beyond it a great plum-colored plain of mesquite.

Save for the busy drummer and his companions in the saloon, Yellow Sky was dozing. The new-comer leaned gracefully upon the bar and recited many tales with the confidence of a bard who has come upon a new field.

"—and at the moment that the old man fell down-stairs with the bureau in his arms, the old woman was coming up with two scuttles of coal, and of course—"

The drummer's tale was interrupted by a young man who suddenly appeared in the open door. He cried: "Scratchy Wilson's drunk, and has turned loose with both hands." The two Mexicans at once set down their glasses and faded out of the rear entrance of the saloon.

The drummer, innocent and jocular, answered: "All right, old man. S'pose he has? Come in and have a drink, anyhow."

But the information had made such an obvious cleft in every skull in the room that the drummer was obliged to see its importance. All had become instantly solemn. "Say," said he, mystified, "what is this?" His three companions made the introductory gesture of eloquent speech; but the young man at the door forestalled them.

"It means, my friend," he answered, as he came into the saloon, "that for the next two hours this town won't be a health resort."

The barkeeper went to the door, and locked and barred it; reaching out of the window, he pulled in heavy wooden shutters, and barred them. Immediately a solemn, chapel-like gloom was upon the place. The drummer was looking from one to another.

"But say," he cried, "what is this, anyhow? You don't mean there is going to be a gun-fight?"

"Don't know whether there'll be a fight or not," answered one man, grimly; "but there'll be some shootin—some good shootin."

The young man who had warned them waved his hand. "Oh, there'll be a fight fast enough, if any one wants it. Anybody can get a fight out there in the street. There's a fight just waiting."

The drummer seemed to be swayed between the interest of a foreigner and a perception of personal danger.

"What did you say his name was?" he asked.

"Scratchy Wilson," they answered in chorus.

"And will he kill anybody? What are you going to do? Does this happen often? Does he rampage around like this once a week or so? Can he break in that door?"

"No; he can't break down that door," replied the barkeeper. "He's tried it three times. But when he comes you'd better lay down on the floor, stranger. He's dead sure to shoot at it, and a bullet may come through."

Thereafter the drummer kept a strict eye upon the door. The time had not yet been called for him to hug the floor, but, as a minor precaution, he sidled near to the wall. "Will he kill anybody?" he said again.

The men laughed low and scornfully at the question.

"He's out to shoot, and He's out for trouble. Don't see any good in experimentin with him."

"But what do you do in a case like this? What do you do?"

A man responded: "Why, he and Jack Potter—"

"But," in chorus the other men interrupted, "Jack Potter's in San Anton."

"Well, who is he? What's he got to do with it?"

"Oh, he's the town marshal. He goes out and fights Scratchy when he gets on one of these tears."

"Wow!" said the drummer, mopping his brow. "Nice job he's got."

The voices had toned away to mere whisperings. The drummer wished to ask further questions, which were born of an increasing anxiety and bewilderment; but when he attempted them, the men merely looked at him in irritation and motioned him to remain silent. A tense waiting hush was upon them. In the deep shadows of the room their eyes shone as they listened for sounds from the street. One man made three gestures at the barkeeper; and the latter, moving like a ghost, handed him a glass and a bottle. The man poured a full glass of whisky, and set down the bottle noiselessly. He gulped the whisky in a swallow, and turned again toward the door in immovable silence. The drummer saw that the barkeeper, without a sound, had taken a Winchester from beneath the bar. Later he saw this individual beckoning to him, so he tiptoed across the room.

"You better come with me back of the bar."

"No, thanks," said the drummer, perspiring; "I'd rather be where I can make a break for the back door."

Whereupon the man of bottles made a kindly but peremptory gesture. The drummer obeyed it, and, finding himself seated on a box with his head below the level of the bar, balm was laid upon his soul at sight of various zinc and copper fittings that bore a resemblance to armor-plate. The barkeeper took a seat comfortably upon an adjacent box.

"You see," he whispered, "this here Scratchy Wilson is a wonder with a gun—a perfect wonder; and when he goes on the wartrail, we hunt our holes—naturally. He's about the last one of the old gang that used to hang out along the river here. He's a terror when he s drunk. When he's sober he's all right—kind of simple—wouldn't hurt a fly—nicest fellow in town. But when he's drunk—whoo!"

There were periods of stillness. "I wish Jack Potter was back from San Anton," said the barkeeper. "He shot Wilson up once,—in the leg,—and he would sail in and pull out the kinks in this thing."

Presently they heard from a distance the sound of a shot, followed by three wild yowls. It instantly removed a bond from the men in the darkened saloon. There was a shuffling of feet. They looked at each other. "Here he comes," they said.

III

A man in a maroon-colored flannel shirt, which had been purchased for purposes of decoration, and made principally by some Jewish women on the East Side of New York, rounded a corner and walked into the middle of the main street of Yellow Sky. In either hand the man held a long, heavy, blue-black revolver. Often he yelled, and these cries rang through a semblance of a deserted village, shrilly flying over the roofs in a volume that seemed to have no relation to the ordinary vocal strength of a man. It was as if the surrounding stillness formed the arch of a tomb over him. These cries of ferocious challenge rang against walls of silence. And his boots had red tops with gilded imprints, of the kind beloved in winter by little sledding boys on the hillsides of New England.

The man's face flamed in a rage begot of whisky. His eyes, rolling, and yet keen for ambush, hunted the still doorways and windows. He walked with the creeping movement of the midnight cat. As it occurred to him, he roared menacing information. The long revolvers in his hands were as easy as straws;

they were moved with an electric swiftness. The little fingers of each hand played sometimes in a musician's way. Plain from the low collar of the shirt, the cords of his neck straightened and sank, straightened and sank, as passion moved him. The only sounds were his terrible invitations. The calm adobes preserved their demeanor at the passing of this small thing in the middle of the street.

There was no offer of fight—no offer of fight. The man called to the sky. There were no attractions. He bellowed and fumed and swayed his revolvers here and everywhere.

The dog of the barkeeper of the Weary Gentleman Saloon had not appreciated the advance of events. He yet lay dozing in front of his master's door. At sight of the dog, the man paused and raised his revolver humorously. At sight of the man, the dog sprang up and walked diagonally away, with a sullen head, and growling. The man yelled, and the dog broke into a gallop. As it was about to enter an alley, there was a loud noise, a whistling, and something spat the ground directly before it. The dog screamed, and, wheeling in terror, galloped headlong in a new direction. Again there was a noise, a whistling, and sand was kicked viciously before it. Fear-stricken, the dog turned and flurried like an animal in a pen. The man stood laughing, his weapons at his hips.

Ultimately the man was attracted by the closed door of the Weary Gentleman Saloon. He went to it, and, hammering with a revolver, demanded drink.

The door remaining imperturbable, he picked a bit of paper from the walk, and nailed it to the framework with a knife. He then turned his back contemptuously upon this popular resort, and, walking to the opposite side of the street, and spinning there on his heel quickly and lithely, fired at the bit of paper. He missed it by a half-inch. He swore at himself, and went away. Later he comfortably fusilladed the windows of his most intimate friend. The man was playing with this town; it was a toy for him.

But still there was no offer of fight. The name of Jack Potter, his ancient antagonist, entered his mind, and he concluded that it would be a glad thing if he should go to Potter's house, and by bombardment induce him to come out and fight. He moved in the direction of his desire, chanting Apache scalp-music.

When he arrived at it, Potter's house presented the same still front as had the other adobes. Taking up a strategic position, the man howled a challenge. But this house regarded him as might a great stone god. It gave no sign. After a decent wait, the man howled further challenges, mingling with them wonderful epithets.

Presently there came the spectacle of a man churning himself into deepest rage over the immobility of a house. He fumed at it as the winter wind attacks a prairie cabin in the North. To the distance there should have gone the sound of a tumult like the fighting of two hundred Mexicans. As necessity bade him, he paused for breath or to reload his revolvers.

IV

Potter and his bride walked sheepishly and with speed. Sometimes they laughed together shamefacedly and low.

"Next corner, dear," he said finally.

They put forth the efforts of a pair walking bowed against a strong wind. Potter was about to raise a finger to point the first appearance of the new home when, as they circled the corner, they came face to face with a man in a maroon-colored shirt, who was feverishly pushing cartridges into a large revolver. Upon the instant the man dropped his revolver to the ground, and, like lightning, whipped another from its holster. The second weapon was aimed at the bridegroom's chest.

There was a silence. Potter's mouth seemed to be merely a grave for his tongue. He exhibited an instinct to at once loosen his arm from the woman's grip, and he dropped the bag to the sand. As for the bride, her face had gone as yellow as old cloth. She was a slave to hideous rites, gazing at the apparitional snake.

The two men faced each other at a distance of three paces. He of the revolver smiled with a new and quiet ferocity.

"Tried to sneak up on me," he said. "Tried to sneak up on me!" His eyes grew more baleful. As Potter made a slight movement, the man thrust his revolver venomously forward. "No; don't you do it, Jack Potter. Don't you move a finger toward a gun just yet. Don't you move an eyelash. The time has come for me to settle with you, and I'm goin' to do it my own way, and loaf along with no interferin'. So if you don't want a gun bent on you, just mind what I tell you."

Potter looked at his enemy. "I ain't got a gun on me, Scratchy," he said. "Honest, I ain't." He was stiffening and steadying, but yet somewhere at the back of his mind a vision of the Pullman floated: the sea-green figured velvet, the shining brass, silver, and glass, the wood that gleamed as darkly brilliant as the surface of a pool of oil—all the glory of the marriage, the environment of the new estate. "You know I fight when it comes to fighting, Scratchy Wilson; but I ain't got a gun on me. You'll have to do all the shootin' yourself."

His enemy's face went livid. He stepped forward, and lashed his weapon to and fro before Potter's chest. "Don't you tell me you ain't got no gun on you, you whelp. Don't tell me no lie like that. There ain't a man in Texas ever seen you without no gun. Don't take me for no kid." His eyes blazed with light, and his throat worked like a pump.

"I ain't takin' you for no kid," answered Potter. His heels had not moved an inch backward. "I'm takin' you for a damn fool. I tell you I ain't got a gun, and I ain't. If you're goin' to shoot me up, you better begin now; you'll never get a chance like this again."

So much enforced reasoning had told on Wilson's rage; he was calmer. "If you ain't got a gun, why ain't you got a gun?" he sneered. "Been to Sunday-school?"

"I ain't got a gun because I've just come from San Anton with my wife. I'm married," said Potter. "And if I'd thought there was going to be any galoots like you prowling around when I brought my wife home, I'd had a gun, and don't you forget it."

"Married!" said Scratchy, not at all comprehending.

"Yes, married. I'm married," said Potter, distinctly.

"Married!" said Scratchy. Seemingly for the first time, he saw the drooping, drowning woman at the other man's side.

"No!" he said. He was like a creature allowed a glimpse of another world. He moved a pace backward, and his arm, with the revolver, dropped to his side. "Is this the lady?" he asked.

"Yes; this is the lady," answered Potter.

There was another period of silence.

"Well," said Wilson at last, slowly, "I s'pose it's all off now."

"It's all off if you say so Scratchy. You know I didn't make the trouble." Potter lifted his valise.

"Well, I 'low it's off, Jack," said Wilson. He was looking at the ground. "Married!" He was not a student of chivalry; it was merely that in the presence of this foreign condition he was a simple child of the earlier plains. He picked up his starboard revolver, and, placing both weapons in their holsters, he went away. His feet made funnel-shaped tracks in the heavy sand.

CARLYLE TRIES POLYGAMY
by William Melvin Kelley

For a while anyway an Africamerican man named Carlyle Bedlow lived in one large, sunny room in a brownstone on lower Edgecombe Avenue in Harlem, U.S.A. Like many men he had a polygamous nature, which did not make him promiscuous. And neither had he married. But over the years he usually seemed to have two or three steady lady friends.

Often they overlapped, and sometimes they repeated. First he would have one woman, for example Glora Glamus. Then he would meet another one, like Senegale Miller. Then he would shuttle back and forth between the two. On the way he might meet a third. Then he would shuttle around among the three, travelling from the Bronx to Manhattan to Brooklyn. Then the first woman would get tired of his intermittency and break it off. Then he would meet another woman shuttling back and forth between the second two. Occasionally he would disappear to his room in Harlem, where he lived alone and never let anyone visit except his brother and his widowed mother, who rarely came because she did not like climbing the three flights of steps to his room.

Carlyle Bedlow kept his room neat and clean. Since he never entertained any women there, he had a firm narrow bed, which he made up into a couch each morning. His clothes he kept in a large closet and three black footlockers. A high-grade Navajo rug (handmade by the Etcitty sisters) covered the polished-wood floor. In the corner near the window sat an EzeeGuy chair, where by sunlight or lamp he would relax and read science-fiction novels, a pile of which he stacked beside the chair.

Sometimes he would look up from his reading and think about the two more or less steady lady friends he had kept for the past ten years. Actually Glora had occupied a place in his heart for about thirty years. In the beginning he loved her madly but could not win her because she loved Carlyle's mentor in the hustling life, the society baker and contract killer C. C. (Cooley) Johnson. Eventually, when she realized that Cooley Johnson would never love anybody, she and Carlyle began a relationship that produced a daughter, Carlotta, now twelve years old. Carlyle and Glora had broken it off fifty times, but had made up fifty-one times. Besides, they both adored Carlotta. So did Carlyle's mother, though she did not like professional barmaid Glora, considering her barky and brassy and boastful.

The second lady friend in Carlyle's life had a child for him as well, an eight-year-old daughter names Mali. He had met Mali's mama, Senegale Miller, at a jump-up given by the Rastafarian bredda who supplied high-quality society clientele, affluent former Woodstockians who had returned to the lap of luxury but secretly still smoked the blessed herb and did not want the world to know it.

Senegale Miller possessed luxuriant glistening black dreadlocks reaching to the small of her back which had never known scissors or comb. Raised in the cockpit country of Arawaka and descended from Maroons (who fought their way out of slavery in the seventeen-thirties), she had not worn shoes until coming to America. She stood six feet tall in her smooth cocoa-buttered chocolate-colored skin and had the grace of a seal in water. Carlyle's mother did not like Senegale either, mostly because she could not understand her thick accent, but, as she did with Carlotta, she showered Mali with gifts.

Carlotta and Mali got along very well, better than most big and little sisters. Sometimes Carlyle borrowed his brother's RoadStar sedan and without telling their mothers took the two girls anywhere they wanted to go, the beach or zoo or circus or rodeo or amusement park. He walked behind them, an unobtrusive shepherd, enjoying the sight of them whispering, cavorting, holding hands.

Recently their mothers had become jealous of each other. They had known of each other for the past three years, when Senegale had tracked him down to Glora's house in the Bronx, demanding money for Mali's school uniforms. Before that, he had kept them separated in different parts of the city, Senegale in Brooklyn and Glora in the Bronx. Once they learned about each other, they did not stop talking and asking about each other.

In the Bronx, Glora might inquire, "When you getting your monkey woman to cut off that bush of hair and get a regular look, baby?"

In Brooklyn, Senegale would comment, "Is only a foolfool woulda make him babymudda to work into said wicked atmosphere, man no see it."

In the Bronx, Glora might wonder, "Why you don't go to court for custody of that cute little Mali, then report that bitch to immigration?"

In Brooklyn, Senegale would ponder, "Why you must keep on with the old woman when you kyan find rest and fulfillment in I-arm of this daughter of King Solomon?"

At times the verbal struggle they waged in his ears became so intense that Carlyle would retreat to his sunny Harlem room and rest in his EzeeGuy until his ears repaired themselves. He would not see either woman for a week. His brother, who knew something of his dilemma, told him that the blessed Koran gave a man permission to maintain four women, which did not help. Carlyle could barely manage two.

"Then you must cut one loose, my brother. Keep the relationship with your offspring, but call it off with one of the mothers." His brother had decided to wait till the Provider sent him a woman, abstaining from sex for several years, though Carlyle suspected he had a woman stashed somewhere. "You must choose!"

But Carlyle loved both women, Glora for her mocha beauty and her fast mouth, Senegal for her chocolate beauty and her independent spirit, and could not choose between them. Reclining in his EzeeGuy, he would puff a spliff and try to envision life without one or the other of them. He had always loved Glora; Senegale had stomped into his life with her goofy believe in the divinity of Ethiopia just when he started to get sour, making him aware of some motivating force in the world besides money. Until Senegale came along he had not known how much he loved Glora, because falling in love with Senegale reminded him that he had love inside himself to give. So suddenly he also found himself in love with Glora again.

Carlyle could not decide between them. But something had to change. Then one day he encountered Brother Ben selling juice and astrology books at the corner of 125th Street and Frederick Douglass, and the brother launched into his tired polygamy rap, which goes:

Vietnam + Homosexuality + Prison + Heroin + AIDS + Crack had so reduced the male Africamerican population as to make polygamy the only way for Africamerican culture to sustain itself. Each man had to accept his responsibility. Each woman had to realize that only by accepting the other woman in her man's life could she get a man to call her own. Then of course once a man had gathered his women together he might organize them to make dried-flower arrangements or some such product—

"But Brother Ben," Carlyle interrupted. "You have a nuclear family under your own roof, a wife you've loved for years and two beautiful daughters like mine. And besides, no other woman would have you!"

Brother Ben blinked but continued his rap undeterred as Carlyle ambled away. But Brother Ben had made one usable point: perhaps Carlyle should bring together his two warring lady friends for a sitdown. Given them the opportunity to say bad things to each other face to face without making Carlyle's brain the battleground. Perhaps they could work out what he could not. At least they might blow off some bad gas.

Carlyle arranged to have both meet him on a Tuesday evening at one of Harlem's few surviving gems, the Golden Grouse Bar Restaurant. He liked breakfast better than dinner at the Grouse but did not expect anybody to eat very much. However, red-clad Glora tipped in first and quick ordered an immense fried-chicken dinner with scalloped potatoes and tossed salad and peach cobbler and the Grouse's special punch. Before the food had arrived, Senegale appeared in olive drab, her dreadlocks wrapped (out and back like a praying mantis) in the Nationalists colors. She carried various tubs of her own I-tall delicacies because she did not trust the cook at the Grouse to keep the bacon grease out of the peanut oil.

The two women sat silently glaring across the table at each other and consumed all that the waitress and Senegal had carried to the table, near the end of the thirty-minute meal Senegale sampling the peach cobbler and Glora quenching her thirst with the homemade ginger beer. Together they covered their belches and tittered.

Then they both put fire under his sorry brown butt! "Thought the sight of this simple country cow pie would do what? But make I tell all the world that I-woman never fear no old higgler till yet, no see it! Sure don't see what jive hustle he think he pulling with this tired B.S. but this sister came a long way to tell eÆvrybody that this just won't hardly go down! Because I-love that I-woman keeping for said man spring from the most high mountain of New Zion! Besides this brother have deluded himself into thinking that because I love him that mean I need him when he be too dim to see I got my own house on Barnes Avenue in the Bronx all bought and paid for with mops and tips, and also got by far the best of his never-do-nothing buttocks in his daughter Carlotta. Which I-sister kyan strenuously affirm and illustrate as him give I-woman nothing of value but sweet likkle Mali, and she quite valu-able." They glowered at him.

So now what, bumbasukka?

"I just wanted to see if we all couldn't maybe find a way to get along," Carlyle said simple. "I can't help myself but I love you both. And I been mainly true to you two for the past ten years." He heard and despised the quite desperation in his voice. "I mean, the kids don't seem to defend each other."

The women agreed. Dem two pickney hitch up like sea and sand, no see it. Looking so cute and fly in they little matching outfits, hooking it up on the phone when this fool think he sneaking them out on the sly to take them someplace like my child don't come tell her mama ev'ry ting that be goin' on, turkey! All the while dem aburn up phone wire, no see it, talkin' bout my sister dis and my sister dat, Carlotta why and Carlotta what for. And many times Carlotta have said, 'Mama, shy can't Mali spend the night?'"

Well they could certainly agree to arrange that. Senegal expressed her gratitude that Mali would spend time on safer Bronx streets than those in the part of Brooklyn in which she presently resided where posses marauded in broad daylight and as soon as she found suitable accommodations, perhaps with members of her extended family in New Jersey, she would willingly offer similar hospitality to Carlotta. Strangely enough, Glora's aforementioned two-family semi-detached featured a smaller second-floor space, which she had recently listed with Sister Edward's Realty, seeking tenants, five hundred dollars a month for two-bedrooms-kitchen-living-room-bath, use of washer-dryer, easy walking distance to the I.R.T.ùbut Senegale knew the way because she had already visited there at least once. They shook on it, bracelets and bangles jangling

On the first of the following month, two jaunty I-dren driving a yellow van, puffing spliffs and blasting St. Donald Drummond and the Skatalites on their trunk-size cassette player, delivered Senegal and Mali Miller, along with two mahogany beds, a sofa and an overstuffed chair, a dish cabinet, a kitchen table and chairs, large cartons of clothes, books, utensils, dishes and pots, a cast-iron Dutchie, tools, raffia, leather hides for belts and sandals, and one calico puss cat named Kiki, to chez Glora Glamus, Bronx, N.Y. Soon the house filled with incessant female activity. Carlotta and Mali and their girlfriends (neighborhood pre-teens quickly forming a crew) seemed to make no distinction upstairs and downstairs, roaming freely throughout every room under the roof, as likely to sleep in one as in the other of their two bedrooms, eating wherever hunger and opportunity struck them, though both avoided Glora's rhubarb pie as well as Senegale's steamed okra. And the two women began to take the step-aerobics class and do weights at the local NU-BODi exercise salon on White Plains Road, working off their stress and excess energy with the rest of the sisters. Around the corner on Paulding Avenue, Carlyle's mother loved living near to both of her two darlings, though she still barely tolerated their mothers.

After completing his hustling chores, Carlyle Bedlow spends more time in his one large room in the brownstone on lower Edgecombe Avenue, Harlem, U.S.A. Since he no longer travels to Brooklyn except on business to the Promenade or Park Slope, and can visit his two daughters at one address, he gets to see them both more often than in the days before polygamy, a definite improvement in his life. But now that his two lady friends live within whispering distance of each other Carlyle finds his sexual style stunted. Whenever he hopes to bed down with one woman, he knows the other woman knows his exact whereabouts and keeps expecting one or the other of the kids to burst through the door. Occasionally he gets over. But more often than not cool winds sweep his loins. The woman load him with lists of things to do and buy. He completes his errands for them, then returns to the solitude and quiet of his room. His brother visits, assuring him that Carlyle has done the honest, manly thing, brought out everything into the open, creating a healthier environment for his children, that with each woman knowing where she fits into the Grand Scheme, they will all live happily ever after. For a while anyway.

THE CASK OF AMONTILLADO

by Edgar Allan Poe

Edgar Allan Poe, master of the macabre, uses settings to achieve a mood of horror and fear. He wants us to feel "creepy," as in the example that follows. Because the story was written over one hundred years ago, many readers are not familiar with some of the references. Amontillado is a fine and rare wine; sherry is a very common, cheap wine. And connoisseurs of wines store them in cellars. In the past, these cellars were often the same caves or rooms in which the bodies of the dead were placed. Called "catacombs," they were dug under the resident's home and were often deep and winding. These places were used to store wine and bodies because of the constant cool temperature, which helped to preserve them. Carnival season, in many parts of the world, is a time of madness, when the crazier side of people is allowed free reign.

The language of the story is especially notable. Though it reflects the formal language of the time, it is also part of Poe's technique for establishing the tone. He was so successful that this kind of formal language has now come to be associated with the classic horror story.

This is one of those stories that reveals more on a second reading. Once you know where it's going, you can better appreciate the irony of the dialogue. Consider, especially, the following:

- *When and where the story occurs; it helps to set the mood.*
- *The setting also refers to a historic tradition and important social conditions; notice what they add to the tale.*
- *The setting changes early on. Notice how that change is pertinent to the story (especially in the way one setting contrasts with the other.*
- *There's a close relationship between the setting and the central idea; can you tell what that is?*
- *The setting (time of the year) also relates to the main character's personality; some might argue that it influenced his behavior.*

The thousand injuries of Fortunato I had borne as I best could, but when he ventured upon insult I vowed revenge. You, who so well know the nature of my soul, will not suppose, however, that I gave utterance to a threat. At length I would be avenged; this was a point definitely settled—but the very definitiveness with which it was resolved precluded the idea of risk. I must not only punish but punish with impunity. A wrong is unredressed when retribution overtakes its redresser. It is equally unredressed when the avenger fails to make himself felt as such to him who has done the wrong.

It must be understood that neither by word nor deed had I given Fortunato cause to doubt my good will. I continued, as was my wont, to smile in his face, and he did not perceive that my smile now was at the thought of his immolation.

He had a weak point—this—Fortunato although in other regards he was a man to be respected and even feared. He prided himself on his connoisseurship in wine. Few Italians have the true virtuoso spirit. For the most part their enthusiasm is adopted to suit the time and opportunity, to practise imposture upon the British and Austrian millionaires. In painting and gemmary, Fortunato, like his countrymen, was a quack, but in the matter of old wines he was sincere. In this respect I did not differ from him materially;—I was skillful in the Italian vintages myself, and bought largely whenever I could.

It was about dusk, one evening during the supreme madness of the carnival season, that I encountered my friend. He accosted me with excessive warmth, for he had been drinking much. The man wore motley. He had on a tight-fitting parti-striped dress, and his head was surmounted by the conical cap and bells. I was so pleased to see him that I thought I should never have done wringing his hand.

I said to him—"My dear Fortunato, you are luckily met. How remarkably well you are looking to-day. But I have received a pipe of what passes for Amontillado, and I have my doubts."

"How?" said he. "Amontillado? A pipe? Impossible! And in the middle of the carnival!"

"I have my doubts," I replied; "and I was silly enough to

pay the full Amontillado price without consulting you in the matter. You were not to be found, and I was fearful of losing a bargain."

"Amontillado!"

"I have my doubts."

"Amontillado!"

"And I must satisfy them."

"Amontillado!"

"As you are engaged, I am on my way to Luchresi. If any one has a critical turn it is he. He will tell me—"

"Luchresi cannot tell Amontillado from Sherry."

"And yet some fools will have it that his taste is a match for your own."

"Come, let us go."

"Whither?"

"To your vaults."

"My friend, no; I will not impose upon your good nature. I perceive you have an engagement. Luchresi—"

"I have no engagement;—come."

"My friend, no. It is not the engagement, but the severe cold with which I perceive you are afflicted. The vaults are insufferably damp. They are encrusted with nitre."

"Let us go, nevertheless. The cold is merely nothing. Amontillado! You have been imposed upon. And as for Luchresi, he cannot distinguish Sherry from Amontillado."

Thus speaking, Fortunato possessed himself of my arm; and putting on a mask of black silk and drawing a roquelaire closely about my person, I suffered him to hurry me to my palazzo.

There were no attendants at home; they had absconded to make merry in honor of the time. I had told them that I should not return until the morning, and had given them explicit orders not to stir from the house. These orders were sufficient, I well knew, to insure their immediate disappearance, one and all, as soon as my back was turned.

I took from their sconces two flambeaux, and giving one to Fortunato, bowed him through several suites of rooms to the archway that led into the vaults. I passed down a long and winding staircase, requesting him to be cautious as he followed. We came at length to the foot of the descent, and stood together upon the damp ground of the catacombs of the Montresors.

The gait of my friend was unsteady, and the bells upon his cap jingled as he strode.

"The pipe," he said.

"It is farther on," said I; "but observe the white web-work which gleams from these cavern walls."

He turned towards me, and looked into my eyes with two filmy orbs that distilled the rheum of intoxication.

"Nitre?" he asked at length.

"Nitre," I replied. "How long have you had that cough?"

"Ugh! ugh! ugh!—ugh! ugh! ugh!—ugh! ugh! ugh!—ugh! ugh! ugh!—ugh! ugh! ugh!"

My poor friend found it impossible to reply for many minutes.

"It is nothing," he said at last.

"Come," I said, with decision, "we will go back; your health is precious. You are rich, respected, admired, beloved; you are happy, as once I was. You are a man to be missed. For me it is no matter. We will go back; you will be ill, and I cannot be responsible. Besides, there is Luchresi—"

"Enough," he said; "the cough is a mere nothing; it will not kill me. I shall not die of a cough."

"True—true," I replied; "and, indeed, I had no intention of alarming you unnecessarily—but you should use all proper caution. A draught of this Medoc will defend us from the damps."

Here I knocked off the neck of a bottle which I drew from a long row of its fellows that lay upon the mould.

"Drink," I said, presenting him the wine.

He raised it to his lips with a leer. He paused and nodded to me familiarly, while his bells jingled.

"I drink," he said, "to the buried that repose around us."

"And I to your long life."

He again took my arm, and we proceeded.

"These vaults," he said, "are extensive."

"The Montresors," I replied, "were a great and numerous family."

"I forget your arms."

"A huge human foot d'or, in a field azure; the foot crushes a serpent rampant whose fangs are imbedded in the heel."

"And the motto?"

"Nemo me impune lacessit." [No one attacks me with impunity.]

"Good!" he said.

The wine sparkled in his eyes and the bells jingled. My own fancy grew warm with the Medoc. We had passed through long walls of piled skeletons, with casks and puncheons intermingling, into the inmost recesses of the catacombs. I paused again, and this time I made bold to seize Fortunato by an arm above the elbow.

"The nitre!" I said; "see, it increases. It hangs like moss upon the vaults. We are below the rivers bed. The drops of moisture trickle among the bones. Come, we will go back ere it is too late. Your cough—"

"It is nothing," he said; "let us go on. But first, another draught of the Medoc."

I broke and reached him a flagon of De Grave. He emptied it at a breath. His eyes flashed with a fierce light. He laughed and threw the bottle upwards with a gesticulation I did not understand.

I looked at him in surprise. He repeated the movement—a grotesque one.

"You do not comprehend?" he said.

"Not I," I replied.

"Then you are not of the brotherhood."

"How?"

"You are not of the masons."

"Yes, yes," I said; "yes, yes."

"You? Impossible! A mason?"

"A mason," I replied.

"A sign," he said, "a sign."

"It is this," I answered, producing from beneath the folds of my roquelaire a trowel.

"You jest," he exclaimed, recoiling a few paces. "But let us proceed to the Amontillado."

"Be it so," I said, replacing the tool beneath the cloak and again offering him my arm. He leaned upon it heavily. We continued our route in search of the Amontillado. We passed through a range of low arches, descended, passed on, and descending again, arrived at a deep crypt, in which the foulness of the air caused our flambeaux rather to glow than flame.

At the most remote end of the crypt there appeared another less spacious. Its walls had been lined with human remains, piled to the vault overhead, in the fashion of the great catacombs of Paris. Three sides of this interior crypt were still ornamented in this manner. From the fourth side the bones had been thrown down, and lay promiscuously upon the earth, forming at one point a mound of some size. Within the wall thus exposed by the displacing of the bones, we perceived a still interior crypt or recess, in depth about four feet, in width three, in height six or seven. It seemed to have been constructed for no special use within itself, but formed merely the interval between two of the colossal supports of the roof of the catacombs, and was backed by one of their circumscribing walls of solid granite.

It was in vain that Fortunato, uplifting his dull torch, endeavored to pry into the depth of the recess. Its termination the feeble light did not enable us to see.

"Proceed," I said; "herein is the Amontillado. As for Luchresi—"

"He is an ignoramus," interrupted my friend, as he stepped unsteadily forward, while I followed immediately at his heels. In an instant he had reached the extremity of the niche, and finding his progress arrested by the rock, stood stupidly bewildered. A moment more and I had fettered him to the granite. In its surface were two iron staples, distant from each other about two feet, horizontally. From one of these depended a short chain, from the other a padlock. Throwing the links about his waist, it was but the work of a few seconds to secure it. He was too much astounded to resist. Withdrawing the key I stepped back from the recess.

"Pass your hand," I said, "over the wall; you cannot help feeling the nitre. Indeed, it is very damp. Once more let me implore you to return. No? Then I must positively leave you. But I must first render you all the little attentions in my power."

"The Amontillado!" ejaculated my friend, not yet recovered from his astonishment.

"True," I replied; "the Amontillado."

As I said these words I busied myself among the pile of bones of which I have before spoken. Throwing them aside, I soon uncovered a quantity of building stone and mortar. With these materials and with the aid of my trowel, I began vigorously to wall up the entrance of the niche.

I had scarcely laid the first tier of the masonry when I discovered that the intoxication of Fortunato had in a great measure worn off. The earliest indication I had of this was a low moaning cry from the depth of the recess. It was not the cry of a drunken man. There was a long and obstinate silence. I laid the second tier, and the third, and the fourth; and then I heard the furious vibrations of the chain. The noise lasted for several minutes, during which, that I might hearken to it with the more satisfaction, I ceased my labors and sat down upon the bones. When at last the clanking subsided, I resumed the trowel, and finished without interruption the fifth, the sixth, and the seventh tier. The wall was now nearly upon a level with my breast. I again paused, and holding the flambeaux over the mason-work, threw a few feeble rays upon the figure within.

A succession of loud and shrill screams, bursting suddenly from the throat of the chained form, seemed to thrust me violently back. For a brief moment I hesitated, I trembled. Unsheathing my rapier, I began to grope with it about the recess; but the thought of an instant reassured me. I placed my hand upon the solid fabric of the catacombs, and felt satisfied. I reapproached the wall; I replied to the yells of him who clamoured. I re-echoed, I aided, I surpassed them in volume and in strength. I did this, and the clamourer grew still.

It was now midnight, and my task was drawing to a close. I had completed the eighth, the ninth and the tenth tier. I had finished a portion of the last and the eleventh; there remained but a single stone to be fitted and plastered in. I struggled with its weight; I placed it partially in its destined position. But now there came from out the niche a low laugh that erected the hairs upon my head. It was succeeded by a sad voice, which I had difficulty in recognizing as that of the noble Fortunato. The voice said—

"Ha! ha! ha!—he! he! he!—a very good joke, indeed—an excellent jest. We will have many a rich laugh about it at the palazzo—he! he! he!—over our wine—he! he! he!"

"The Amontillado," I said.

"He! he! he!—he! he! he!—yes, the Amontillado. But is it not getting late? Will not they be awaiting us at the palazzo, the Lady Fortunato and the rest? Let us be gone."

"Yes," I said, "let us be gone."

"For the love of God, Montresor!"

"Yes," I said, "for the love of God."

But to these words I hearkened in vain for a reply. I grew impatient. I called aloud—

"Fortunato!"

No answer. I called again—

"Fortunato!"

No answer still. I thrust a torch through the remaining aperture and let it fall within. There came forth in return only a jingling of the bells. My heart grew sick; it was the dampness of the catacombs that made it so. I hastened to make an end of my labour. I forced the last stone into its position; I plastered it up. Against the new masonry I re-erected the old rampart of bones. For the half of a century no mortal has disturbed them. In pace requiescat! [Rest in Peace.]

THE CHRYSANTHEMUMS
by John Steinbeck

As our reading experience expands, we become more conscious of each writer's "style," his or her own particular and unique use of language. While not every author's style is easily identified, with extensive reading you can learn to recognize the work of many of them.

As you read "The Chrysanthemums," try to recall the examples provided from the textbook. Steinbeck has an extraordinary command of the language and uses it to full advantage. Symbolism, syntax, dialogue, and the artful choice of words lead carefully to the ironic ending.

Pay careful attention to Steinbeck's adjectives, similes, metaphors, and descriptions. The words used to describe the setting and the characters are carefully selected to reinforce the themes of frustration and isolation, as does the dialogue, which contrasts with the author's descriptions of the characters.

Read carefully, and look for these particular devices:

- *Universal symbols: Steinbeck uses quite a few; see if you can determine their function.*
- *Symbols created by the author: Steinbeck also creates original symbols. See if you can identify any.*
- *Even the title has symbolic significance (beyond the simple fact that the main character is growing chrysanthemums).*

The high grey-flannel fog of winter closed off the Salinas Valley from the sky and from all the rest of the world. On every side it sat like a lid on the mountains and made of the great valley a closed pot. On the broad, level land floor the gang ploughs bit deep and left the black earth shining like metal where the shares had cut. On the foot-hill ranches across the Salinas River, the yellow stubble fields seemed to be bathed in pale cold sunshine, but there was no sunshine in the valley now in December. The thick willow scrub along the river flamed with sharp and positive yellow leaves.

It was a time of quiet and of waiting. The air was cold and tender. A light wind blew up from the southwest so that the farmers were mildly hopeful of a good rain before long; but fog and rain do not go together.

Across the river, on Henry Allen's foot-hill ranch there was little work to be done, for the hay was cut and stored and the orchards were ploughed up to receive the rain deeply when it should come. The cattle on the higher slopes were becoming shaggy and rough-coated.

Elisa Allen, working in her flower garden, looked down across the yard and saw Henry, her husband, talking to two men in business suits. The three of them stood by the tractor-shed, each man with one foot on the side of the little Fordson. They smoked cigarettes and studied the machine as they talked.

Elisa watched them for a moment and then went back to her work. She was thirty-five. Her face was lean and strong and her eyes were as clear as water. Her figure looked blocked and heavy in her gardening costume, a man's black hat pulled low down over her eyes, clod-hopper shoes, a figured print dress almost completely covered by a big corduroy apron with four big pockets to hold the snips, the trowel and scratcher, the seeds and the knife she worked with. She wore heavy leather gloves to protect her hands while she worked.

She was cutting down the old year's chrysanthemum stalks with a pair of short and powerful scissors. She looked down toward the men by the tractor-shed now and then. Her face was eager and mature and handsome; even her work with the scissors was overeager, over-powerful. The chrysanthemum stems seemed too small and easy for her energy.

She brushed a cloud of hair out of her eyes with the back of her glove, and left a smudge of earth on her cheek in doing it. Behind her stood the neat white farmhouse with red geraniums close-banked around it as high as the windows. It was a hard-swept-looking little house, with hard-polished windows, and a clean mud-mat on the front steps.

Elisa cast another glance toward the tractor-shed. The strangers were getting into their Ford coup. She took off a glove and put her strong fingers down into the forest of new green chrysanthemum sprouts that were growing round the old roots. She spread the leaves and looked down among the close-growing stems. No aphids were there, no sow bugs or snails or cutworms. Her terrier fingers destroyed such pests before they could get started.

Elisa started at the sound of her husband's voice. He had come near quietly, and he leaned over the wire fence that protected her flower garden from cattle and dogs and chickens.

"At it again," he said. "You've got a strong new crop coming."

Elisa straightened her back and pulled on the gardening glove again. "Yes. They'll be strong this coming year." In her tone and on her face there was a little smugness.

"You've got a gift with things," Henry observed. "Some of those yellow chrysanthemums you had this year were ten inches across. I wish you'd work out in the orchard and raise some apples that big."

Her eyes sharpened. "Maybe I could do it, too. I've a gift with things, all right. My mother had it. She could stick anything in the ground and make it grow. She said it was having planter's hands that knew how to do it."

"Well, it sure works with flowers," he said.

"Henry, who were those men you were talking to?"

"Why, sure, that's what I came to tell you. They were from the Western Meat Company. I sold those thirty head of three-year-old steers. Got nearly my own price, too."

"Good," she said. "Good for you."

"And I thought," he continued, "I thought how it's Saturday afternoon, and we might go into Salinas for dinner at a restaurant, and then to a picture show—to celebrate, you see."

"Good," she repeated. "Oh, yes. That will be good."

Henry put on his joking tone. "There's fights tonight. How'd you like to go to the fights?"

"Oh, no," she said breathlessly. "No, I wouldn't like fights."

"Just fooling, Elisa. We'll go to a movie. Let's see. It's two now. I'm going to take Scotty and bring down those steers from the hill. It'll take us maybe two hours. We'll go in town about five and have dinner at the Cominos Hotel. Like that?"

"Of course I'll like it. It's good to eat away from home."

"All right then. I'll go get up a couple of horses."

She said: "I'll have plenty of time to transplant some of these sets, I guess.

"She heard her husband calling Scotty down by the barn. And a little later she saw the two men ride up the pale yellow hillside in search of the steers.

There was a little square sandy bed kept for rooting the chrysanthemums. With her trowel she turned the soil over and over, and smoothed it and patted it firm. Then she dug ten parallel trenches to receive the sets. Back at the chrysanthemum bed she pulled out the little crisp shoots, trimmed off the leaves of each one with her scissors and laid it on a small orderly pile.

A squeak of wheels and plod of hoofs came from the road. Elisa looked up. The country road ran along the dense bank of willows and cottonwoods that bordered the river, and up this road came a curious vehicle, curiously drawn. It was an old spring-wagon, with a round canvas top on it like the cover of a prairie schooner. It was drawn by an old bay horse and a little gray-and-white burro. A big stubble-bearded man sat between the cover flaps and drove the crawling team. Underneath the wagon, between the hind wheels, a lean and rangy mongrel dog walked sedately. Words were painted on the canvas, in clumsy, crooked letters. "Pots, pans, knives, scissors, lawn mores, Fixed." Two rows of articles, and the triumphantly definitive "Fixed" below. The black paint had run down in little sharp points beneath each letter.

Elisa, squatting on the ground, watched to see the crazy, loose-jointed wagon pass by. But it didn't pass. It turned into the farm road in front of her house, crooked old wheels skirling and squeaking. The rangy dog darted from between the wheels and ran ahead. Instantly the two ranch shepherds flew out at him. Then all three stopped, and with stiff and quivering tails, with taut straight legs, with ambassadorial dignity, they slowly circled, sniffing daintily. The caravan pulled up to Elisa's wire fence and stopped. Now the newcomer dog, feeling outnumbered, lowered his tail and retired under the wagon with raised hackles and bared teeth.

The man on the wagon seat called out: "That's a bad dog in a fight when he gets started."

Elisa laughed. "I see he is. How soon does he generally get started?"

The man caught up her laughter and echoed it heartily. "Sometimes not for weeks and weeks," he said. He climbed stiffly down, over the wheel. The horse and the donkey drooped like unwatered flowers.

Elisa saw that he was a very big man. Although his hair and beard were graying, he did not look old. His worn black suit was wrinkled and spotted with grease. The laughter had disappeared from his face and eyes the moment his laughing voice ceased. His eyes were dark, and they were full of the brooding that gets in the eyes of teamsters and of sailors. The calloused hands he rested on the wire fence were cracked, and every crack was a black line. He took off his battered hat.

"I'm off my general road, ma'am," he said. "Does this dirt road cut over across the river to the Los Angeles highway?"

Elisa stood up and shoved the thick scissors in her apron pocket. "Well, yes, it does, but it winds around and then fords the river. I don't think your team could pull through the sand."

He replied with some asperity: "It might surprise you what them beasts can pull through."

"When they get started?" she asked.

He smiled for a second. "Yes. When they get started."

"Well," said Elisa, "I think you'll save time if you go back to the Salinas road and pick up the highway there."

He drew a big finger down the chicken wire and made it sing. "I ain't in any hurry, ma'am. I go from Seattle to San Diego and back every year. Takes all my time. About six months each way. I aim to follow nice weather."

Elisa took off her gloves and stuffed them in the apron pocket with the scissors. She touched the under edge of her man's hat, searching for fugitive hairs. "That sounds like a nice kind of way to live." she said.

He leaned confidentially over the fence. "Maybe you noticed the writing on my wagon. I mend pots and sharpen knives and scissors. You got any of them things to do?"

"Oh, no," she said quickly. "Nothing like that." Her eyes hardened with resistance.

"Scissors is the worst thing," he explained. "Most people just ruin scissors trying to sharpen em, but I know how. I got a special tool. It's a little bobbit kind of thing, and patented. But it sure does the trick."

"No. My scissors are all sharp."

"All right, then. Take a pot," he continued earnestly, "a bent pot, or a pot with a hole. I can make it like new so you don't have to buy no new ones. That's a saving for you."

"No," she said shortly. "I tell you I have nothing like that for you to do."

His face fell to an exaggerated sadness. His voice took on a whining undertone. "I ain't had a thing to do today. Maybe I won't have no supper tonight. You see I'm off my regular road. I know folks on the highway clear from Seattle to San Diego. They save their things for me to sharpen up because they know I do it so good and save them money."

"I'm sorry," Elisa said irritably. "I haven't anything for you to do."

His eyes left her face and fell to searching the ground. They roamed about until they came to the chrysanthemum bed where she had been working. "What's them plants, ma'am?"

The irritation and resistance melted from Elisa's face. "Oh, those are chrysanthemums, giant whites and yellows. I raise them every year, bigger than anybody around here."

"Kind of a long-stemmed flower? Looks like a quick puff of colored smoke?" he asked.

"That's it. What a nice way to describe them."

"They smell kind of nasty till you get used to them," he said.

"Its a good bitter smell," she retorted, "not nasty at all."

He changed his tone quickly. "I like the smell myself."

"I had ten-inch blooms this year," she said.

The man leaned farther over the fence. "Look. I know a lady down the road a piece, has got the nicest garden you ever seen. Got nearly every kind of flower but no chrysanthemums. Last time I was mending a copper-bottom washtub for her (that's a hard job but I do it good), she said to me: 'If you ever run acrost some nice chrysanthemums I wish you'd try to get me a few seeds.' That's what she told me."

Elisa's eyes grew alert and eager. "She couldn't have known much about chrysanthemums. You can raise them from seed, but it's much easier to root the little sprouts you see here."

"Oh," he said. "I s'pose I can't take none to her, then."

"Why yes you can," Elisa cried. "I can put some in damp sand, and you can carry them right along with you. They'll take root in the pot if you keep them damp. And then she can transplant them."

"She'd sure like to have some, ma'am. You say they're nice ones?"

"Beautiful," she said. "Oh, beautiful." Her eyes shone. She tore off the battered hat and shook out her dark pretty hair. "I'll put them in a flower pot, and you can take them right with you. Come into the yard."

While the man came through the picket gate Elisa ran excitedly along the geranium-bordered path to the back of the house. And she returned carrying a big red flower pot. The gloves were forgotten now. She kneeled on the ground by the starting bed and dug up the sandy soil with her fingers and scooped it into the bright new flower pot. Then she picked up the little pile of shoots she had prepared. With her strong fingers she pressed them into the sand and tamped around them with her knuckles. The man stood over her. "I'll tell you what to do," she said. "You remember so you can tell the lady."

"Yes, I'll try to remember."

"Well, look. These will take root in about a month. Then she must set them out, about a foot apart in good rich earth like this, see?" She lifted a handful of dark soil for him to look at. "They'll grow fast and tall. Now remember this: In July tell her to cut them down, about eight inches from the ground."

"Before they bloom?" he asked.

"Yes, before they bloom." Her face was tight with eagerness. "They'll grow right up again. About the last of September the buds will start."

She stopped and seemed perplexed. "It's the budding that takes the most care," she said hesitantly. "I don't know how to tell you." She looked deep into his eyes, searchingly. Her mouth opened a little, and she seemed to be listening. "I'll try to tell you," she said. "Did you ever hear of planting hands?"

"Can't say I have, ma'am."

"Well, I can only tell you what it feels like. It's when you're picking off the buds you don't want. Everything goes right down into your fingertips. You watch your fingers work. They do it themselves. You can feel how it is. They pick and pick the buds. They never make a mistake. They're with the plant. Do you see? Your fingers and the plant. You can feel that, right up your arm. They know. They never make a mistake. You can feel it. When you're like that you can't do anything wrong. Do you see that? Can you understand that?"

She was kneeling on the ground looking up at him. Her breast swelled passionately.

The man's eyes narrowed. He looked away self-consciously.

"Maybe I know," he said. "Sometimes in the night in the wagon there—"

Elisa's voice grew husky. She broke in on him: "I've never lived as you do, but I know what you mean. When the night is dark—why, the stars are sharp-pointed, and there's quiet. Why, you rise up and up! Every pointed star gets driven into your body. It's like that. Hot and sharp and—lovely."

Kneeling there, her hand went out toward his legs in the greasy black trousers. Her hesitant fingers almost touched the cloth. Then her hand dropped to the ground. She crouched low like a fawning dog.

He said: "It's nice, just like you say. Only when you don't have no dinner, it ain't."

She stood up then, very straight, and her face was ashamed. She held the flower pot out to him and placed it gently in his arms. "Here. Put it in your wagon, on the seat, where you can watch it. Maybe I can find something for you to do."

At the back of the house she dug in the can pile and found two old and battered aluminum saucepans. She carried them back and gave them to him. "Here, maybe you can fix these."

His manner changed. He became professional. "Good as new I can fix them." At the back of his wagon he set a little anvil, and out of an oily tool-box dug a small machine hammer. Elisa came through the gate to watch him while he pounded out the dents in the kettles. His mouth grew sure and knowing. At a difficult part of the work he sucked his underlip.

"You sleep right in the wagon?" Elisa asked.

"Right in the wagon, ma'am. Rain or shine I'm dry as a cow in there."

"It must be nice," she said. "It must be very nice. I wish women could do such things."

"It ain't the right kind of a life for a woman."

Her upper lip raised a little, showing her teeth. "How do you know? How can you tell?" she said.

"I don't know, ma'am," he protested. "Of course I don't know. Now here's your kettles, done. You don't have to buy no new ones."

"How much?"

"Oh, fifty cents'll do. I keep my prices down and my work good. That's why I have all them satisfied customers up and down the highway."

Elisa brought him a fifty-cent piece from the house and dropped it in his hand. "You might be surprised to have a rival some time. I can sharpen scissors, too. And I can beat the dents out of little pots. I could show you what a woman might do."

He put his hammer back in the oily box and shoved the little anvil out of sight. "It would be a lonely life for a woman, ma'am, and a scary life, too, with animals creeping under the wagon all night." He climbed over the single-tree, steadying himself with a hand on the burros white rump. He settled himself in the seat, picked up the lines. "Thank you kindly, ma'am," he said. "I'll do like you told me; I'll go back and catch the Salinas road."

"Mind," she called, "if you're long in getting there, keep the sand damp."

"Sand, ma'am...Sand? Oh, sure. You mean around the chrysanthemums. Sure I will." He clucked his tongue. The beasts leaned luxuriously into their collars. The mongrel dog took his place between the back wheels. The wagon turned and crawled out the entrance road and back the way it had come, along the river.

Elisa stood in front of her wire fence watching the slow progress of the caravan. Her shoulders were straight, her head thrown back, her eyes half-closed, so that the scene came vaguely into them. Her lips moved silently, forming the words "Good-bye—good-bye." Then she whispered: "That's a bright direction. There's a glowing there." The sound of her whisper startled her. She shook herself free and looked about to see whether anyone had been listening. Only the dogs had heard. They lifted their heads toward her from their sleeping in the dust, and then stretched out their chins and settled asleep again. Elisa turned and ran hurriedly into the house.

In the kitchen she reached behind the stove and felt the water tank. It was full of hot water from the noonday cooking. In the bathroom she tore off her soiled clothes and flung them into the corner. And then she scrubbed herself with a little block of pumice, legs and thighs, loins and chest and arms, until her skin was scratched and red. When she had dried herself she stood in front of a mirror in her bedroom and looked at her body. She tightened her stomach and threw out her chest. She turned and looked over her shoulder at her back.

After a while she began to dress, slowly. She put on her newest underclothing and her nicest stockings and the dress which was the symbol of her prettiness. She worked carefully on her hair, pencilled her eyebrows and rouged her lips.

Before she was finished she heard the little thunder of hoofs and the shouts of Henry and his helper as they drove the red steers into the corral. She heard the gate bang shut and set herself for Henry's arrival.

His step sounded on the porch. He entered the house calling: "Elisa, where are you?"

"In my room, dressing. I'm not ready. There's hot water for your bath. Hurry up. It's getting late."

When she heard him splashing in the tub, Elisa laid his dark suit on the bed, and shirt and socks and tie beside it. She stood his polished shoes on the floor beside the bed. Then she went to the porch and sat primly and stiffly down. She looked toward the river road where the willow-line was still yellow with frosted leaves so that under the high grey fog they seemed a thin band of sunshine. This was the only color in the grey afternoon. She sat unmoving for a long time. Her eyes blinked rarely.

Henry came banging out of the door, shoving his tie inside his vest as he came. Elisa stiffened and her face grew tight. Henry stopped short and looked at her. "Why—why, Elisa. You look so nice!"

"Nice? You think I look nice? What do you mean by 'nice'?"

Henry blundered on. "I don't know. I mean you look different, strong and happy."

"I am strong? Yes, strong. What do you mean 'strong'?"

He looked bewildered. "You're playing some kind of a game," he said helplessly. "It's a kind of a play. You look strong enough to break a calf over your knee, happy enough to eat it like a watermelon."

For a second she lost her rigidity. "Henry! Don't talk like that. You didn't know what you said." She grew complete again. "I'm strong," she boasted. "I never knew before how strong."

Henry looked down toward the tractor-shed, and when he brought his eyes back to her, they were his own again. "I'll get out the car. You can put on your coat while I'm starting."

Elisa went into the house. She heard him drive to the gate and idle down his motor, and then she took a long time to put on her hat. She pulled it here and pressed it there. When Henry turned the motor off she slipped into her coat and went out.

The little roadster bounced along on the dirt road by the river, raising the birds and driving the rabbits into the brush. Two cranes flapped heavily over the willow-line and dropped into the river bed.

Far ahead on the road Elisa saw a dark speck. She knew.

She tried not to look as they passed it, but her eyes would not obey. She whispered to herself sadly: "He might have thrown them off the road. That wouldn't have been much trouble, not very much. But he kept the pot," she explained. "He had to keep the pot. That's why he couldn't get them off the road."

The roadster turned a bend and she saw the caravan ahead. She swung full around toward her husband so she could not see the little covered wagon and the mis-matched team as the car passed them.

In a moment it was over. The thing was done. She did not look back.

She said loudly, to be heard over the motor: "It will be good, tonight, a good dinner."

"Now you've changed again," Henry complained. He took one hand from the wheel and patted her knee. "I ought to take you in to dinner oftener. It would be good for both of us. We get so heavy out on the ranch."

"Henry," she asked, "could we have wine at dinner?"

"Sure we could. Say! That will be fine."

She was silent for a while; then she said: "Henry, at those prizefights, do the men hurt each other very much?"

"Sometimes a little, not often. Why?"

"Well, I've read how they break noses, and blood runs down their chests. I've read how the fighting gloves get heavy and soggy with blood."

He looked around at her. "What's the matter, Elisa? I didn't know you read things like that." He brought the car to a stop, then turned to the right over the Salinas River bridge.

"Do any women ever go to the fights?" she asked.

"Oh, sure, some. What's the matter, Elisa? Do you want to go? I don't think you'd like it, but I'll take you if you really want to go."

She relaxed limply in the seat. "Oh, no. No. I don't want to go. I'm sure I don't." Her face was turned away from him. "It will be enough if we can have wine. It will be plenty." She turned up her coat collar so he could not see that she was crying weakly—like an old woman.

DESIREE'S BABY

by Kate Chopin

The author intentionally creates characters and a conflict, chooses a particular point of view and setting, and carefully selects the story's language to control the reader's attitude and give a story it's specific tone.

The following example, a story about a couple living in the 1800s, makes a clear statement about the bigotry of that time and, perhaps, our own. The discussion of the plot in Chapter Three explains how this story uses the flashback technique to set up the circumstances that are critical to the surprise ending. A slow, careful reading of the first six paragraphs yields clues to that ending. Each item is important and has an impact on the development of the central idea.

Because the story is set in Louisiana, the French influence is evident. Words like "corbielle" and "cochon de lait" and expressions like "mais si" not only locate the story, but also help establish the tone. ("Corbielle" are wedding presents; "cochon de lait" translates literally as "suckling pig," but is used affectionately here; "mais si" literally means "but, yes," but is better translated as "of course.") Chopin's diction, though more than one hundred years old, helps to establish the social class of the characters. As you read, keep these points in mind:

- *The language establishes a close relationship between the setting and the tone; look for examples.*
- *Polite expressions contrast significantly with the harsh nature of the content of some remarks; how does this contribute to the tone?*
- *Is any element emphasized more than the others? And if so, how does it affect the tone?*
- *There's a change in the tone, from the beginning to the end of the story; what purpose does it serve?*

As the day was pleasant, Madame Valmond drove over to L'Abri to see Desiree and the baby.

It made her laugh to think of Desiree with a baby. Why, it seemed but yesterday that Desiree was little more than a baby herself; when Monsieur in riding through the gateway of Valmond had found her lying asleep in the shadow of the big stone pillar.

The little one awoke in his arms and began to cry for "Dada." That was as much as she could do or say. Some people thought she might have strayed there of her own accord, for she was of the toddling age. The prevailing belief was that she had been purposely left by a party of Texans, whose canvas-covered wagon, late in the day, had crossed the ferry that Coton Mas kept, just below the plantation. In time Madame Valmond abandoned every speculation but the one that Desiree had been sent to her by a beneficent Providence to be the child of her affection, seeing that she was without child of the flesh. For the girl grew to be beautiful and gentle, affectionate and sincere,—the idol of Valmond.

It was no wonder, when she stood one day against the stone pillar in whose shadow she had lain asleep, eighteen years before, that Armand Aubigny riding by and seeing her there, had fallen in love with her. That was the way all the Aubignys fell in love, as if struck by a pistol shot. The wonder was that he had not loved her before; for he had known her since his father brought him home from Paris, a boy of eight, after his mother died there. The passion that awoke in him that day, when he saw her at the gate, swept along like an avalanche, or like a prairie fire, or like anything that drives headlong over all obstacles.

Monsieur Valmond grew practical and wanted things well considered; that is, the girl's obscure origin. Armand looked into her eyes and did not care. He was reminded that she was nameless. What did it matter about a name when he could give her one of the oldest and proudest in Louisiana? He ordered the corbeille from Paris, and contained himself with what patience he could until it arrived; then they were married.

Madame Valmond had not seen Desiree and the baby for four weeks. When she reached L'Abri she shuddered at the first sight of it, as she always did. It was a sad looking place, which for many years had not known the gentle presence of a mistress, old Monsieur Aubigny having married and buried his wife in France, and she having loved her own land too well ever to leave it. The roof came down steep and black like a cowl, reaching out beyond the wide galleries that encircled the yellow stuccoed house. Big, solemn oaks grew close to it, and their thick-leaved, far-reaching branches shadowed it like a pall. Young Aubignys rule was a strict one, too, and under it his negroes had forgotten how to be gay, as they had been during the old master's easy-going and indulgent lifetime.

The young mother was recovering slowly, and lay full length, in her soft white muslins and laces, upon a couch. The baby was beside her, upon her arm, where he had fallen asleep, at her breast. The yellow nurse woman sat beside a window fanning herself.

Madame Valmond bent her portly figure over Desiree and kissed her, holding her an instant tenderly in her arms. Then she turned to the child.

"This is not the baby!" she exclaimed, in startled tones. French was the language spoken at Valmond in those days.

"I knew you would be astonished," laughed Desiree, "at the way he has grown. The little cochon de lait! Look at his legs, mamma, and his hands and fingernails—real fingernails. Zandrine had to cut them this morning. Isn't it true, Zandrine?"

The woman bowed her turbaned head majestically, "Mais si, Madame."

"And the way he cries," went on Desiree, "is deafening. Armand heard him the other day as far away as La Blanches' cabin."

Madame Valmond had never removed her eyes from the child. She lifted it and walked with it over to the window that was lightest. She scanned the baby narrowly, then looked as searchingly at Zandrine, whose face was turned to gaze across the fields.

"Yes, the child has grown, has changed," said Madame Valmond, slowly, as she replaced it beside its mother. "What does Armand say?"

Desiree's face became suffused with a glow that was happiness itself.

"Oh, Armand is the proudest father in the parish, I believe, chiefly because it is a boy, to bear his name; though he says not,—that he would have loved a girl as well. But I know it isn't true. I know he says that to please me. And mamma," she added, drawing Madame Valmond's head down to her and speaking in a whisper, "he hasn't punished one of them—not one of them—since the baby is born. Even Negrillon, who pretended to have burnt his leg that he might rest from work—he only laughed, and said Negrillon was a great scamp. Oh, mamma, I'm so happy; it frightens me."

What Desiree said was true. Marriage, and later the birth of his son had softened Armand Aubigny's imperious and exacting nature greatly. This was what made the gentle Desiree so happy, for she loved him desperately. When he frowned she trembled, but loved him. When he smiled, she asked no greater blessing of God. But Armand's dark, handsome face had not often been disfigured by frowns since the day he fell in love with her.

When the baby was about three months old, Desiree awoke one day to the conviction that there was something in the air menacing her peace. It was at first too subtle to grasp. It had only been a disquieting suggestion; an air of mystery among the blacks; unexpected visits from far-off neighbors who could hardly account for their coming. Then a strange, an awful change in her husband's manner, which she dared not ask him to explain. When he spoke to her, it was with averted eyes, from which the old love-light seemed to have gone out. He absented himself from home; and when there, avoided her presence and that of her child, without excuse. And the very spirit of Satan seemed suddenly to take hold of him in his dealings with the slaves. Desiree was miserable enough to die.

She sat in her room, one hot afternoon, in her peignoir, listlessly drawing through her fingers the strands of her long, silky brown hair that hung about her shoulders. The baby, half naked, lay asleep upon her own great mahogany bed, that was like a sumptuous throne, with its satin-lined half-canopy. One of La Blanches' little quadroon boys—half naked too—stood fanning the child slowly with a fan of peacock feathers. Desiree's eyes had been fixed absently and sadly upon the baby, while she was striving to penetrate the threatening mist that she felt closing about her. She looked from her child to the boy who stood beside him, and back again; over and over. "Ah!" It was a cry that she could not help; which she was not conscious of having uttered. The blood turned like ice in her veins, and a clammy moisture gathered upon her face.

She tried to speak to the little quadroon boy; but no sound would come, at first. When he heard his name uttered, he looked up, and his mistress was pointing to the door. He laid aside the great, soft fan, and obediently stole away, over the polished floor, on his bare tiptoes.

She stayed motionless, with gaze riveted upon her child, and her face the picture of fright.

Presently her husband entered the room, and without noticing her, went to a table and began to search among some papers which covered it.

"Armand," she called to him, in a voice which must have stabbed him, if he was human. But he did not notice. "Armand," she said again. Then she rose and tottered towards him. "Armand," she panted once more, clutching his arm, "look at our child. What does it mean? Tell me."

He coldly but gently loosened her fingers from about his arm and thrust the hand away from him. "Tell me what it means!" she cried despairingly.

"It means," he answered lightly, "that the child is not white; it means that you are not white."

A quick conception of all that this accusation meant for her nerved her with unwonted courage to deny it. "It is a lie; it is not true, I am white! Look at my hair, it is brown; and my eyes are gray, Armand, you know they are gray. And my skin is fair," seizing his wrist.

"Look at my hand; whiter than yours, Armand," she laughed hysterically.

"As white as La Blanche's," he returned cruelly; and went away leaving her alone with their child.

When she could hold a pen in her hand, she sent a despairing letter to Madame Valmond.

"My mother, they tell me I am not white. Armand has told me I am not white. For Gods sake tell them it is not true. You must know it is not true. I shall die. I must die. I cannot be so unhappy, and live."

The answer that came was as brief:

"My own Desiree: Come home to Valmond; back to your mother who loves you. Come with your child."

When the letter reached Desiree she went with it to her husband's study, and laid it open upon the desk before which he sat. She was like a stone image: silent, white, motionless after she placed it there.

In silence he ran his cold eyes over the written words. He said nothing. "Shall I go, Armand?" she asked in tones sharp with agonized suspense.

"Yes, go."

"Do you want me to go?"

"Yes. I want you to go."

He thought Almighty God had dealt cruelly and unjustly with him; and felt, somehow, that he was paying Him back in kind when he stabbed thus into his wife's soul. Moreover he no longer loved her, because of the unconscious injury she had brought upon his home and his name.

She turned away like one stunned by a blow, and walked slowly towards the door, hoping he would call her back.

"Good-by, Armand," she moaned.

He did not answer her. That was his last blow at fate.

Desiree went in search of her child. Zandrine was pacing the sombre gallery with it. She took the little one from the nurse's arms with no word of explanation, and descending the steps, walked away, under the live-oak branches.

It was an October afternoon; the sun was just sinking. Out in the still fields the negroes were picking cotton.

Desiree had not changed the thin white garment nor the slippers which she wore. Her hair was uncovered and the sun's rays brought a golden gleam from its brown meshes. She did not take the broad, beaten road which led to the far-off plantation of Valmond. She walked across a deserted field, where the stubble bruised her tender feet, so delicately shod, and tore her thin gown to shreds.

She disappeared among the reeds and willows that grew thick along the banks of the deep, sluggish bayou; and she did not come back again.

Some weeks later there was a curious scene enacted at L'Abri. In the centre of the smoothly swept back yard was a great bonfire. Armand Aubigny sat in the wide hallway that commanded a view of the spectacle; and it was he who dealt out to a half dozen negroes the material which kept this fire ablaze.

A graceful cradle of willow, with all its dainty furnishings, was laid upon the pyre, which had already been fed with the richness of a priceless layette. Then there were silk gowns, and velvet and satin ones added to these; laces, too, and embroideries; bonnets and gloves; for the corbeille had been of rare quality.

The last thing to go was a tiny bundle of letters; innocent little scribblings that Desiree had sent to him during the days of their espousal. There was the remnant of one back in the drawer from which he took them. But it was not Desiree's; it was part of an old letter from his mother to his father. He read it. She was thanking God for the blessing of her husband's love:—

"But, above all," she wrote, "night and day, I thank the good God for having so arranged our lives that our dear Armand will never know that his mother, who adores him, belongs to the race that is cursed with the brand of slavery."

THE POSSIBILITY OF EVIL
by Shirley Jackson

Miss Adela Strangeworth came daintily along Main Street on her way to the grocery. The sun was shining, the air was fresh and clear after the night's heavy rain, and everything in Miss Strangeworth's little town looked washed and bright. Miss Strangeworth took deep breaths and thought that there was nothing in the world like a fragrant summer day.

She knew everyone in town, of course; she was fond of telling strangers—tourists who sometimes passed through the town and stopped to admire Miss Strangeworth's roses—that she had never spent more than a day outside this town in all her long life. She was seventy-one, Miss Strangeworth told the tourists, with a pretty little dimple showing by her lip, and she sometimes found herself thinking that the town belong to her. "My grandfather built the first house on Pleasant Street," she would say, opening her blue eyes wide with the wonder of it. "This house, right here. My family has lived here for better than a hundred years. My grandmother planted these roses, and my mother tended them, just as I do. I've watched my town grow; I can remember when Mr. Lewis, Senior, opened the grocery store, and the year the river flooded out the shanties on the low road, and the excitement when some young folks wanted to move the park over to the space in front of where the new post office is today. They wanted to put up a statue of Ethan Allen." Miss Strangeworth would frown a little and sound stern, "But it should have been a statue of my grandfather. There wouldn't have been a town here at all if it hadn't been for my grandfather and the lumber mill."

Miss Strangeworth never gave away any of her roses, although the tourists often asked. The roses belonged on Pleasant Street, and it bothered Miss Strangeworth to think of people wanting to carry them away, to take them into strange towns and down strange streets. When the new minister came, and the ladies were gathering flowers to decorate the church, Miss Strangeworth sent over a great basket of gladioli; when she picked the roses at all, she set them in bowls and vases around the inside of the house her grandfather had built.

Walking down Main Street on a summer morning, Miss Strangeworth had to stop every minute or so to say good morning to someone or to ask after someone's health. When she came into the grocery, half a dozen people turned away from the shelves and the counters to wave at her or call out good morning.

"And good morning to you, too, Mr. Lewis," Miss Strangeworth said at last. The Lewis family had been in the town almost as long as the Strangeworths; but the day young Lewis left high school and went to work in the grocery, Miss Strangeworth had stopped calling him Tommy and started calling him Mr. Lewis, and he had stopped calling her Addie and started calling her Miss Strangeworth. They had been in high school together, and had gone to picnics together, and to high-school dances and basketball games; but now Mr. Lewis was behind the counter in the grocery, and Miss Strangeworth was living alone in the Strangeworth house on Pleasant Street.

"Good morning," Mr. Lewis said, and added politely, "Lovely day."

"It is a very nice day," Miss Strangeworth said, as though she had only just decided that it would do after all. "I would like a chop, please, Mr. Lewis, a small, lean veal chop. Are those strawberries from Arthur Parker's garden? They're early this year."

"He brought them in this morning," Mr. Lewis said.

"I shall have a box," Miss Strangeworth said. Mr. Lewis looked worried, she thought, and for a minute she hesitated, but then she decided surely he could not be worried over the strawberries. He looked very tired indeed. He was usually so chipper, Miss Strangeworth thought, and almost commented, but it was far too personal a subject to be introduced to Mr. Lewis, the grocer, so she only said, "And a can of cat food and, I think, a tomato."

Silently, Mr. Lewis assembled her order on the counter, and waited. Miss Strangeworth looked at him curiously and then said, "It's Tuesday, Mr. Lewis. You forgot to remind me."

"Did I? Sorry."

"Imagine your forgetting that I always buy my tea on Tuesday," Miss Strangeworth said gently. "A quarter pound of tea, please, Mr. Lewis."

"Is that all, Miss Strangeworth?"

"Yes, thank you, Mr. Lewis. Such a lovely day, isn't it?

"Lovely," Mr. Lewis said.

Miss Strangeworth moved slightly to make room for Mrs. Harper at the counter. "Morning, Adela," Mrs. Harper said, and Miss Strangeworth said, "Good morning, Martha."

"Lovely day," Mrs. Harper said, and Miss Strangeworth said, "Yes lovely," and Mr. Lewis, under Mrs. Harper's glance, nodded.

"Ran out of sugar for my cake frosting," Mrs. Harper explained. Her hand shook slightly as she opened her pocketbook. Miss Strangeworth wondered, glancing at her quickly, if she had been taking proper care of herself. Martha Harper was not as young as she used to be, Miss Strangeworth thought. She probably could use a good strong tonic.

"Martha," she said, "you don't look well."

"I'm perfectly all right," Mrs. Harper said shortly. She handed her money to Mr. Lewis, took her change and her sugar, and went out without speaking again. Looking after her, Miss Strangeworth shook her head slightly. Martha definitely did not look well.

Carrying her little bag of groceries, Miss Strangeworth came out of the store into the bright sunlight and stopped to smile down on the Crane baby. Don and Helen Crane were really the two most infatuated young parents she had ever known, she thought indulgently, looking at the delicately embroidered baby cap and the lace-edged carriage cover.

"That little girl is going to grow up expecting luxury all her life," she said to Helen Crane.

Helen laughed. "That's the way we want her to feel," she said. "Like a princess."

"A princess can see a lot of trouble sometimes," Miss Strangeworth said dryly. "How old is Her Highness now?"

"Six months next Tuesday," Helen Crane said, looking down with rapt wonder at her child. "I've been worrying, though, about her. Don't you think she ought to move around more? Try to sit up, for instance?"

"For plain and fancy worrying," Miss Strangeworth said, amused, "give me a new mother every time."

"She just seems slow," Helen Crane said.

"Nonsense. All babies are different. Some of them develop much more quickly than others."

"That's what my mother says." Helen Crane laughed, looking a little bit ashamed.

"I suppose you've got young Don all upset about the fact that his daughter is already six months old and hasn't yet begun to learn to dance?"

"I haven't mentioned it to him. I suppose she's just so precious that I worry about her all the time."

"Well, apologize to her right now," Miss Strangeworth said. "She is probably worrying about why you keep jumping around all the time." Smiling to herself and shaking her old head, she went on down the sunny street, stopping once to ask little Billy Moore why he wasn't out riding in his daddy's shiny new car, and talking for a few minutes outside the library with Miss Chandler, the librarian, about the new novels to be ordered and paid for by the annual library appropriation. Miss Chandler seemed absent-minded and very much as though she were thinking about something else. Miss Strangeworth noticed that Miss Chandler had not taken much trouble with her hair that morning, and sighed. Miss Strangeworth hated sloppiness.

Many people seemed disturbed recently, Miss Strangeworth thought. Only yesterday the Stewarts' fifteen-year-old Linda had run crying down her own front walk and all the way to school, not caring who saw her. People around town thought she might have had a fight with the Harris boy, but they showed up together at the soda shop after school as usual, both of them looking grim and bleak. Trouble at home, people concluded, and sighed over the problems of trying to raise kids right these days.

From halfway down the block Miss Strangeworth could catch the heavy scent of her roses, and she moved a little more quickly. The perfume of roses meant home, and home meant the Strangeworth House on Pleasant Street. Miss Strangeworth stopped at her own front gate, as she always did, and looked with deep pleasure at her house, with the red and pink and white roses massed along the narrow lawn, and the ramblers going up along the porch; and the neat, the unbelievable trim lines of the house itself, with its slimness and its washed white look. Every window sparkled, every curtain hung stiff and straight, and even the stones of the front walk were swept and clear. People around town wondered how old Miss Strangeworth managed to keep the house looking the way it did, and there was a legend about a tourist once mistaking it for the local museum and going all through the place without finding out about his mistake. But the town was proud of Miss Strangeworth and her roses and her house. They had all grown together.

Miss Strangeworth went up her front steps, unlocked her front door with her key, and went into the kitchen to put away her groceries. She debated about having a cup of tea and then decided that it was too close to midday dinnertime; she would not have the appetite for her little chop if she had tea now. Instead she went into the light, lovely sitting room, which still glowed from the hands of her mother and her grandmother, who had covered the chairs with bright chintz and hung the curtains. All the furniture was spare and shining, and the round hooked rugs on the floor had been the work of Miss Strangeworth's grandmother and her mother. Miss Strangeworth had put a bowl of her red roses on the low table before the window, and the room was full of their scent.

Miss Strangeworth went to the narrow desk in the corner and unlocked it with her key. She never knew when she might feel like writing letters, so she kept her notepaper inside and the desk locked. Miss Strangeworth's usual stationery was heavy and cream-colored, with STRANGEWORTH HOUSE engraved across the top, but, when she felt like writing her other letters, Miss Strangeworth used a pad of various-colored paper bought from the local newspaper shop. It was almost a town joke, that colored paper, layered in pink and green and blue and yellow; everyone in town bought it and used it for odd, informal notes and shopping lists. It was usual to remark, upon receiving a note written on a blue page, that so-and-so would be needing a new pad soon; here she was, down to the blue already. Everyone used the matching envelopes for tucking away recipes, or keeping odd little things in, or even to hold cookies in the school lunch boxes. Mr. Lewis sometimes gave them to the children for carrying home penny candy.

Although Miss Strangeworth's desk held a trimmed quill pen which had belonged to her grandfather, and a gold-frosted fountain pen which had belonged to her father, Miss Strangeworth always used a dull stub of pencil when she wrote her letters, and she printed them in a childish block print. After thinking for a minute, although she had been phrasing the letter in the back of her mind all the way home, she wrote on a pink sheet: DIDN'T YOU EVER SEE AN IDIOT CHILD BEFORE? SOME PEOPLE JUST SHOULDN'T HAVE CHILDREN SHOULD THEY?

She was pleased with the letter. She was fond of doing things exactly right. When she made a mistake, as she sometimes did, or when the letters were not spaced nicely on the page, she had to take the discarded page to the kitchen stove and burn it at once. Miss Strangeworth never delayed when things had to be done.

After thinking for a minute, she decided that she would like to write another letter, perhaps to go to Mrs. Harper, to follow up the ones she had already mailed. She selected a green sheet this time and wrote quickly: HAVE YOU FOUND OUT YET WHAT THEY WERE ALL LAUGHING ABOUT AFTER YOU LEFT THE BRIDGE CLUB ON THURSDAY? OR IS THE WIFE REALLY ALWAYS THE LAST ONE TO KNOW?

Miss Strangeworth never concerned herself with facts; her letters all dealt with the more negotiable stuff of suspicion. Mr. Lewis would never have imagined for a minute that his grandson might be lifting petty cash from the store register if he had not had one of Miss Strangeworth's letters. Miss Chandler, the librarian, and Linda Stewart's parents would have gone unsuspectingly ahead with their lives, never aware of possible evil lurking nearby, if Miss Strangeworth had not sent letters opening their eyes. Miss Strangeworth would have been genuinely shocked if there had been anything between Linda Stewart and the Harris boy, but, as long as evil existed unchecked in the world, it was Miss Strangeworth's duty to keep her town alert to it. It was far more sensible for Miss Chandler to wonder what Mr. Shelley's first wife had really died of than to take a chance on not knowing. There were so many wicked people in the world and only one Strangeworth left in the town. Besides, Miss Strangeworth liked writing her letters.

She addressed an envelope to Don Crane after a moment's thought, wondering curiously if he would show the letter to his wife, and using a pink envelope to match the pink paper. Then she addressed a second envelope, green, to Mrs. Harper. Then an idea came to her and she selected a blue sheet and wrote: YOU NEVER KNOW ABOUT DOCTORS. REMEMBER THAT THEY'RE ONLY HUMAN AND NEED MONEY LIKE THE REST OF US. SUPPOSE THE KNIFE SLIPPED ACCIDENTALLY. WOULD DR. BURNS GET HIS FEE AND A LITTLE EXTRA FROM THAT NEPHEW OF YOURS?

She addressed the blue envelope to old Mrs. Foster, who was having an operation next month. She had thought of writing one more letter, to the head of the school board, asking how a chemistry teacher like Billy Moore's father could afford a new convertible, but, all at once, she was tired of writing letters. The three she had done would do for one day. She could write more tomorrow; it was not as though they all had to be done at once.

She had been writing her letters sometimes two or three every day for a week, sometimes no more than one in a month—for the past year. She never got any answers, of course, because she never signed her name. If she had been asked, she would have said that her name, Adela Strangeworth, a name honored in the town for so many years, did not belong on such trash. The town where she lived had to be kept clean and sweet, but people everywhere were lustful and evil and degraded, and needed to be watched; the world was so large, and there was only one Strangeworth left in it. Miss Strangeworth sighed, locked her desk, and put the letters into her big black leather pocketbook, to be mailed when she took her evening walk.

She broiled her little chop nicely, and had a sliced tomato and a good cup of tea ready when she sat down to her midday dinner at the table in her dining room, which could be opened to seat twenty-two, with a second table, if necessary, in the hall. Sitting in the warm sunlight that came through the tall windows of the dining room, seeing her roses massed outside, handling the heavy, old silverware and the fine translucent china, Miss Strangeworth was pleased; she would not have cared to be doing anything else. People must live graciously, after all, she thought, and sipped her tea. Afterward, when her plate and cup and saucer were washed and dried and put back onto the shelves where they belonged, and her silverware was back in the mahogany silver chest, Miss Strangeworth went up the graceful staircase and into her bedroom, which was the front room overlooking the roses, and had been her mother's and her grandmother's. Their Crown Derby dresser set and furs had been kept here, their fans and silver-backed brushes and their own bowls of roses; Miss Strangeworth kept a bowl of white roses on the bed table.

She drew the shades, took the rose satin spread from the bed, slipped out of her dress and her shoes, and lay down tiredly. She knew that no doorbell or phone would ring; no one in town would dare to disturb Miss Strangeworth during her afternoon nap. She slept, deep in the rich smell of roses.

After her nap she worked in her garden for a little while, sparing herself because of the heat; then she came in to her supper. She ate asparagus from her own garden, with sweet-butter sauce and a soft-boiled egg, and, while she had her supper, she listened to a late-evening news broadcast and then to a program of classical music on her small radio. After her dishes were done and her kitchen set in order, she took up her hat—Miss Strangeworth's hats were proverbial in the town; people believed that she had inherited them from her mother and her grandmother—and, locking the front door of her house behind her, set off on her evening walk, pocketbook under her arm. She nodded to Linda Stewart's father, who was washing his car in the pleasantly cool evening. She thought that he looked troubled.

There was only one place in town where she could mail her letters, and that was the new post office, shiny with red brick and silver letters. Although Miss Strangeworth had never given the matter any particular thought, she had always made a point of mailing her letters very secretly; it would, of course, not have been very wise to let anyone see her mail them. Consequently, she timed her walk so she could reach the post office just as darkness was starting to dim the outlines of the trees and the shapes of people's faces, although no one could ever mistake Miss Strangeworth, with her dainty walk and her rustling skirts.

There was always a group of young people around the post office, the very youngest roller-skating upon its driveway, which went all the way around the building and was the only smooth road in town; and the slighter older ones already knowing how to gather in small groups and chatter and laugh and make great, excited plans for going across the street to the soda shop in a minute or two. Miss Strangeworth had never had any self-consciousness before the children. She did not feel that any of them were staring at her unduly or longing to laugh at her; it would have been most reprehensible for their parents to permit their children to mock Miss Strangeworth of Pleasant Street. Most of the children stood back respectfully as Miss Strangeworth passed, silenced briefly in her presence, and some of the older children greeted her, saying soberly, "Hello, Miss Strangeworth."

Miss Strangeworth smiled at them and quickly went on. It had been a long time since she had known the name of every child in town. The mail slot was in the door of the post office. The children stood away as Miss Strangeworth approached it, seemingly surprised anyone should want to use the post office after it had been officially closed up for the night and turned over to the children. Miss Strangeworth stood by the door, opening her black pocketbook to take out the letters, and heard a voice which she knew at once to be Linda Stewart's. Poor little Linda was crying again, and Miss Strangeworth listened carefully. This was, after all, her town, and these were her people; if one of them was in trouble, she ought to know about it.

"I can't tell you, Dave," Linda was saying—so she was talking to the Harris boy, as Miss Strangeworth had supposed—"I just can't. It's just nasty."

"But why won't your father let me come around any more? What on earth did I do?

"I can't tell you. I just wouldn't tell you for anything. You've got to have a dirty, dirty mind for things like that."

"But something's happened. You've been crying and crying, and your father is all upset. Why can't I know about it, too? Aren't I like one of the family?"

"Not any more, Dave, not any more. You're not to come near our house again, my father said so. He said he'd horsewhip you. That's all I can tell you: You're not to come near our house any more."

"But I didn't do anything."

"Just the same, my father said…"

Miss Strangeworth sighed and turned away. There was so much evil in people. Even in a charming little town like this one, there was still so much evil in people.

She slipped her letters into the slot, and two of them fell inside. The third caught on the edge and fell outside, onto the ground at Miss Strangeworth's feet. She did not notice it because she was wondering whether a letter to the Harris boy's father might not be of some service in wiping out this potential badness. Wearily Miss Strangeworth turned to go home to her quiet bed in her lovely house, and never heard the Harris boy calling to her to say that she had dropped something.

"Old lady Strangeworth's getting deaf," he said, looking after her and holding in his hand the letter he had picked up.

"Well, who cares?" Linda said. "Who cares any more, anyway?"

"It's for Don Crane," the Harris boy said, "this letter. She dropped a letter addressed to Don Crane. Might as well take it on over. We pass his house anyway." He laughed. "Maybe it's got a check or something in it and he'd be just as glad to get it tonight instead of tomorrow."

"Catch old lady Strangeworth sending anybody a check," Linda said. "Throw it in the post office. Why do anyone a favor?" She sniffled. "Doesn't seem to me anybody around here cares about us," she said. "Why should we care about them?"

"I'll take it over anyway," the Harris boy said. "Maybe it's good news for them. Maybe they need something happy tonight, too. Like us."

Sadly, holding hands, they wandered off down the dark street, the Harris boy carrying Miss Strangeworth's pink envelope in his hand.

Miss Strangeworth awakened the next morning with a feeling of intense happiness and, for a minute wondered why, and then remembered that this morning three people would open her letters. Harsh, perhaps, at first, but wickedness was never easily banished, and a clean heart was a scoured heart. She washed her soft old face and brushed her teeth, still sound in spite of her seventy-one years, and dressed herself carefully in her sweet, soft clothes and buttoned shoes. Then, coming downstairs and reflecting that perhaps a little waffle would be agreeable for breakfast in the sunny dining room, she found the mail on the hall floor and bent to pick it up. A bill, the morning paper, a letter in a green envelope that looked oddly familiar. Miss Strangeworth stood perfectly still for a minute, looking down at the green envelope with the penciled printing, and thought: It looks like one of my letters. Was one of my letters sent back? No, because no one would know where to send it. How did this get here?

Miss Strangeworth was a Strangeworth of Pleasant Street. Her hand did not shake as she opened the envelope and unfolded the sheet of green paper inside. She began to cry silently for the wickedness of the world when she read the words: LOOK OUT AT WHAT USED TO BE YOUR ROSES.

I'M A FOOL
by Sherwood Anderson

I'm a Fool—From *The Dial* by Sherwood Anderson, The Dial Publishing Co., Inc. 1922.

It was a hard jolt for me, one of the most bitterest I ever had to face. And it all came about through my own foolishness, too. Even yet sometimes, when I think of it, I want to cry or swear or kick myself. Perhaps, even now, after all this time, there will be a kind of satisfaction in making myself look cheap by telling of it.

It began at three o'clock one October afternoon as I sat in the grandstand at the fall trotting and pacing meet at Sandusky, Ohio.

To tell the truth, I felt a little foolish that I should be sitting in the grandstand at all. During the summer before I had left my home town with Harry Whitehead and, with a nigger named Burt, had taken a job as swipe with one of the two horses Harry was campaigning through the fall race meets that year. Mother cried and my sister Mildred, who wanted to get a job as a school teacher in our town that fall, stormed and scolded about the house all during the week before I left. They both thought it something disgraceful that one of our family should take a place as a swipe with race horses. I've an idea Mildred thought my taking the place would stand in the way of her getting the job she'd been working so long for.

But after all I had to work, and there was no other work to be got. A big lumbering fellow of nineteen couldn't just hang around the house and I had got too big to mow people's lawns and sell newspapers. Little chaps who could get next to people's sympathies by their sizes were always getting jobs away from me. There was one fellow who kept saying to everyone who wanted a lawn mowed or a cistern cleaned, that he was saving money to work his way through college, and I used to lay awake nights thinking up ways to injure him without being found out. I kept thinking of wagons running over him and bricks falling on his head as he walked along the street. But never mind him.

I got the place with Harry and I liked Burt fine. We got along splendid together. He was a big nigger with a lazy sprawling body and soft, kind eyes, and when it came to a fight he could hit like Jack Johnson. He had Bucephalus, a big black pacing stallion that could do 2.09 or 2.10, if he had to, and I had a little gelding named Doctor Fritz that never lost a race all fall when Harry wanted him to win.

We set out from home late in July in a box car with the two horses and after that, until late November, we kept moving along to the race meets and the fairs. It was a peachy time for me, I'll say that. Sometimes now I think that boys who are raised regular in houses, and never have a fine nigger like Burt for a best friend, and go to high schools and college, and never steal anything, or get drunk a little, or learn to swear from fellows who know how, or come walking up in front of a grandstand in their shirt sleeves and with dirty horsey pants on when the races are going on and the grandstand is full of people all dressed up—What's the use of talking about it? Such fellows don't know nothing at all. They've never had no opportunity.

But I did. Burt taught me how to rub down a horse and put the bandages on after a race and steam a horse out and a lot of valuable things for any man to know. He could wrap a bandage on a horse's leg so smooth that if it had been the same color you would think it was his skin, and I guess he'd have been a big driver, too, and got to the top like Murphy and Walter Cox and the others if he hadn't been black.

Gee whizz, it was fun. You got to a county seat town, maybe say on a Saturday or Sunday, and the fair began the next Tuesday and lasted until Friday afternoon. Doctor Fritz would be, say in the 2.25 trot on Tuesday afternoon and on Thursday afternoon Bucephalus would knock 'em cold in the "free-for-all" pace. It left you a lot of time to hang around and listen to horse talk, and see Burt knock some yap cold that got too gay, and you'd find out about horses and men and pick up a lot of stuff you could use all the rest of your life, if you had some sense and salted down what you heard and felt and saw.

And then at the end of the week when the race meet was over, and Harry had run home to tend up to his livery stable business, you and Burt hitched the two horses to carts and drove slow and steady across country, to the place for the next meeting, so as to not over-heat the horses, etc., etc., you know.

Gee whizz, Gosh amighty, the nice hickorynut and beechnut and oaks and other kinds of trees along the roads, all brown and red, and the good smells, and Burt singing a song that was called "Deep River," and the country girls at the windows of houses and everything. You can stick your colleges up your nose for all me. I guess I know where I got my education.

Why, one of those little burgs of towns you come to on the way, say now on a Saturday afternoon, and Burt says, "Let's lay up here." And you did.

And you took the horses to a livery stable and fed them, and you got your good clothes out of a box and put them on.

And the town was full of farmers gaping, because they could see you were race horse people, and the kids maybe never see a nigger before and was afraid and run away when the two of us walked down their main street.

And that was before prohibition and all that foolishness, and so you went into a saloon, the two of you, and all the yaps come and stood around, and there was always someone pretended he was horsey and knew things and spoke up and began asking questions, and all you did was to lie and lie all you could about what horses you had, and I said, I owned them, and then some fellow said, "Will you have a drink of whiskey?" and Burt knocked his eye out the way he could say, off-hand like, "Oh well, all right, I'm agreeable to a little nip. I'll split a quart with you." Gee whizz.

But that isn't what I want to tell my story about. We got home late in November and I promised mother I'd quit the race horses for good. There's a lot of things you've got to promise a mother because she don't know any better.

And so, there not being any work in our town any more than when I left there to go to the races, I went off to Sandusky and got a pretty good place taking care of horses for a man who owned a teaming and delivery and storage and coal and real estate business there. It was a pretty good place with good eats, and a day off each week, and sleeping on a cot in a big barn, and mostly just shovelling in hay and oats to a lot of big good-enough skates of horses, that couldn't have trotted a race with a toad. I wasn't dissatisfied and I could send money home.

And then, as I started to tell you, the fall races come to Sandusky and I got the day off and I went. I left the job at noon and had on my good clothes and my new brown derby hat, I'd just bought the Saturday before, and a stand-up collar.

First of all I went down-town and walked about with the dudes. I've always thought to myself, "put up a good front" and so I did it. I had forty dollars in my pocket and so I went into the West House, a big hotel, and walked up to the cigar stand. "Give me three twenty-five cent cigars," I said. There was a lot of horsemen and strangers and dressed-up people from other towns standing around in the lobby and in the bar, and I mingled amongst them. In the bar there was a fellow with a cane and a Windsor tie on, that it made me sick to look at him. I like a man to be a man and dress up, but not to go put on that kind of airs. So I pushed him aside, kind of rough, and had me a drink of whiskey. And then he looked at me, as though he thought maybe he'd get gay, but he changed his mind and didn't say anything. And then I had another drink of whiskey, just to show him something, and went out and had a hack out to the races, all to myself, and when I got there I bought myself the best seat I could get up in the grandstand, but didn't go in for any of these boxes. That's putting on too many airs.

And so there I was, sitting up in the grandstand as gay as you please and looking down on the swipes coming out with their horses, and with their dirty horsey pants on and the horse blankets swung over their shoulders, same as I had been doing all the year before. I liked one thing about the same as the other, sitting up there and feeling grand and being down there and looking up at the yaps and feeling grander and more important, too. One thing's about as good as another, if you take it just right. I've often said that.

Well, right in front of me, in the grandstand that day, there was a fellow with a couple of girls and they was about my age. The young fellow was a nice guy all right. He was the kind maybe that goes to college and then comes to be a lawyer or maybe a newspaper editor or something like that, but he wasn't stuck on himself. There are some of that kind are all right and he was one of the ones.

He had his sister with him and another girl and the sister looked around over his shoulder, accidental at first, not intending to start anything—she wasn't that kind—and her eyes and mine happened to meet.

You know how it is. Gee, she was a peach! She had on a soft dress, kind of a blue stuff and it looked carelessly made, but was well sewed and made and everything. I knew that much. I blushed when she looked right at me and so did she. She was the nicest girl I've ever seen in my life. She wasn't stuck on herself and she could talk proper grammar without being like a school teacher or something like that. What I mean is, she was O.K. I think maybe her father was well-to-do, but not rich to make her chesty because she was his daughter, as some are. Maybe he owned a drug store or a drygoods store in their home town, or something like that. She never told me and I never asked.

My own people are all O.K. too, when you come to that. My grandfather was Welsh and over in the old country, in Wales he was—but never mind that.

The first heat of the first race come off and the young fellow setting there with the two girls left them and went down to make a bet. I knew what he was up to, but he didn't talk big and noisy and let everyone around know he was a sport, as some do. He wasn't that kind. Well, he come back and I heard him tell the two girls what horse he'd bet on, and when the heat was trotted they all half got to their feet and acted in the excited, sweaty way people do when they've got money down on a race, and the horse they bet on is up there pretty close at the end, and they think maybe he'll come on with a rush, but he never does because he hasn't got the old juice in him, come right down to it.

And then, pretty soon, the horses came out for the 2.18 pace and there was a horse in it I knew. He was a horse Bob French had in his string but Bob didn't own him. He was a horse owned by a Mr. Mathers down at Marietta, Ohio.

This Mr. Mathers had a lot of money and owned some coal mines or something, and he had a swell place out in the country, and he was stuck on race horses, but was a Presbyterian or something, and I think more than likely his wife was one, too, maybe a stiffer one than himself. So he never raced his horses hisself, and the story round the Ohio race tracks was that when one of his horses got ready to go to the races he turned him over to Bob French and pretended to his wife he was sold.

So Bob had the horses and he did pretty much as he pleased and you can't blame Bob, at least, I never did. Sometimes he was out to win and sometimes he wasn't. I never cared much about that when I was swiping a horse. What I did want to know was that my horse had the speed and could go out in front, if you wanted him to.

And, as I'm telling you, there was Bob in this race with one of Mr. Mathers' horses, was named "About Ben Ahem" or something like that, and was fast as a streak. He was a gelding and had a mark of 2.21, but could step in .08 or .09.

Because when Burt and I were out, as I've told you, the year before, there was a nigger, Burt knew, worked for Mr. Mathers and we went out there one day when we didn't have no race on at the Marietta Fair and our boss Harry was gone home.

And so everyone was gone to the fair but just this one nigger and he took us all through Mr. Mathers' swell house and he and Burt tapped a bottle of wine Mr. Mathers had hid in his bedroom, back in a closet, without his wife knowing, and he showed us this Ahem horse. Burt was always stuck on being a driver but didn't have much chance to get to the top, being a nigger, and he and the other nigger gulped that whole bottle of wine and Burt got a little lit up.

So the nigger let Burt take this About Ben Ahem and step him a mile in a track Mr. Mathers had all to himself, right there on the farm. And Mr. Mathers had one child, a daughter, kinda sick and not very good looking, and she came home and we had to hustle and get About Ben Ahem stuck back in the barn.

I'm only telling you to get everything straight. At Sandusky, that afternoon I was at the fair, this young fellow with the two girls was fussed, being with the girls and losing his bet. You know how a fellow is that way. One of them was his girl and the other his sister. I had figured that out.

"Gee whizz," I says to myself, "I'm going to give him the dope."

He was mighty nice when I touched him on the shoulder. He and the girls were nice to me right from the start and clear to the end. I'm not blaming them.

And so he leaned back and I give him the dope on About Ben Ahem. "Don't bet a cent on this first heat because he'll go like an oxen hitched to a plow, but when the first heat is over go right down and lay on your pile." That's what I told him.

Well, I never saw a fellow treat any one sweller. There was a fat man sitting beside the little girl, that had looked at me twice by this time, and I at her, and both blushing, and what did he do but have the nerve to turn and ask the fat man to get up and change places with me so I could set with his crowd.

Gee whizz, craps amighty. There I was. What a chump I was to go and get gay up there in the West House bar, and just because that dude was standing there with a cane and that kind of a necktie on, to go and get all balled up and drink that whiskey, just to show off.

Of course she would know, me setting right beside her and letting her smell of my breath. I could have kicked myself right down out of that grandstand and all around that race track and made a faster record than most of the skates of horses they had there that year.

Because that girl wasn't any mutt of a girl. What wouldn't I have give right then for a stick of chewing gum to chew, or a lozenger, or some liquorice, or most anything. I was glad I had those twenty-five cent cigars in my pocket and right away I give that fellow one and lit one myself. Then that fat man got up and we changed places and there I was, plunked right down beside her.

They introduced themselves and the fellow's best girl, he had with him, was named Miss Elinor Woodbury, and her father was a manufacturer of barrels from a place called Tiffin, Ohio. And the fellow himself was named Wilbur Wessen and his sister was Miss Lucy Wessen.

I suppose it was their having such swell names got me off my trolley. A fellow, just because he has been a swipe with a race horse, and works taking care of horses for a man in the teaming, delivery, and storage business, isn't any better or worse than any one else. I've often thought that, and said it too.

But you know how a fellow is. There's something in that kind of nice clothes, and the kind of nice eyes she had, and the way she had looked at me, awhile before, over her brother's shoulder, and me looking back at her, and both of us blushing.

I couldn't show her up for a boob, could I?

I made a fool of myself, that's what I did. I said my name was Walter Mathers from Marietta, Ohio, and then I told all three of them the smashingest lie you ever heard. What I said was that my father owned the horse About Ben Ahem and that he had let him out to this Bob French for racing purposes, because our family was proud and had never gone into racing that way, in our own name, I mean. Then I had got started and they were all leaning over and listening, and Miss Lucy Wessen's eyes were shining, and I went the whole hog.

I told about our place down at Marietta, and about the big stables and the grand brick house we had on a hill, up above the Ohio River, but I knew enough not to do it in no bragging way. What I did was to start things and then let them drag the rest out of me. I acted just as reluctant to tell as I could. Our family hasn't got any barrel factory, and, since I've known us, we've always been pretty poor, but not asking anything of any one at that, and my grandfather, over in Wales—but never mind that.

We set there talking like we had known each other for years and years, and I went and told them that my father had been expecting maybe this Bob French wasn't on the square, and had sent me up to Sandusky on the sly to find out what I could.

And I bluffed it through I had found out all about the 2.18 pace, in which About Ben Ahem was to start.

I said he would lose the first heat by pacing like a lame cow and then he would come back and skin em alive after that. And to back up what I said I took thirty dollars out of my pocket and handed it to Mr. Wilbur Wessen and asked him, would he mind, after the first heat, to go down and place it on About Ben

Ahem for whatever odds he could get. What I said was that I didn't want Bob French to see me and none of the swipes.

Sure enough the first heat come off and About Ben Ahem went off his stride, up the back stretch, and looked like a wooden horse or a sick one, and come in to be last. Then this Wilbur Wessen went down to the betting place under the grandstand and there I was with the two girls, and when that Miss Woodbury was looking the other way once, Lucy Wessen kinda, with her shoulder you know, kinda touched me. Not just tucking down, I don't mean. You know how a woman can do. They get close, but not getting gay either. You know what they do. Gee whizz.

And then they give me a jolt. What they had done, when I didn't know, was to get together, and they had decided Wilbur Wessen would bet fifty dollars, and the two girls had gone and put in ten dollars each, of their own money, too. I was sick then, but I was sicker later.

About the gelding, About Ben Ahem, and their winning their money, I wasn't worried a lot about that. It came out O.K. Ahem stepped the next three heats like a bushel of spoiled eggs going to market before they could be found out, and Wilbur Wessen had got nine to two for the money. There was something else eating at me.

Because Wilbur come back, after he had bet the money, and after that he spent most of his time talking to that Miss Woodbury, and Lucy Wessen and I was left alone together like on a desert island. Gee, if I'd only been on the square or if there had been any way of getting myself on the square. There ain't any Walter Mathers, like I said to her and them, and there hasn't ever been one, but if there was, I bet I'd go to Marietta, Ohio, and shoot him to-morrow.

There I was, big boob that I am. Pretty soon the race was over, and Wilbur had gone down and collected our money, and we had a hack down-town, and he stood us a swell supper at the West House, and a bottle of champagne beside.

And I was with that girl and she wasn't saying much, and I wasn't saying much either. One thing I know. She wasn't stuck on me because of the lie about my father being rich and all that. There's a way you know...Craps amighty. There's a kind of girl, you see just once in your life, and if you don't get busy and make hay, then you're gone for good and all, and might as well go jump off a bridge. They give you a look from inside of them somewhere, and it ain't no vamping, and what it means is—you want that girl to be your wife, and you want nice things around her like flowers and swell clothes, and you want her to have the kids you're going to have, and you want good music played and no rag time. Gee whizz.

There's a place over near Sandusky, across a kind of bay, and its called Cedar Point. And after we had supper we went over to it in a launch, all by ourselves. Wilbur and Miss Lucy and that Miss Woodbury had to catch a ten o'clock train back to Tiffin, Ohio, because, when you're out with girls like that you can't get careless and miss any trains and stay out all night, like you can with some kinds of Janes.

And Wilbur blowed himself to the launch and it cost him fifteen cold plunks, but I wouldn't never have knew if I hadn't listened. He wasn't no tin horn kind of a sport.

Over at the Cedar Point place, we didn't stay around where there was a gang of common kind of cattle at all.

There was big dance halls and dining places for yaps, and there was a beach you could walk along and get where it was dark, and we went there.

She didn't talk hardly at all and neither did I, and I was thinking how glad I was my mother was all right, and always made us kids learn to eat with a fork at a table, and not swill soup, and not be noisy and rough like a gang you see around a race track that way.

Then Wilbur and his girl went away up the beach and Lucy and I sat down in a dark place, where there was some roots of old trees, the water had washed up, and after that the time, till we had to go back in the launch and they had to catch their trains, wasn't nothing at all. It went like winking your eye.

Here's how it was. The place we were setting in was dark, like I said, and there was the roots from that old stump sticking up like arms, and there was a watery smell, and the night was like—as if you could put your hand out and feel it—so warm and soft and dark and sweet like an orange.

I most cried and I most swore and I most jumped up and danced, I was so mad and happy and sad.

When Wilbur come back from being alone with his girl, and she saw him coming, Lucy she says, "we got to go to the train now," and she was most crying too, but she never knew nothing I knew, and she couldn't be so all busted up. And then, before Wilbur and Miss Woodbury got up to where we was, she put her face up and kissed me quick and put her head up against me and she was all quivering and—Gee whizz.

Sometimes I hope I have cancer and die. I guess you know what I mean. We went in the launch across the bay to the train like that, and it was dark, too. She whispered and said it was like she and I could get out of the boat and walk on the water, and it sounded foolish, but I knew what she meant.

And then quick we were right at the depot, and there was a big gang of yaps, the kind that goes to the fairs, and crowded and milling around like cattle, and how could I tell her? "It won't be long because you'll write and I'll write to you." That's all she said.

I got a chance like a hay barn afire. A swell chance I got.

And maybe she would write me, down at Marietta that way, and the letter would come back, and stamped on the front of it by the U.S.A. "there ain't any such guy," or something like that, whatever they stamp on a letter that way.

And me trying to pass myself off for a bigbug and a swell—to her, as decent a little body as God ever made. Craps amighty—a swell chance I got!

And then the train come in, and she got on it, and Wilbur Wessen he come and shook hands with me, and that Miss Woodbury was nice, too, and bowed to me, and I at her, and the train went and I busted out and cried like a kid.

Gee, I could have run after that train and made Dan Patch look like a freight train after a wreck but, socks amighty, what was the use? Did you ever see such a fool?

I'll bet you what—if I had an arm broke right now or a train had run over my foot—I wouldn't go to no doctor at all. I'd go set down and let her hurt and hurt—that's what I'd do.

I'll bet you what—if I hadn't a drunk that booze I'd never been such a boob as to go tell such a lie—that couldn't never be made straight to a lady like her.

I wish I had that fellow right here that had on a Windsor tie and carried a cane. I'd smash him for fair. Gosh darn his eyes. He's a big fool—that's what he is.

And if I'm not another you just go find me one and I'll quit working and be a bum and give him my job. I don't care nothing for working, and earning money, and saving it for no such boob as myself.

THE MOST DANGEROUS GAME
by Richard Connell

"Off there to the right—somewhere—is a large island," said Whitney. "It's rather a mystery—"

"What island is it?" Rainsford asked.

"The old charts call it 'Ship-Trap Island,'" Whitney replied. "A suggestive name, isn't it? Sailors have a curious dread of the place. I don't know why. Some superstition—"

"Can't see it," remarked Rainsford, trying to peer through the dank tropical night that was palpable as it pressed its thick warm blackness in upon the yacht.

"You've good eyes," said Whitney, with a laugh, "and I've seen you pick off a moose moving in the brown fall bush at four hundred yards, but even you can't see four miles or so through a moonless Caribbean night."

"Nor four yards," admitted Rainsford. "Ugh! It's like moist black velvet."

"It will be light in Rio," promised Whitney. "We should make it in a few days. I hope the jaguar guns have come from Purdeys. We should have some good hunting up the Amazon. Great sport, hunting."

"The best sport in the world," agreed Rainsford.

"For the hunter," amended Whitney. "Not for the jaguar."

"Don't talk rot, Whitney," said Rainsford. "You're a big-game hunter, not a philosopher. Who cares how a jaguar feels?"

"Perhaps the jaguar does," observed Whitney.

"Bah! They've no understanding."

"Even so, I rather think they understand one thing—fear. The fear of pain and the fear of death."

"Nonsense," laughed Rainsford. "This hot weather is making you soft, Whitney. Be a realist. The world is made up of two classes—the hunters and the huntees. Luckily, you and I are the hunters. Do you think we've passed that island yet?"

"I can't tell in the dark. I hope so."

"Why?" asked Rainsford.

"The place has a reputation—a bad one."

"Cannibals?" suggested Rainsford.

"Hardly. Even cannibals wouldn't live in such a God-forsaken place. But it's gotten into sailor lore, somehow. Didn't you notice that the crew's nerves seemed a bit jumpy to-day?"

"They were a bit strange, now you mention it. Even Captain Nielsen—"

"Yes, even that tough-minded old Swede, who'd go up to the devil himself and ask him for a light. Those fishy blue eyes held a look I never saw there before. All I could get out of him was: 'This place has an evil name among seafaring men, sir.' Then he said to me, very gravely: 'Don't you feel anything?'—as if the air about us was actually poisonous. Now, you mustn't laugh when I tell you this—I did feel something like a sudden chill."

"There was no breeze. The sea was as flat as a plate-glass window. We were drawing near the island then. What I felt was a—a mental chill; a sort of sudden dread."

"Pure imagination," said Rainsford. "One superstitious sailor can taint the whole ship's company with his fear."

"Maybe. But sometimes I think sailors have an extra sense that tells them when they are in danger. Sometimes I think evil is a tangible thing—with wave lengths, just as sound and light have. An evil place can, so to speak, broadcast vibrations of evil. Anyhow, I'm glad we're getting out of this zone. Well, I think I'll turn in now, Rainsford."

"I'm not sleepy," said Rainsford. "I'm going to smoke another pipe on the after deck."

"Good night, then, Rainsford. See you at breakfast."

"Right. Good night, Whitney."

There was no sound in the night as Rainsford sat there, but the muffled throb of the engine that drove the yacht swiftly through the darkness, and the swish and ripple of the wash of the propeller.

Rainsford, reclining in a steamer chair, indolently puffed on his favorite brier. The sensuous drowsiness of the night was on him. "It's so dark," he thought, "that I could sleep without closing my eyes; the night would be my eyelids—"

An abrupt sound startled him. Off to the right he heard it, and his ears, expert in such matters, could not be mistaken. Again he heard the sound, and again. Somewhere, off in the blackness, someone had fired a gun three times.

Rainsford sprang up and moved quickly to the rail, mystified. He strained his eyes in the direction from which the reports had come, but it was like trying to see through a blanket. He leaped upon the rail and balanced himself there, to get greater elevation; his pipe, striking a rope, was knocked from his mouth. He lunged for it; a short, hoarse cry came from his lips as he realized he had reached too far and had lost his balance. The cry was pinched off short as the blood-warm waters of the Caribbean Sea closed over his head.

He struggled up to the surface and tried to cry out, but the wash from the speeding yacht slapped him in the face and the salt water in his open mouth made him gag and strangle. Desperately he struck out with strong strokes after the receding lights of the yacht, but he stopped before he had swum fifty feet. A certain cool-headedness had come to him; it was not the first time he had been in a tight place. There was a chance that his cries could be heard by some one aboard the yacht, but that chance was slender, and grew more slender as the yacht raced on. He wrestled himself out of his clothes, and shouted with all his power. The lights of the yacht became faint and ever-vanishing fireflies; then they were blotted out entirely by the night.

Rainsford remembered the shots. They had come from the right, and doggedly he swam in that direction, swimming with slow, deliberate strokes, conserving his strength. For a seemingly endless time he fought the sea. He began to count his strokes; he could do possibly a hundred more and then—

Rainsford heard a sound. It came out of the darkness, a high screaming sound, the sound of an animal in an extremity of anguish and terror.

He did not recognize the animal that made the sound; he did not try to; with fresh vitality he swam toward the sound. He heard it again; then it was cut short by another noise, crisp, staccato.

"Pistol shot," muttered Rainsford, swimming on.

Ten minutes of determined effort brought another sound to his ears—the most welcome he had ever heard—the muttering and growling of the sea breaking on a rocky shore. He was almost on the rocks before he saw them; on a night less calm he would have been shattered against them. With his remaining strength he dragged himself from the swirling waters. Jagged crags appeared to jut into the opaqueness, he forced himself upward, hand over hand. Gasping, his hands raw, he reached a flat place at the top. Dense jungle came down to the very edge of the cliffs. What perils that tangle of trees and underbrush might hold for him did not concern Rainsford just then. All he knew was that he was safe from his enemy, the sea, and that utter weariness was on him. He flung himself down at the jungle edge and tumbled headlong into the deepest sleep of his life.

When he opened his eyes he knew from the position of the sun that it was late in the afternoon. Sleep had given him new vigor; a sharp hunger was picking at him. He looked about him, almost cheerfully.

"Where there are pistol shots, there are men. Where there are men, there is food," he thought. But what kind of men, he wondered, in so forbidding a place? An unbroken front of snarled and ragged jungle fringed the shore.

He saw no sign of a trail through the closely knit web of weeds and trees; it was easier to go along the shore, and Rainsford floundered along by the water. Not far from where he had landed, he stopped.

Some wounded thing, by the evidence a large animal, had thrashed about in the underbrush; the jungle weeds were crushed down and the moss was lacerated; one patch of weeds was stained crimson. A small, glittering object not far away caught Rainsford's eye and he picked it up. It was an empty cartridge.

"A twenty-two," he remarked. "That's odd. It must have been a fairly large animal, too. The hunter had his nerve with him to tackle it with a light gun. It's clear that the brute put up a fight. I suppose the first three shots I heard was when the hunter flushed his quarry and wounded it. The last shot was when he trailed it here and finished it."

He examined the ground closely and found what he had hoped to find—the print of hunting boots. They pointed along the cliff in the direction he had been going. Eagerly he hurried along, now slipping on a rotten log or a loose stone, but making headway; night was beginning to settle down on the island.

Bleak darkness was blacking out the sea and jungle when Rainsford sighted the lights. He came upon them as he turned a crook in the coast line, and his first thought was that he had come upon a village, for there were many lights. But as he forged along he saw to his great astonishment that all the lights were in one enormous building—a lofty structure with pointed towers plunging upward into the gloom. His eyes made out the shadowy outlines of a palatial chateau; it was set on a high bluff, and on three sides of its cliffs dived down to where the sea licked greedy lips in the shadows.

"Mirage," thought Rainsford. But it was no mirage, he found, when he opened the tall spiked iron gate. The stone steps were real enough; the massive door with a leering gargoyle for a knocker was real enough; yet about it all hung an air of unreality.

He lifted the knocker, and it creaked up stiffly, as if it had never before been used. He let it fall, and it startled him with its booming loudness. He thought he heard steps within; the door remained closed. Again Rainsford lifted the heavy knocker, and let it fall. The door opened then, opened as suddenly as if it were on a spring, and Rainsford stood blinking in the river of glaring gold light that poured out. The first thing Rainsford's eyes discerned was the largest man Rainsford had ever seen—a gigantic creature, solidly made and black-bearded to the waist. In his hand, the man held a long-barreled revolver, and he was pointing it straight at Rainsford's heart.

Out of the snarl of beard two small eyes regarded Rainsford.

"Don't be alarmed," said Rainsford, with a smile which he hoped was disarming. "I'm no robber. I fell off a yacht. My name is Sanger Rainsford of New York City."

The menacing look in the eyes did not change. The revolver pointed as rigidly as if the giant were a statue. He gave no sign that he understood Rainsford's words, or that he had even heard them. He was dressed in uniform, a black uniform trimmed with gray astrakhan.

"I'm Sanger Rainsford of New York," Rainsford began again. "I fell off a yacht. I am hungry."

The man's only answer was to raise with his thumb the hammer of his revolver. Then Rainsford saw the man's free hand go to his forehead in a military salute, and he saw him click his heels together and stand at attention. Another man was coming down the broad marble steps, an erect, slender man in evening clothes. He advanced to Rainsford and held out his hand.

In a cultivated voice marked by a slight accent that gave it added precision and deliberateness, he said: "It is a very great pleasure and honor to welcome Mr. Sanger Rainsford, the celebrated hunter, to my home."

Automatically Rainsford shook the man's hand.

"I've read your book about hunting snow leopards[1] in Tibet, you see," explained the man. "I am General Zaroff."

Rainsford's first impression was that the man was singularly handsome; his second was that there was an original, almost bizarre quality about the general's face. He was a tall man past middle age, for his hair was a vivid white; but his thick eyebrows and pointed military mustache were as black as the night from which Rainsford had come. His eyes, too, were black and very bright. He had high cheek bones, a sharp-cut nose, a spare, dark face, the face of a man used to giving orders, the face of an aristocrat. Turning to the giant in uniform, the general made a sign. The giant put away his pistol, saluted, withdrew.

"Ivan is an incredibly strong fellow," remarked the general, "but he has the misfortune to be deaf and dumb. A simple fellow, but, I'm afraid, like all his race, a bit of a savage."

"Is he Russian?"

"He is a Cossack,[2]" said the general, and his smile showed red lips and pointed teeth. "So am I."

---

[1]The ounce, native to the Himalayas, and quite rare.

[2]From the southern part of European Russia, the Cossacks were known as exceptionally fine horsemen and light cavalrymen and, under the Czars, were feared for their ruthless raids.

"Come," he said, "we shouldn't be chatting here. We can talk later. Now you want clothes, food, rest. You shall have them. This is a most restful spot."

Ivan had reappeared, and the general spoke to him with lips that moved but gave forth no sound.

"Follow Ivan, if you please, Mr. Rainsford," said the general. "I was about to have my dinner when you came. I'll wait for you. You'll find that my clothes will fit you, I think."

It was to a huge, beam-ceilinged bedroom with a canopied bed big enough for six men that Rainsford followed the silent giant. Ivan laid out an evening suit, and Rainsford, as he put it on, noticed that it came from a London tailor who ordinarily cut and sewed for none below the rank of duke.

The dining room to which Ivan conducted him was in many ways remarkable. There was a medieval magnificence about it; it suggested a baronial hall of feudal times with its oaken panels, its high ceiling, its vast refectory table where twoscore men could sit down to eat. About the hall were the mounted heads of many animals—lions, tigers, elephants, moose, bears; larger or more perfect specimens Rainsford had never seen. At the great table the general was sitting, alone.

"You'll have a cocktail, Mr. Rainsford," he suggested. The cocktail was surpassingly good; and, Rainsford noted, the table appointments were of the finest—the linen, the crystal, the silver, the china.

They were eating borsch, the rich, red soup with whipped cream so dear to Russian palates. Half apologetically General Zaroff said: "We do our best to preserve the amenities of civilization here. Please forgive any lapses. We are well off the beaten track, you know. Do you think the champagne has suffered from its long ocean trip?"

"Not in the least," declared Rainsford. He was finding the general a most thoughtful and affable host, a true cosmopolite. But there was one small trait of the general's that made Rainsford uncomfortable. Whenever he looked up from his plate, he found the general studying him, appraising him narrowly.

"Perhaps," said General Zaroff, "you were surprised that I recognized your name. You see, I read all books on hunting published in English, French, and Russian. I have but one passion in my life, Mr. Rainsford, and it is the hunt."

"You have some wonderful heads here," said Rainsford as he ate a particularly well-cooked filet mignon. "That Cape buffalo[3] is the largest I ever saw."

"Oh, that fellow. Yes, he was a monster."

"Did he charge you?"

"Hurled me against a tree," said the general. "Fractured my skull. But I got the brute."

"I've always thought," said Rainsford, "that the Cape buffalo is the most dangerous of all big game."

For a moment the general did not reply; he was smiling his curious red-lipped smile. Then he said slowly: "No. You are wrong, sir. The Cape buffalo is not the most dangerous big game." He sipped his wine. "Here in my preserve on this island," he said in the same slow tone, "I hunt more dangerous game."

Rainsford expressed his surprise. "Is there big game on this island?"

The general nodded. "The biggest."

"Really?"

"Oh, it isn't here naturally, of course. I have to stock the island."

"What have you imported, general?" Rainsford asked. "Tigers?"

The general smiled. "No," he said. "Hunting tigers ceased to interest me some years ago. I exhausted their possibilities, you see. No thrill left in tigers, no real danger. I live for danger, Mr. Rainsford."

The general took from his pocket a gold cigaret case and offered his guest a long black cigaret with a silver tip; it was perfumed and gave off a smell like incense.

"We will have some capital hunting, you and I," said the general. "I shall be most glad to have your society."

"But what game—" began Rainsford.

"I'll tell you," said the general. "You will be amused, I know. I think I may say, in all modesty, that I have done a rare

[3]Big, quick, intelligent, when separated from the herd, a rogue, one of the most dangerous African game animals.

thing. I have invented a new sensation. May I pour you another glass of port, Mr. Rainsford?"

"Thank you, general."

The general filled both glasses, and said: "God makes some men poets. Some He makes kings, some beggars. Me He made a hunter. My hand was made for the trigger, my father said. He was a very rich man with a quarter of a million acres in the Crimea, and he was an ardent sportsman. When I was only five years old he gave me a little gun, specially made in Moscow for me, to shoot sparrows with. When I shot some of his prize turkeys with it, he did not punish me; he complimented me on my marksmanship. I killed my first bear in the Caucasus when I was ten. My whole life has been one prolonged hunt. I went into the army—it was expected of noblemen's sons—and for a time commanded a division of Cossack cavalry, but my real interest was always the hunt. I have hunted every kind of game in every land. It would be impossible for me to tell you how many animals I have killed."

The general puffed at his cigaret.

"After the debacle in Russia[4] I left the country, for it was imprudent for an officer of the Czar to stay there. Many noble Russians lost everything. I, luckily, had invested heavily in American securities, so I shall never have to open a tea room in Monte Carlo or drive a taxi in Paris. Naturally, I continued to hunt—grizzlies in your Rockies, crocodiles in the Ganges, rhinoceroses in East Africa. It was in Africa that the Cape buffalo hit me and laid me up for six months. As soon as I recovered I started for the Amazon to hunt jaguars, for I had heard they were unusually cunning. They weren't." The Cossack sighed. "They were no match at all for a hunter with his wits about him, and a high-powered rifle. I was bitterly disappointed. I was lying in my tent with a splitting headache one night when a terrible thought pushed its way into my mind. Hunting was beginning to bore me! And hunting, remember, had been my life. I have heard that in America business men often go to pieces when they give up the business that has been their life."

"Yes, that's so," said Rainsford.

[4]The revolution of 1917 that overthrew the Czar and prepared the way for communist rule.

The general smiled. "I had no wish to go to pieces," he said. "I must do something. Now, mine is an analytical mind, Mr. Rainsford. Doubtless that is why I enjoy the problems of the chase."

"No doubt, General Zaroff."

"So," continued the general, "I asked myself why the hunt no longer fascinated me. You are much younger than I am, Mr. Rainsford, and have not hunted as much, but you perhaps can guess the answer."

"What was it?"

"Simply this: hunting had ceased to be what you call 'a sporting proposition.' It had become too easy. I always got my quarry. Always. There is no greater bore than perfection."

The general lit a fresh cigaret.

"No animal had a chance with me any more. That is no boast; it is a mathematical certainty. The animal had nothing but his legs and his instinct. Instinct is no match for reason. When I thought of this it was a tragic moment for me, I can tell you."

Rainsford leaned across the table, absorbed in what his host was saying.

"It came to me as an inspiration what I must do," the general went on.

"And that was?"

The general smiled the quiet smile of one who has faced an obstacle and surmounted it with success. "I had to invent a new animal to hunt," he said.

"A new animal? You're joking."

"Not at all," said the general. "I never joke about hunting. I needed a new animal. I found one. So I bought this island, built this house, and here I do my hunting. The island is perfect for my purposes—there are jungles with a maze of trails in them, hills, swamps—"

"But the animal, General Zaroff?"

"Oh," said the general, "it supplies me with the most exciting hunting in the world. No other hunting compares with it for an instant. Every day I hunt, and I never grow bored now, for I have a quarry with which I can match my wits."

Rainsford's bewilderment showed in his face.

"I wanted the ideal animal to hunt," explained the general. "So I said: 'What are the attributes of an ideal quarry?' And the answer was, of course: 'it must have courage, cunning, and, above all, it must be able to reason.'"

"But no animal can reason," objected Rainsford.

"My dear fellow," said the general, "there is one that can."

"But you can't mean—" gasped Rainsford.

"And why not?"

"I can't believe you are serious, General Zaroff. This is a grisly joke."

"Why should I not be serious? I am speaking of hunting."

"Hunting? Good God, General Zaroff, what you speak of is murder."

The general laughed with entire good nature. He regarded Rainsford quizzically. "I refuse to believe that so modern and civilized a young man as you seem to be harbors romantic ideas about the value of human life. Surely your experiences in the war—"

"Did not make me condone cold-blooded murder," finished Rainsford stiffly.

Laughter shook the general. "How extraordinarily droll you are!" he said. "One does not expect nowadays to find a young man of the educated class, even in America, with such a naive, and, if I may say so, mid-Victorian point of view. It's like finding a snuff-box in a limousine. Ah, well, doubtless you had Puritan ancestors. So many Americans appear to have had. I'll wager you'll forget your notions when you go hunting with me. You've a genuine new thrill in store for you, Mr. Rainsford."

"Thank you, I'm a hunter, not a murderer."

"Dear me," said the general, quite unruffled, "again that unpleasant word. But I think I can show you that your scruples are quite ill founded."

"Yes?"

"Life is for the strong, to be lived by the strong, and, if need be, taken by the strong. The weak of the world were put here to give the strong pleasure. I am strong. Why should I not use my gift? If I wish to hunt, why should I not? I hunt the scum of the earth—sailors from tramp ships—lascars, blacks, Chinese, whites, mongrels—a thoroughbred horse or hound is worth more than a score of them."

"But they are men," said Rainsford hotly.

"Precisely," said the general. "That is why I use them. It gives me pleasure. They can reason, after a fashion. So they are dangerous."

"But where do you get them?"

The general's left eyelid fluttered down in a wink. "This island is called Ship-Trap," he answered. "Sometimes an angry god of the high seas sends them to me. Sometimes, when Providence is not so kind, I help Providence a bit. Come to the window with me."

Rainsford went to the window and looked out toward the sea.

"Watch! Out there!" exclaimed the general, pointing into the night. Rainsford's eyes saw only blackness, and then, as the general pressed a button, far out to sea Rainsford saw the flash of lights.

The general chuckled. "They indicate a channel," he said, "where there's none: giant rocks with razor edges crouch like a sea monster with wide-open jaws. They can crush a ship as easily as I crush this nut." He dropped a walnut on the hardwood floor and brought his heel grinding down on it. "Oh, yes," he said, casually, as if in answer to a question, "I have electricity. We try to be civilized here."

"Civilized? And you shoot down men?"

A trace of anger was in the general's black eyes, but it was there for but a second, and he said, in his most pleasant manner: "Dear me, what a righteous young man you are! I assure you I do not do the thing you suggest. That would be barbarous. I treat these visitors with every consideration. They get plenty of good food and exercise. They get into splendid physical condition. You shall see for yourself to-morrow."

"What do you mean?"

"We'll visit my training school," smiled the general. "It's in the cellar. I have about a dozen pupils down there now. They're from the Spanish bark San Lucar that had the bad luck to go on the rocks out there. A very inferior lot, I regret to say. Poor specimens and more accustomed to the deck than to the jungle."

He raised his hand, and Ivan, who served as waiter, brought thick Turkish coffee. Rainsford, with an effort, held his tongue in check.

"It's a game, you see," pursued the general blandly. "I suggest to one of them that we go hunting. I give him a supply of food and an excellent hunting knife. I give him three hours start. I am to follow, armed only with a pistol of the smallest caliber and range. If my quarry eludes me for three whole days, he wins the game. If I find him"—the general smiled—"he loses."

"Suppose he refuses to be hunted?"

"Oh," said the general, "I give him his option, of course. He need not play that game if he doesn't wish to. If he does not wish to hunt, I turn him over to Ivan. Ivan once had the honor of serving as official knouter to the Great White Czar, and he has his own ideas of sport. Invariably, Mr. Rainsford, invariably they choose the hunt."

"And if they win?"

The smile on the generals face widened. "To date I have not lost," he said.

Then he added, hastily: "I don't wish you to think me a braggart, Mr. Rainsford. Many of them afford only the most elementary sort of problem. Occasionally I strike a tartar. One almost did win. I eventually had to use the dogs."

"The dogs?"

"This way, please. I'll show you."

The general steered Rainsford to a window. The lights from the windows sent a flickering illumination that made grotesque patterns on the courtyard below, and Rainsford could see moving about there a dozen or so huge black shapes; as they turned toward him, their eyes glittered greenly.

"A rather good lot, I think," observed the general. "They are let out at seven every night. If anyone should try to get into my house—or out of it—something extremely regrettable would occur to him." He hummed a snatch of song from the Folies Bergre.[5]

"And now," said the general, "I want to show you my new collection of heads. Will you come with me to the library?"

[5]Paris theatre and music hall that in 1918 reestablished itself as the scene for revues, spectaculars, etc.

"I hope," said Rainsford, "that you will excuse me tonight, General Zaroff. I'm really not feeling at all well."

"Ah, indeed?" the general inquired solicitously. "Well, I suppose that's only natural, after your long swim. You need a good, restful night's sleep. Tomorrow you'll feel like a new man, I'll wager. Then we'll hunt, eh? I've one rather promising prospect—"

Rainsford was hurrying from the room.

"Sorry you can't go with me tonight," called the general. "I expect rather fair sport—a big, strong black. He looks resourceful—Well, good night, Mr. Rainsford; I hope you have a good night's rest."

The bed was good, and the pajamas of the softest silk, and he was tired in every fiber of his being, but nevertheless Rainsford could not quiet his brain with the opiate of sleep. He lay, eyes wide open. Once he thought he heard stealthy steps in the corridor outside his room. He sought to throw open the door; it would not open. He went to the window and looked out. His room was high up in one of the towers. The lights of the chateau were out now, and it was dark and silent, but there was a fragment of sallow moon, and by its wan light he could see, dimly, the courtyard; there, weaving in and out in the pattern of shadow, were black, noiseless forms; the hounds heard him at the window and looked up, expectantly, with their green eyes. Rainsford went back to the bed and lay down. By many methods he tried to put himself to sleep. He had achieved a doze when, just as morning began to come, he heard, far off in the jungle, the faint report of a pistol.

General Zaroff did not appear until luncheon. He was dressed faultlessly in the tweeds of a country squire. He was solicitous about the state of Rainsford's health.

"As for me," sighed the general, "I do not feel so well. I am worried, Mr. Rainsford. Last night I detected traces of my old complaint."

To Rainsford's questioning glance the general said: "Ennui. Boredom."

Then, taking a second helping of Crepes Suzette, the general explained: "The hunting was not good last night. The fellow lost his head. He made a straight trail that offered no problems at all. That's the trouble with these sailors; they have dull brains to begin with, and they do not know how to get about in the woods. They do excessively stupid and obvious things. It's most annoying. Will you have another glass of Chablis, Mr. Rainsford?"

"General," said Rainsford firmly, "I wish to leave this island at once."

The general raised his thickets of eyebrows; he seemed hurt. "But, my dear fellow," the general protested, "you've only just come. You've had no hunting—"

"I wish to go today," said Rainsford. He saw the dead black eyes of the general on him, studying him. General Zaroff's face suddenly brightened.

He filled Rainsford's glass with venerable Chablis from a dusty bottle.

"Tonight," said the general, "we will hunt—you and I."

Rainsford shook his head. "No, general," he said. "I will not hunt."

The general shrugged his shoulders and delicately ate a hothouse grape. "As you wish, my friend," he said. "The choice rests entirely with you. But may I not venture to suggest that you will find my idea of sport more diverting than Ivan's?"

He nodded toward the corner to where the giant stood, scowling, his thick arms crossed on his hogshead of chest.

"You don't mean—" cried Rainsford.

"My dear fellow," said the general, "have I not told you I always mean what I say about hunting? This is really an inspiration. I drink to a foeman worthy of my steel—at last."

The general raised his glass, but Rainsford sat staring at him.

"You'll find this game worth playing," the general said enthusiastically. "Your brain against mine. Your woodcraft against mine. Your strength and stamina against mine. Outdoor chess! And the stake is not without value, eh?"

"And if I win—" began Rainsford huskily.

"I'll cheerfully acknowledge myself defeated if I do not find you by midnight of the third day," said General Zaroff. "My sloop will place you on the mainland near a town."

The general read what Rainsford was thinking.

"Oh, you can trust me," said the Cossack. "I will give you my word as a gentleman and a sportsman. Of course you, in turn, must agree to say nothing of your visit here."

"I'll agree to nothing of the kind," said Rainsford.

"Oh," said the general, "in that case—but why discuss that now? Three days hence we can discuss it over a bottle of Veuve Cliquot,[6] unless—"

The general sipped his wine.

Then a businesslike air animated him. "Ivan," he said to Rainsford, "will supply you with hunting clothes, food, a knife. I suggest you wear moccasins; they leave a poorer trail. I suggest, too, that you avoid the big swamp in the southeast corner of the island. We call it Death Swamp. There's quicksand there. One foolish fellow tried it. The deplorable part of it was that Lazarus followed him. You can imagine my feelings, Mr. Rainsford. I loved Lazarus; he was the finest hound in my pack. Well, I must beg you to excuse me now. I always take a siesta after lunch. You'll hardly have time for a nap, I fear. You'll want to start, no doubt. I shall not follow till dusk. Hunting at night is so much more exciting than by day, don't you think? Au revoir, Mr. Rainsford, au revoir."

General Zaroff, with a deep, courtly bow, strolled from the room.

From another door came Ivan. Under one arm he carried khaki hunting clothes, a haversack of food, a leather sheath containing a long-bladed hunting knife; his right hand rested on a cocked revolver thrust in the crimson sash about his waist....

Rainsford had fought his way through the bush for two hours. "I must keep my nerve. I must keep my nerve," he said through tight teeth.

He had not been entirely clear-headed when the chateau gates snapped shut behind him. His whole idea at first was to put distance between himself and General Zaroff, and, to this end, he had plunged along, spurred on by the sharp rowels of something very like panic. Now he had got a grip on himself, had stopped, and was taking stock of himself and the situation.

[6]A fine champagne; Chablis is a very dry white Burgandy table wine; Chambertin is a highly esteemed red Burgandy wine.

He saw that straight flight was futile; inevitably it would bring him face to face with the sea. He was in a picture with a frame of water, and his operations, clearly, must take place within that frame.

"I'll give him a trail to follow," muttered Rainsford, and he struck off from the rude paths he had been following into the trackless wilderness. He executed a series of intricate loops; he doubled on his trail again and again, recalling all the lore of the fox hunt, and all the dodges of the fox. Night found him leg-weary, with hands and face lashed by the branches, on a thickly wooded ridge. He knew it would be insane to blunder on through the dark, even if he had the strength. His need for rest was imperative and he thought: "I have played the fox, now I must play the cat of the fable.[7]" A big tree with a thick trunk and outspread branches was nearby, and, taking care to leave not the slightest mark, he climbed up into the crotch, and stretching out on one of the broad limbs, after a fashion, rested. Rest brought him new confidence and almost a feeling of security. Even so zealous a hunter as General Zaroff could not trace him there, he told himself; only the devil himself could follow that complicated trail through the jungle after dark. But, perhaps, the general was a devil—

An apprehensive night crawled slowly by like a wounded snake, and sleep did not visit Rainsford, although the silence of a dead world was on the jungle. Toward morning when a dingy gray was varnishing the sky, the cry of some startled bird focused Rainsford's attention in that direction. Something was coming through the bush, coming slowly, carefully, coming by the same winding way Rainsford had come. He flattened himself down on the limb, and through a screen of leaves almost as thick as tapestry, he watched. The thing that was approaching was a man.

It was General Zaroff. He made his way along with his eyes fixed in utmost concentration on the ground before him. He paused, almost beneath the tree, dropped to his knees and studied the ground. Rainsford's impulse was to hurl himself down

---

[7]The fox boasts of his many tricks to elude the hounds; the cat knows only one—to climb the nearest tree—but that is worth more than all of the fox's tricks.

like a panther, but he saw the general's right hand held something metallic—a small automatic pistol.

The hunter shook his head several times, as if he were puzzled. Then he straightened up and took from his case one of his black cigarets; its pungent incense-like smoke floated up to Rainsford's nostrils.

Rainsford held his breath. The general's eyes had left the ground and were traveling inch by inch up the tree. Rainsford froze there, every muscle tensed for a spring. But the sharp eyes of the hunter stopped before they reached the limb where Rainsford lay; a smile spread over his brown face. Very deliberately he blew a smoke ring into the air; then he turned his back on the tree and walked carelessly away, back along the trail he had come. The swish of the underbrush against his hunting boots grew fainter and fainter.

The pent-up air burst hotly from Rainsford's lungs. His first thought made him feel sick and numb. The general could follow a trail through the woods at night; he could follow an extremely difficult trail; he must have uncanny powers; only by the merest chance had the Cossack failed to see his quarry.

Rainsford's second thought was even more terrible. It sent a shudder of cold horror through his whole being. Why had the general smiled? Why had he turned back?

Rainsford did not want to believe what his reason told him was true, but the truth was as evident as the sun that had by now pushed through the morning mists. The general was playing with him! The general was saving him for another day's sport! The Cossack was the cat; he was the mouse.[8] Then it was that Rainsford knew the full meaning of terror.

"I will not lose my nerve. I will not."

He slid down from the tree, and struck off again into the woods. His face was set and he forced the machinery of his mind to function. Three hundred yards from his hiding place he stopped where a huge dead tree leaned precariously on a smaller, living one. Throwing off his sack of food, Rainsford took his knife from its sheath and began to work with all his energy.

---

[8]A cat, sure of his prey, plays with a mouse before killing him.

The job was finished at last, and he threw himself down behind a fallen log a hundred feet away. He did not have to wait long. The cat was coming again to play with the mouse.

Following the trail with the sureness of a bloodhound, came General Zaroff. Nothing escaped those searching black eyes, no crushed blade of grass, no bent twig, no mark, no matter how faint, in the moss. So intent was the Cossack on his stalking that he was upon the thing Rainsford had made before he saw it. His foot touched the protruding bough that was the trigger. Even as he touched it, the general sensed his danger and leaped back with the agility of an ape. But he was not quite quick enough; the dead tree, delicately adjusted to rest on the cut living one, crashed down and struck the general a glancing blow on the shoulder as it fell; but for his alertness, he must have been smashed beneath it. He staggered, but he did not fall; nor did he drop his revolver. He stood there, rubbing his injured shoulder, and Rainsford, with fear again gripping his heart, heard the general's mocking laugh ring through the jungle.

"Rainsford," called the general, "if you are within the sound of my voice, as I suppose you are, let me congratulate you. Not many men know how to make a Malay man-catcher. Luckily, for me, I, too, have hunted in Malacca. You are proving interesting, Mr. Rainsford. I am going now to have my wound dressed; it's only a slight one. But I shall be back. I shall be back."

When the general, nursing his bruised shoulder, had gone, Rainsford took up his flight again. It was flight now, a desperate, hopeless flight, that carried him on for some hours. Dusk came, then darkness, and still he pressed on. The ground grew softer under his moccasins; the vegetation grew ranker, denser; insects bit him savagely. Then, as he stepped forward, his foot sank into the ooze. He tried to wrench it back, but the muck sucked viciously at his foot as if it were a giant leech. With a violent effort, he tore loose. He knew where he was now. Death Swamp and its quicksand.

His hands were tight closed as if his nerve were something tangible that some one in the darkness was trying to tear from his grip. The softness of the earth had given him an idea. He stepped back from the quicksand a dozen feet or so, and, like some huge prehistoric beaver, he began to dig.

Rainsford had dug himself in in France[9] when a second's delay meant death. That had been a placid pastime compared to his digging now. The pit grew deeper; when it was above his shoulders, he climbed out and from some hard saplings cut stakes and sharpened them to a fine point. These stakes he planted in the bottom of the pit with the points sticking up. With flying fingers he wove a rough carpet of weeds and branches and with it he covered the mouth of the pit. Then, wet with sweat and aching with tiredness, he crouched behind the stump of a lightning-charred tree.

He knew his pursuer was coming; he heard the padding sound of feet on the soft earth, and the night breeze brought him the perfume of the general's cigaret. It seemed to Rainsford that the general was coming with unusual swiftness; he was not feeling his way along, foot by foot. Rainsford, crouching there, could not see the general, nor could he see the pit. He lived a year in a minute. Then he felt an impulse to cry aloud with joy, for he heard the sharp crackle of the breaking branches as the cover of the pit gave way; he heard the sharp scream of pain as the pointed stakes found their mark. He leaped up from his place of concealment. Then he cowered back. Three feet from the pit a man was standing, with an electric torch in his hand.

"You've done well, Rainsford," the voice of the general called. "Your Burmese tiger pit has claimed one of my best dogs. Again you score. I think, Mr. Rainsford, I'll see what you can do against my whole pack. I'm going home for a rest now. Thank you for a most amusing evening."

At daybreak Rainsford, lying near the swamp, was awakened by the sound that made him know that he had new things to learn about fear. It was a distant sound, faint and wavering, but he knew it. It was the baying of a pack of hounds.

Rainsford knew he could do one of two things. He could stay where he was and wait. That was suicide. He could flee.

---

[9]During World War I, he had quickly dug a hole or trench to shelter himself from exploding shells, bullets, etc.

That was postponing the inevitable. For a moment he stood there, thinking. An idea that held a wild chance came to him, and, tightening his belt, he headed away from the swamp.

The baying of the hounds drew nearer, then still nearer, nearer, ever nearer. On a ridge Rainsford climbed a tree. Down a watercourse, not a quarter of a mile away, he could see the bush moving. Straining his eyes, he saw the lean figure of General Zaroff; just ahead of him Rainsford made out another figure whose wide shoulders surged through the tall jungle weeds; it was the giant Ivan, and he seemed pulled forward by some unseen force; Rainsford knew that Ivan must be holding the pack in leash.

They would be on him any minute now. His mind worked frantically. He thought of a native trick he had learned in Uganda. He slid down the tree. He caught hold of a springy young sapling and to it he fastened his hunting knife, with the blade pointing down the trail; with a bit of wild grapevine he tied back the sapling. Then he ran for his life. The hounds raised their voices as they hit the fresh scent. Rainsford knew now how an animal at bay feels.

He had to stop to get his breath. The baying of the hounds stopped abruptly, and Rainsford's heart stopped, too. They must have reached the knife.

He shinnied excitedly up a tree and looked back. His pursuers had stopped. But the hope that was in Rainsford's brain when he climbed died, for he saw in the shallow valley that General Zaroff was still on his feet. But Ivan was not. The knife, driven by the recoil of the springing tree, had not wholly failed.

"Nerve, nerve, nerve!" he panted, as he dashed along. A blue gap showed between the trees dead ahead. Ever nearer drew the hounds. Rainsford forced himself on toward that gap. He reached it. It was the shore of the sea. Across a cove he could see the gloomy gray stone of the chateau. Twenty feet below him the sea rumbled and hissed. Rainsford hesitated. He heard the hounds. Then he leaped far out into the sea....

When the general and his pack reached the place by the sea, the Cossack stopped. For some minutes he stood regarding the blue-green expanse of water. He shrugged his shoulders. Then he sat down, took a drink of brandy from a silver flask, lit a perfumed cigaret, and hummed a bit from Madame Butterfly.

General Zaroff had an exceedingly good dinner in his great paneled dining hall that evening. With it he had a bottle of Pol Roger and half a bottle of Chambertin. Two slight annoyances kept him from perfect enjoyment. One was the thought that it would be difficult to replace Ivan; the other was that his quarry had escaped him; of course the American hadn't played the game—so thought the general as he tasted his after-dinner liqueur. In his library he read, to soothe himself, from the works of Marcus Aurelius.[10] At ten he went up to his bedroom. He was deliciously tired, he said to himself, as he locked himself in. There was a little moonlight, so, before turning on his light, he went to the window and looked down at the courtyard. He could see the great hounds, and he called: "Better luck another time," to them. Then he switched on the light.

A man, who had been hiding in the curtains of the bed, was standing there.

"Rainsford!" screamed the general. "How in God's name did you get here?"

"Swam," said Rainsford. "I found it quicker than walking through the jungle."

The general sucked in his breath and smiled. "I congratulate you," he said. "You have won the game."

Rainsford did not smile. "I am still a beast at bay," he said, in a low, hoarse voice. "Get ready, General Zaroff."

The general made one of his deepest bows. "I see," he said. "Splendid! One of us is to furnish a repast for the hounds. The other will sleep in this very excellent bed. On guard, Rainsford...."

He had never slept in a better bed, Rainsford decided.

---

[10]Roman emperor (A.D. 161-180), Stoic philosopher, writer, and humanitarian who, though good to the poor and opposed to the cruelty of gladiatorial shows, persecuted early Christians.

THE GIRLS IN THEIR SUMMER DRESSES
by Irwin Shaw

Fifth Avenue was shining in the sun when they left the Brevoort. The sun was warm, even though it was February, and everything looked like Sunday morning—the buses and the well-dressed people walking slowly in couples and the quiet buildings with the windows closed.

Michael held Frances' arm tightly as they walked toward Washington Square in the sunlight. They walked lightly, almost smiling, because they had slept late and had a good breakfast and it was Sunday. Michael unbuttoned his coat and let it flap around him in the mild wind.

"Look out," Frances said as they crossed Eighth Street. "You'll break your neck." Michael laughed and Frances laughed with him.

"She's not so pretty," Frances said. "Anyway, not pretty enough to take a chance of breaking your neck."

Michael laughed again. "How did you know I was looking at her?"

Frances cocked her head to one side and smiled at her husband under the brim of her hat. "Mike, darling," she said.

"O.K.," he said. "Excuse me."

Frances patted his arm lightly and pulled him along a little faster toward Washington Square. "Let's not see anybody all day," she said. "Let's just hang around with each other. You and me. We're always up to our neck in people, drinking their Scotch or drinking our Scotch; we only see each other in bed. I want to go out with my husband all day long. I want him to talk only to me and listen only to me."

"What's to stop us?" Michael asked.

"The Stevensons. They want us to drop by around one o'clock and they'll drive us into the country."

"The cunning Stevensons," Mike said. "Transparent. They can whistle. They can go driving in the country by themselves."

"Is it a date?"

"It's a date."

Frances leaned over and kissed him on the tip of the ear.

"Darling," Michael said, "this is Fifth Avenue."

"Let me arrange a program," Frances said. "A planned Sunday in New York for a young couple with money to throw away."

"Go easy."

"First let's go to the Metropolitan Museum of Art," Frances suggested, because Michael had said during the week he wanted to go. "I haven't been there in three years and there're at least ten pictures I want to see again. Then we can take the bus down to Radio City and watch them skate. And later we'll go down to Cavanaghs and get a steak as big as a blacksmith's apron, with a bottle of wine, and after that there's a French picture at the Filmarte that everybody says—say, are you listening to me?"

"Sure," he said. He took his eyes off the hatless girl with the dark hair, cut dancer-style like a helmet, who was walking past him.

"That's the program for the day," Frances said flatly. "Or maybe you'd just rather walk up and down Fifth Avenue."

"No," Michael said. "Not at all."

"You always look at other women," Frances said. "Everywhere. Every damned place we go."

"No, darling," Michael said, "I look at everything. God gave me eyes and I look at women and men in subway excavations and moving pictures and the little flowers of the field. I casually inspect the universe."

"You ought to see the look in your eye," Frances said, "as you casually inspect the universe on Fifth Avenue."

"I'm a happily married man." Michael pressed her elbow tenderly. "Example for the whole twentieth century—Mr. and

Mrs. Mike Loomis. Hey, let's have a drink," he said, stopping.

"We just had breakfast."

"Now listen, darling," Mike said, choosing his words with care, "it's a nice day and we both felt good and there's no reason why we have to break it up. Let's have a nice Sunday."

"All right. I don't know why I started this. Let's drop it. Let's have a good time."

They joined hands consciously and walked without talking among the baby carriages and the old Italian men in their Sunday clothes and the young women with Scotties in Washington Square Park.

"At least once a year everyone should go to the Metropolitan Museum of Art," Frances said after a while, her tone a good imitation of the tone she had used at breakfast and at the beginning of their walk. "And it's nice on Sunday. There're a lot of people looking at the pictures and you get the feeling maybe Art isn't on the decline in New York City, after all—"

"I want to tell you something," Michael said very seriously."I have not touched another woman. Not once. In all the five years."

"All right," Frances said.

"You believe that, don't you?"

"All right."

They walked between the crowded benches, under the scrubby city-park trees.

"I try not to notice it," Frances said, "but I feel rotten inside, in my stomach, when we pass a woman and you look at her and I see that look in your eye and that's the way you looked at me the first time. In Alice Maxwell's house. Standing there in the living room, next to the radio, with a green hat on and all those people."

"I remember the hat," Michael said.

"The same look," Frances said. "And it makes me feel bad. It makes me feel terrible."

"Sh-h-h, please, darling, sh-h-h."

"I think I would like a drink now," Frances said.

They walked over to a bar on Eighth Street, not saying anything. Michael automatically helping her over curbstones and guiding her past automobiles. They sat near a window in the bar and the sun streamed in and there was a small, cheerful fire in the fireplace. A little Japanese waiter came over and put down some pretzels and smiled happily at them.

"What do you order after breakfast?" Michael asked.

"Brandy, I suppose," Frances said.

"Courvoisier," Michael told the waiter, "Two Courvoisiers."

The waiter came with the glasses and they sat drinking the brandy in the sunlight. Michael finished half his and drank a little water.

"I look at women," he said. "Correct. I don't say it's wrong or right. I look at them. If I pass them on the street and I don't look at them, I'm fooling you, I'm fooling myself."

"You look at them as though you want them," Frances said, playing with her brandy glass. "Every one of them."

"In a way," Michael said, speaking softly and not to his wife, "in a way that's true. I don't do anything about it, but it's true."

"I know it. That's why I feel bad."

"Another brandy," Michael called. "Waiter, two more brandies."

He sighed and closed his eyes and rubbed them gently with his fingertips. "I love the way women look. One of the things I like best about New York is the battalions of women. When I first came to New York from Ohio that was the first thing I noticed, the million wonderful women, all over the city. I walked around with my heart in my throat."

"A kid," Frances said. "That's a kid's feeling."

"Guess again," Michael said. "Guess again. I'm older now. I'm a man getting near middle age, putting on a little fat, and I still love to walk along Fifth Avenue at three o'clock on the east side of the street between Fiftieth and the Fifty-seventh Streets. They're all out then, shopping, in their furs and their crazy hats, everything all concentrated from all over the world into seven blocks—the best furs, the best clothes, the handsomest women, out to spend money and feeling good about it."

The Japanese waiter put the two drinks down, smiling with great happiness.

"Everything is all right? Everything is wonderful," Michael said.

"If it's just a couple of fur coats," Frances said, "and forty-five dollar hats—"

"It's not the fur coats. Or the hats. That's just the scenery for that particular kind of women. Understand," he said, "you don't have to listen to this."

"I want to listen."

"I like the girls in the offices. Neat, with their eyeglasses, smart, chipper, knowing what everything is about. I like the girls on Forty-fourth Street at lunchtime, the actresses, all dressed up on nothing a week. I like the salesgirls in the stores, paying attention to you first because you're a man, leaving lady customers waiting. I got all this stuff accumulated in me because I've been thinking about it for ten years and now you've asked for it and here it is."

"Go ahead," Frances said.

"When I think of New York City, I think of all the girls on parade in the city. I don't know whether it's something special with me or whether every man in the city walks around with the same feeling inside him, but I feel as though I'm at a picnic in this city. I like to sit near the women in the theatres, the famous beauties who've taken six hours to get ready and look at it. And the young girls at the football games, with the red cheeks, and when the warm weather comes, the girls in their summer dresses." He finished his drink. "That's the story."

Frances finished her drink and swallowed two or three times extra. "You say you love me?"

"I love you."

"I'm pretty, too," Frances said. "As pretty as any of them."

"You're beautiful," Michael said.

"I'm good for you," Frances said, pleading. "I've made a good wife, a good housekeeper, a good friend. I'd do any damn thing for you."

"I know," Michael said. He put his hand out and grasped hers.

"You'd like to be free to—" Frances said.

"Sh-h-h."

"Tell the truth." She took her hand away from under his.

Michael flicked the edge of his glass with his finger. "O.K.," he said gently. "Sometimes I feel I would like to be free."

"Well," Frances said, "any time you say."

"Don't be foolish." Michael swung his chair around to her side of the table and patted her thigh.

She began to cry silently into her handkerchief, bent over just enough so that nobody else in the bar would notice. "Someday," she said, crying, "you're going to make a move."

Michael didn't say anything. He sat watching the bartender slowly peel a lemon.

"Aren't you?" Frances asked harshly. "Come on, tell me. Talk. Aren't you?"

"Maybe," Michael said. He moved his chair back again. "How the hell do I know?"

"You know," Frances persisted. "Don't you know?"

"Yes," Michael said after a while, "I know."

Frances stopped crying then. Two or three snuffles into the handkerchief and she put it away and her face didn't tell anything to anybody. "At least do me one favor," she said.

"Sure."

"Stop talking about how pretty this woman is or that one. Nice eyes, nice breasts, a pretty figure, good voice." She mimicked his voice. "Keep it to yourself. I'm not interested."

Michael waved to the waiter. "I'll keep it to myself," he said.

Frances flicked the corners of her eyes. "Another brandy," she told the waiter.

"Two," Michael said.

"Yes, Ma'am, yes, sir," said the waiter, backing away.

Frances regarded Michael coolly across the table. "Do you want me to call the Stevensons?" she asked. "It'll be nice in the country."

"Sure," Michael said. "Call them."

She got up from the table and walked across the room toward the telephone. Michael watched her walk, thinking what a pretty girl, what nice legs.

HEY, JOE
by Ben Neihart

Joe was newly sixteen. He had the rosy aspect, and the swagger, and the skinny arms, and the bad reputation. He was a brooder, a magazine reader, a swaying dancer at mellow, jazzy rap parties. He kept his hair cut short like the other smoked-out newbies at Metaire Park Country Day, and the only shoes he wore were black suède Pumas.

School had just let out for the Labor Day weekend, so Joe was home, changing clothes, in a hurry to be gone before his mother returned from work. He hated to leave her alone on a Friday night, with her books and the cell phone. He hated the actual leave-taking most of all—her quick kiss, the sound of the front door's bolt lock when he closed it behind him. He wished she didn't spend so much time by herself. Why didn't she hang with her old friends? She was always working—at Tulane Medical Center, in the fund-raising office, asking doctors and scientists and presidents of Corporation Whatever for money. "It's gonna suck the life right out of me," she sometimes joked. Joe hated her saying that, because he could see that it was true; in the past year, it seemed, skin and muscle hung more loosely on her frame, and on her face, even though she did exercises in the high-ceilinged ballroom of the New Orleans Athletic Center, downtown.

He wandered about the living room, looking for his glasses, which he wore only at home. They were hidden somewhere beneath the spoils of his mom's latest shopping spree. On the floor were neat piles of new compact disks, hard-cover novels by European women with killer black hairdos, and shoeboxes. Slung over the furniture were silk blouses, palazzo pants in four shades of cream, and bras and panties, all of them with price tags still attached.

"And the value of this showcase is..." Joe said, and then he hurried down the hall to the bathroom.

In his underwear, he crouched over the bathroom sink. It was his pond, shell-shaped, with separate faucets for hot and cold water. The mirror was steamproof, and flattering; it put your face at a remove, so you weren't right on top of yourself as you did your routine. He squirted some Dial onto a washcloth and worked up a lather to freshen his underarms. He rubbed on some deodorant next, then washed his face and brushed his teeth.

He went into his mom's bedroom. As always, it was neatly set up for when she would come home this evening. The king-size bed was made; a pair of jeans and an immaculate white T-shirt and fresh panties lay on the pillow; the blinds were closed to keep the room cool in the late-summer sunlight. Joe liked the feel of the wood floor under his bare feet. He hopped onto the doctor's-office scale beside the dresser. One hundred twenty pounds. Good, he told himself, lean and portable.

He pulled his mom's door shut on his way to his own bedroom, the smallest room of the house—even smaller than the bathroom. He liked the fact that when he lay down to sleep he could touch the walls on either side of his bed. On weekend mornings, his mom would come into the room to wake him up early so they could spend the morning together in the back yard, sitting on the stone benches in her little rock garden. Between them, they'd drink a pitcher of orange juice, and then Joe would go inside to fix enormous tumblers of iced tea, to clear the thickness from their throats. It was as if they hadn't missed each other in the comings and goings of the week. Long, contented silences; bare feet stretching in the dewy grass; the sun pumping higher into the sky.

Now Joe pulled the front off one of his waist-high Sony speakers, which had been hollowed out to hold his business, the top-shelf weed he imported from Gainesville and sold to his friends. He unrolled a zip-lock freezer bag and took a deep breath of the sweet, fearsome herb. He took a pinch to roll a quick joint. Time to give fashion, he thought. He lit up and collapsed onto his bed. He didn't have to turn on his stereo; music presented itself, as if it had lain dormant in the joint: "Nickel bag, a nickel bag…"

As he got stoned, he looked at his hands, which were covered with scars. His legs and feet were, too. Each scar was the proof of a mountain-bike tumble, or, in one case, a skid across the coral beach on Fitzroy Island in the Great Barrier Reef, where they had gone last Christmas—Joe, his mom, and his dad, just before he died. They had pushed Daddy's wheelchair to the edge of the Coral Sea. "A sea like green milk," Daddy had said. Joe and his mom hurtled past the breaking waves and dove head on, grasping handfuls of water, racing, floating. When they were finished, they stood beside Daddy, dripping onto his sunburned legs and shoulders. "Oh," he said. "Oh, does that feel good."

Now Joe heard the mail truck stop outside. Friday was a magazine day. He drew himself out of bed, sprayed some Lysol around. He locked up the house and galloped down the driveway. The mailbox was rooted in a pile of pink, round stones. Joe kicked them with his toe. He left the bills and letters in the box and pulled out the new Vogue. He sat down on the slope of curb where his driveway met the street. He'd wait here, he decided, for his ride to the Quarter, where it was his habit to spend Friday nights.

He set the magazine on his bare legs and took stock of the cover. The model was the angel of Joe's life. Her name was Linda, and the cattish regard of her eyes could pull you out of a funk. Joe had been following her career for five years now. In interviews, Linda said that all she had ever wanted to be was a model; she didn't want to be an actress or a singer or a politician, and she didn't want to talk about her charities or whatever, and she talked to her mom every day, and they talked about modelling, because that was Linda's job.

On this cover, Linda sat in the grass; she wore a grape velvet dress that was tight in the bodice. The lightest strands of her hair—the color of Coke in a glass full of melting ice—caught the sun, reminding Joe of the old Dutch society paintings that he had admired in his "World of Art: The Netherlands" class. In those paintings the background was usually dark—an inky, enamel cloud—to set off the lighter wires of the subject's hair and her lucent, honeycomb ruff and her knot of blue pearls.

He looked into Linda's eyes and tried to imitate her smile. He pressed his knees together and palmed the hair on his legs as if smoothing a skirt. Then he noticed the small type near the bottom of the cover: "LINDA EVANGELISTA IN LOVE." He turned to the table of contents. He felt as if the boundary between his fingers and the page were disintegrating. There! He paged through the dark-hued Steven Meisel photographs, and then he stopped. A two-page spread of Linda, wearing a gray cropped sweater. She lay beneath her boyfriend, Kyle, the actor from "Twin Peaks," on a blanket that was suffused with morning sunlight. They were kissing, openmouthed. Her hand—with polished, short nails—gently held the side of his neck.

"Work it, Linda," Joe said happily, and then he lay back on the driveway, holding the magazine to his chest. Music billowed from the house next door, where a former friend of his, Al Theim, lived—a Michael Bolton number, sung as if the singer had taken an Uplift enema. Joe howled along in a fake, sour-bellied voice: "Nothing cures a broken heart like time, love, and tenderness."

It was just like Al Theim to broadcast that kind of shit. Joe couldn't believe he'd once been in love with the guy. They used to spend afternoons together listening to Al's older brother's leftover records from the early eighties: A Flock of Seagulls, Visage, Ultravox. The singers wore makeup, and their hair was swept up in whoopie curls and banglets, but the songs, Joe thought, were some songs. Longing vocals on top of wet, sparkly keyboards: "Ultraviolet, radio lights, telecommunication..."

One warm October evening, almost four years earlier, Joe's mom had taken Joe and Al to Scream in the Dark, a haunted house set up in two gaping, connected barns, across the Mississippi, in Algiers. Christian kids dressed from top to bottom in hunter-orange directed the parking, took admission money, and made you sign an injury-release form. It felt like summer: it was seventy-four degrees out in the early evening. Joe and Al wore matching, tartan-plaid, flimsy cotton shorts. Even their thin, hairless legs matched.

"What kind of movie is this?" Joe's mom asked, bending over a picnic table to sign her form. Despite Joe's warning, she'd got herself up in a long black dress.

Joe went first, on his hands and knees into the entrance tunnel. Al followed, and then Joe's mom, her knees bound up in the dress. At the end of the tunnel was a ladder. Joe climbed to the second level, a pitch-dark room of indeterminate size, at the far end of which flashed the strobe-lit entrance to the next room. He ventured forward; Al and Mom followed.

"I thought it was going to be a movie," Mom said, and they all laughed. Then, in the dark, someone touched Joe's shoulder.

He shouted, "Al! That's not funny."

"I didn't do anything," Al whispered.

"Someone touched me," Mom said. "Run!"

Joe hurried through the lightlessness, his forearms braced in front of him, into the following room. The floor and walls and ceiling were painted in a black-and-white checkerboard pattern; the strobe light worked its distortions. Joe looked over his shoulder at his mom and laughed. She chanced a smile. The kids in front of him were trying to get to the other side of the room, but they couldn't walk straight. The floor was a sharp pyramid, and you slid backward as you got closer to the peak. Joe looked over his shoulder. The wall behind his mother was moving. There was a man in a checkerboard costume, face painted white, sliding along the wall. He reached out to touch her. Joe took her hand and dragged her into the next room.

Here, in a hyped-up jungle, where the recorded sounds of squawking birds and giggling monkeys played deafeningly, Joe's mom disappeared; she had found the emergency exit and run out. Joe could hear her shouting, "I thought it was a movie!" The floor was made of foam rubber, and covered with rolling, shin-high hurdles. Al took Joe's hand. A gorilla watched them from behind a vivid palm tree, the outline of which was glowing purple.

Al could distinguish the hurdles from the flat stretches, but Joe, at first, couldn't; he perceived, instead, only the fluorescent foliage painted on the foam. Al shouted "Jump!" at each hurdle.

There was nothing like holding Al's warm, sweaty hand. At what looked to be the final hurdle, Joe made himself fall, and pulled Al with him. They wriggled to the wall, Joe's head propped on the foam hurdle, Al's head on Joe's chest. They watched the jumble of flapping shirts and jeans, listened to the screams and laughter.

Al touched Joe's face. "I like you," he said.

"I like you more than that," Joe said.

"How much?"

Their voices stayed in the space between their faces, and Joe found himself close to tears. "More than I like anyone," he said. "All day in school, I think about you." Birds called. The gorilla moved closer, then paused.

"Man, that makes me feel good," Al said. "Say it again."

And then there had been a kiss.

Now, spread out on his driveway, Joe shuddered and shut his eyes tight. The memory had returned with unwelcome carnal immediacy. Al Theim hadn't meant a word he said, Joe thought. Al Theim was just some wack softhearted guy who blew a few sentences out of his mouth. And so were the handful of guys he'd met since. Bullshitters. Maybe I'm not trying hard enough, he thought. Maybe tonight I'll talk to every person I see on Decatur Street, just bust up to them on the sidewalk and introduce myself. He shifted his head on its bed of grass clippings and loose gravel, and then he fell asleep.

He awoke to the whoop of an approaching car horn. He cracked open his eyes and just barely lifted his head to see who it was. A top-dollar car, reflecting sunlight, so he couldn't make out its color. Friends? Family? He dropped his head back and shut his eyes.

The car pulled onto the driveway beside him, purred for a moment, and then went silent.

The door opened, and his mother said, "Wake up, I'm home."

"Hey," Joe said.

She walked around the car, the soles of her low heels scratching the macadam. She came to his spot beside the mailbox and crouched down next to him. "Where you going tonight?"

"Out with friends."

"O.K., I won't ask." She settled onto her knees and smoothed her lemony cotton lap.

"I said out with friends."

"I said I won't ask."

Joe struggled to sit, propping himself up on one elbow. He looked at his mother's shoes, at her hose and her dress, at her knuckly hands and freckled arms—the freckles from long hours of weekend sunbathing. He knew why she liked the heat beating down on her, emptying her thoughts. He appreciated as much as she did the sensation of spilling a glass of iced tea down your throat as you lay, nearly still, on a chair in your own backyard.

Joe could tell that she was tired. It was Friday. It had been a long week. He put his hand on the side of her face. Her skin was soft, and cold from the car's A.C. "Stay with me a minute," he said. "Let's hang out for a minute."

She tilted her head to the side, catching his hand between her cheek and shoulder and holding it there. "You talk," she said. "I'd be so grateful."

INFLEXIBLE LOGIC
by Russell Maloney

When the six chimpanzees came into his life, Mr. Bainbridge was thirty-eight years old. He was a bachelor and lived comfortably in a remote part of Connecticut, in a large old house with a carriage drive, a conservatory, a tennis court, and a well-selected library. His income was derived from impeccably situated real estate in New York City, and he spent it soberly, in a manner which could give offence to nobody. Once a year, late in April, his tennis court was resurfaced, and after that anybody in the neighborhood was welcome to use it; his monthly statement from Brentanos seldom ran below seventy-five dollars; every third year, in November, he turned in his old Cadillac coup for a new one; he ordered his cigars, which were mild and rather moderately priced, in shipments of one thousand from a tobacconist in Havana; because of the international situation he had cancelled arrangements to travel abroad, and after due thought had decided to spend his travelling allowance on wines, which seemed likely to get scarcer and more expensive if the war lasted. On the whole, Mr. Bainbridge's life was deliberately, and not too unsuccessfully, modelled after that of an English country gentleman of the late eighteenth century, a gentleman interested in the arts and in the expansion of science, and so sure of himself that he didn't care if some people thought him eccentric.

Mr. Bainbridge had many friends in New York, and he spent several days of the month in the city, staying at his club and looking around. Sometimes he called up a girl and took her out to a theatre and a night club. Sometimes he and a couple of classmates got a little tight and went to a prizefight. Mr. Bainbridge also looked in now and then at some of the conservative art galleries, and liked occasionally to go to a concert. And he liked cocktail parties, too, because of the fine footling conversation and the extraordinary number of pretty girls who had nothing else to do with the rest of their evening. It was at a New York cocktail party, however, that Mr. Bainbridge kept his preliminary appointment with doom. At one of the parties given by Hobie Packard, the stockbroker, he learned about the theory of the six chimpanzees.

It was almost six-forty. The people who had intended to have one drink and go had already gone, and the people who intended to stay were fortifying themselves with slightly dried canapés and talking animatedly. A group of stage and radio people had coagulated in one corner, near Packard's Capehart, and were wrangling about various methods of cheating the Collector of Internal Revenue. In another corner was a group of stockbrokers, talking about the greatest stockbroker of them all, Gauguin. Little Marcia Lupton was sitting with a young man, saying earnestly, "Do you really want to know what my greatest ambition is? I want to be myself," and Mr. Bainbridge smiled gently, thinking of the time Marcia had said that to him. Then he heard the voice of Bernard Weiss, the critic, saying, "Of course he wrote one good novel. It's not surprising. After all, we know that if six chimpanzees were set to work pounding six typewriters at random, they would, in a million years, write all the books in the British Museum."

Mr. Bainbridge drifted over to Weiss and was introduced to Weiss's companion, a Mr. Noble. "What's this about a million chimpanzees, Weiss?" he asked.

"Six chimpanzees," Mr. Weiss said. "It's an old cliché of the mathematicians. I thought everybody was told about it in school. Law of averages, you know, or maybe it's permutation and combination. The six chimps, just pounding away at the typewriter keys, would be bound to copy out all the books ever written by man. There are only so many possible combinations of letters and numerals, and they'd produce all of them—see? Of course they'd also turn out a mountain of gibberish, but they'd work the books in, too. All the books in the British Museum."

Mr. Bainbridge was delighted; this was the sort of talk he liked to hear when he came to New York. "Well, but look here," he said, just to keep up his part in the foolish conversation, "what if one of the chimpanzees finally did duplicate a book, right down to the last period, but left that off? Would that count?"

"I suppose not. Probably the chimpanzee would get around to doing the book again, and put the period in."

"What nonsense!" Mr. Noble cried.

"It may be nonsense, but Sir James Jeans believes it," Mr. Weiss said, huffily. "Jeans or Lancelot Hogben. I know I ran across it quite recently."

Mr. Bainbridge was impressed. He read quite a bit of popular science, and both Jeans and Hogben were in his library. "Is that so?" he murmured, no longer feeling frivolous. "Wonder if it has ever actually been tried? I mean has anybody ever put six chimpanzees in a room with six typewriters and a lot of paper?"

Mr. Weiss glanced at Mr. Bainbridges empty cocktail glass and said drily, "Probably not."

Nine weeks later, on a winter evening, Mr. Bainbridge was sitting in his study with his friend James Mallard, an assistant professor of mathematics at New Haven. He was plainly nervous as he poured himself a drink and said, "Mallard, I've asked you to come here—Brandy? Cigar?—for a particular reason. You remember that I wrote you some time ago, asking your opinion of...of a certain mathematical hypothesis or supposition."

"Yes," Professor Mallard said, briskly. "I remember perfectly. About the six chimpanzees and the British Museum. And I told you it was a perfectly sound popularization of a principle known to every schoolboy who had studied the science of probabilities."

"Precisely," Mr. Bainbridge said. "Well, Mallard, I made up my mind.... It was not difficult for me, because I have, in spite of that fellow in the White House, been able to give something every year to the Museum of Natural History, and they were naturally glad to oblige me.... And after all, the only contribution a layman can make to the progress of science is to assist with the drudgery of experiment.... In short, I—"

"I suppose you're trying to tell me that you have procured six chimpanzees and set them to work at typewriters in order to see whether they will eventually write all the books in the British Museum. Is that it?"

"Yes, that's it," Mr. Bainbridge said. "What a mind you have, Mallard. Six fine young males, in perfect condition. I had a—I suppose you'd call it a dormitory—built out in back of the stable. The typewriters are in the conservatory. It's light and airy in there, and I moved most of the plants out. Mr. North, the man who owns the circus, very obligingly let me engage one of his best animal men. Really, it was no trouble at all."

Professor Mallard smiled indulgently. "After all, such a thing is not unheard of," he said. "I seem to remember that a man at some university put his graduate students to work flipping coins, to see if heads and tails came up an equal number of times. Of course they did."

Mr. Bainbridge looked at his friend very queerly. "Then you believe that any such principle of the science of probabilities will stand up under an actual test?"

"Certainly."

"You had better see for yourself." Mr. Bainbridge led Professor Mallard downstairs, along a corridor, through a disused music room, and into a large conservatory. The middle of the floor had been cleared of plants and was occupied by a row of six typewriter tables, each one supporting a hooded machine. At the left of each typewriter was a neat stack of yellow copy paper. Empty wastebaskets were under each table. The chairs were the unpadded, spring-backed kind favored by experienced stenographers. A large bunch of ripe bananas was hanging in one corner, and in another stood a Great Bear water-cooler and a rack of Lily cups. Six piles of typescript, each about a foot high, were ranged along the wall on an improvised shelf. Mr. Bainbridge picked up one of the piles, which he could just conveniently lift, and set it on a table before Professor Mallard. "The output to date of Chimpanzee A, known as Bill," he said simply.

"'"Oliver Twist," by Charles Dickens,'" Professor Mallard read out. He read the first and second pages of the manuscript, then feverishly leafed through to the end. "You mean to tell me," he said, "that this chimpanzee has written—"

"Word for word and comma for comma," said Mr. Bainbridge. "Young, my butler, and I took turns comparing it with the edition I own. Having finished 'Oliver Twist,' Bill is, as you see, starting the sociological works of Vilfredo Pareto, in Italian. At the rate he has been going, it should keep him busy for the rest of the month."

"And all the chimpanzees"—Professor Mallard was pale, and enunciated with difficulty—"they aren't all—"

"Oh, yes, all writing books which I have every reason to believe are in the British Museum. The prose of John Donne, some Anatole France, Conan Doyle, Galen, the collected plays of Somerset Maugham, Marcel Proust, the memoirs of the late Marie of Rumania, and a monograph by a Dr. Wiley on the marsh grasses of Maine and Massachusetts. I can sum it up for you, Mallard, by telling you that since I started this experiment, four weeks and some days ago, none of the chimpanzees has spoiled a single sheet of paper."

Professor Mallard straightened up, passed his handkerchief across his brow, and took a deep breath. "I apologize for my weakness," he said. "It was simply the sudden shock. No, looking at the thing scientifically—and I hope I am at least as capable of that as the next man—there is nothing marvelous about the situation. These chimpanzees, or a succession of similar teams of chimpanzees, would in a million years write all the books in the British Museum. I told you some time ago that I believed that statement. Why should my belief be altered by the fact that they produced some of the books at the very outset? After all, I should not be very much surprised if I tossed a coin a hundred times and it came up heads every time. I know that if I kept at it long enough, the ratio would reduce itself to an exact fifty per cent. Rest assured, these chimpanzees will begin to compose gibberish quite soon. It is bound to happen. Science tells us so. Meanwhile, I advise you to keep this experiment secret. Uninformed people might create a sensation if they knew."

"I will, indeed," Mr. Bainbridge said. "And I'm very grateful for your rational analysis. It reassures me. And now, before you go, you must hear the new Schnabel records that arrived today."

During the succeeding three months, Professor Mallard got into the habit of telephoning Mr. Bainbridge every Friday afternoon at five-thirty, immediately after leaving his seminar room. The Professor would say, "Well?," and Mr. Bainbridge would reply, "They're still at it, Mallard. Haven't spoiled a sheet of paper yet." If Mr. Bainbridge had to go out on Friday afternoon, he would leave a written message with his butler, who would read it to Professor Mallard: "Mr. Bainbridge says we now have Trevelyan's 'Life of Macaulay,' the Confessions of St. Augustine, 'Vanity Fair,' part of Irving's 'Life of George Washington,' the Book of the Dead, and some speeches delivered in Parliament in opposition to the Corn Laws, sir." Professor Mallard would reply, with a hint of a snarl in his voice, "Tell him to remember what I predicted," and hang up with a clash.

The eleventh Friday that Professor Mallard telephoned, Mr. Bainbridge said, "No change. I have had to store the bulk of the manuscript in the cellar. I would have burned it, except that it probably has some scientific value."

"How dare you talk of scientific value?" The voice from New Haven roared faintly in the receiver. "Scientific value! You—you—chimpanzee!" There were further inarticulate sputterings, and Mr. Bainbridge hung up with a disturbed expression. "I am afraid Mallard is overtaxing himself," he murmured.

Next day, however, he was pleasantly surprised. He was leafing through a manuscript that had been completed the previous day by Chimpanzee D, Corky. It was the complete diary of Samuel Pepys, and Mr. Bainbridge was chuckling over the naughty passages, which were omitted in his own edition, when Professor Mallard was shown into the room. "I have come to apologize for my outrageous conduct on the telephone yesterday," the Professor said.

"Please don't think of it any more. I know you have many things on your mind," Mr. Bainbridge said. "Would you like a drink?"

"A large whiskey, straight, please," Professor Mallard said. "I got rather cold driving down. No change, I presume?"

"No, none. Chimpanzee F, Dinty, is just finishing John Florio's translation of Montaigne's essays, but there is no other news of interest."

Professor Mallard squared his shoulders and tossed off his drink in one astonishing gulp. "I should like to see them at work," he said. "Would I disturb them, do you think?"

"Not at all. As a matter of fact, I usually look in on them around this time of day. Dinty may have finished his Montaigne by now, and it is always interesting to see them start a new work. I would have thought that they would continue on the same sheet of paper, but they don't, you know. Always a fresh sheet, and the title in capitals."

Professor Mallard, without apology, poured another drink and slugged it down. "Lead on," he said.

It was dusk in the conservatory, and the chimpanzees were typing by the light of student lamps clamped to their desks. The keeper lounged in a corner, eating a banana and reading Billboard. "You might as well take an hour or so off," Mr. Bainbridge said. The man left.

Professor Mallard, who had not taken off his overcoat, stood with his hands in his pockets, looking at the busy chimpanzees. "I wonder if you know, Bainbridge, that the science of probabilities takes everything into account," he said, in a queer, tight voice. "It is certainly almost beyond the bounds of credibility that these chimpanzees should write books without a single error, but that abnormality may be corrected by—these!" He took his hands from his pockets, and each one held a .38 revolver. "Stand back out of harm's way!" he shouted.

"Mallard! Stop it!" The revolvers barked, first the right hand, then the left, then the right. Two chimpanzees fell, and a third reeled into a corner. Mr. Bainbridge seized his friend's arm and wrested one of the weapons from him.

"Now I am armed, too, Mallard, and I advise you to stop!" he cried. Professor Mallard's answer was to draw a bead on Chimpanzee E and shoot him dead. Mr. Bainbridge made a rush, and Professor Mallard fired at him. Mr. Bainbridge, in his quick death agony, tightened his finger on the trigger of his revolver. It went off, and Professor Mallard went down. On his hands and knees he fired at the two chimpanzees which were still unhurt, and then collapsed.

There was nobody to hear his last words. "The human equation...always the enemy of science..." he panted. "This time... vice versa...I, a mere mortal...savior of science...deserve a Nobel...."

When the old butler came running into the conservatory to investigate the noises, his eyes were met by a truly appalling sight. The student lamps were shattered, but a newly risen moon shone in through the conservatory windows on the corpses of the two gentlemen, each clutching a smoking revolver. Five of the chimpanzees were dead. The sixth was Chimpanzee F. His right arm disabled, obviously bleeding to death, he was slumped before his typewriter. Painfully, with his left hand, he took from the machine the completed last page of Florio's Montaigne. Groping for a fresh sheet, he inserted it, and typed with one finger, "UNCLE TOM'S CABIN, by Harriet Beecher Stowe. Chapte...." Then he, too, was dead.

THE SECRET LIFE OF WALTER MITTY
by James Thurber

This story is a superb example of the use of the limited omniscient point of view. The contrast of Mitty's thoughts, his daydreaming, with his humdrum everyday life creates the humor and irony of this story; without this contrast, the story has no meaning. As you read, pay close attention to the following:

- *The relationship between the central idea and the point of view is critical. If a different point of view were used, more than likely the central idea would be lost.*
- *The connection between the narrative voice and the language of that voice; the point of view is what makes that connection.*
- *When you finish, ask yourself "How would the story change if a different point of view were used?"*
- *The point of view in the story is inconsistent, it shifts back and forth from Mitty's mind to the "real" world. Why is that necessary?*

"We're going through!" The Commander's voice was like thin ice breaking. He wore his full-dress uniform, with the heavily braided white cap pulled down rakishly over one cold gray eye. "We can't make it, sir. It's spoiling for a hurricane, if you ask me." "I'm not asking you, Lieutenant Berg," said the Commander. "Throw on the power lights! Rev her up to 8,500! Were going through!" The pounding of the cylinders increased: ta-pocketa-pocketa-pocketa-pocketa-pocketa. The Commander stared at the ice forming on the pilot window. He walked over and twisted a row of complicated dials. "Switch on No. 8 auxiliary!" he shouted. "Switch on No. 8 auxiliary!" repeated

Lieutenant Berg. "Full strength in No. 3 turret!" shouted the Commander. "Full strength in No. 3 turret!" The crew, bending to their various tasks in the huge, hurtling eight-engined Navy hydroplane, looked at each other and grinned. "The Old Man'll get us through," they said to one another. "The Old Man ain't afraid of Hell!"...

"Not so fast! You're driving too fast!" said Mrs. Mitty. "What are you driving so fast for?"

"Hmm?" said Walter Mitty. He looked at his wife, in the seat beside him, with shocked astonishment. She seemed grossly unfamiliar, like a strange woman who had yelled at him in a crowd. "You were up to fifty-five," she said. "You know I don't like to go more than forty. You were up to fifty-five." Walter Mitty drove on toward Waterbury in silence, the roaring of the SN202 through the worst storm in twenty years of Navy flying fading in the remote, intimate airways of his mind. "You're tensed up again," said Mrs. Mitty. "It's one of your days. I wish you'd let Dr. Renshaw look you over."

Walter Mitty stopped the car in front of the building where his wife went to have her hair done. "Remember to get those overshoes while I'm having my hair done," she said. "I don't need overshoes," said Mitty. She put her mirror back into her bag. "We've been all through that," she said, getting out of the car. "You're not a young man any longer." He raced the engine a little. "Why don't you wear your gloves? Have you lost your gloves?" Walter Mitty reached in a pocket and brought out the gloves. He put them on, but after she had turned and gone into the building and he had driven on to a red light, he took them off again. "Pick it up, brother!" snapped a cop as the light changed, and Mitty hastily pulled on his gloves and lurched ahead. He drove around the streets aimlessly for a time, and then he drove past the hospital on his way to the parking lot.

..."It's the millionaire banker, Wellington McCall," said the pretty nurse. "Yes?" said Walter Mitty, removing his gloves slowly. "Who has the case?" "Dr. Renshaw and Dr. Benbow, but there are two specialists here, Dr. Remington from New York and Mr. Pritchard-Mitford from London. He flew over." A door opened down a long, cool corridor and Dr. Renshaw came out. He looked distraught and haggard. "Hello, Mitty," he said.

"We're having the devil's own time with McMillan, the millionaire banker and close personal friend of Roosevelt. Obstreosis of the ductal tract. Tertiary. Wish you'd take a look at him." "Glad to," said Mitty.

In the operating room there were whispered introductions: "Dr. Remington, Dr. Mitty. Mr. Pritchard-Mitford, Dr. Mitty." "I've read your book on streptothricosis," said Pritchard-Mitford, shaking hands. "A brilliant performance, sir." "Thank you," said Walter Mitty. "Didn't know you were in the States, Mitty," grumbled Remington. "Coals to Newcastle, bringing Mitford and me up here for a tertiary." "You are very kind," said Mitty. A huge, complicated machine, connected to the operating table, with many tubes and wires, began at this moment to go pocketa-pocketa-pocketa.

"The new anesthetizer is giving away!" shouted an intern. "There is no one in the East who knows how to fix it!" "Quiet, man!" said Mitty, in a low, cool voice. He sprang to the machine, which was now going pocketa-pocketa-queep-pocketa-queep. He began fingering delicately a row of glistening dials: "Give me a fountain pen!" he snapped. Someone handed him a fountain pen. He pulled a faulty piston out of the machine and inserted the pen in its place. "That will hold for ten minutes," he said. "Get on with the operation." A nurse hurried over and whispered to Renshaw, and Mitty saw the man turn pale. "Coreopsis has set in," said Renshaw nervously. "If you would take over, Mitty?" Mitty looked at him and at the craven figure of Benbow, who drank, and at the grave uncertain faces of the two great specialists. "If you wish," he said. They slipped a white gown on him; he adjusted a mask and drew on thin gloves; nurses handed him shining…

"Back it up, Mac! Look out for that Buick!" Walter Mitty jammed on the brakes. "Wrong lane, Mac," said the parking-lot attendant, looking at Mitty closely. "Gee. Yeh," muttered Mitty. He began cautiously to back out of the lane marked "Exit Only." "Leave her sit there," said the attendant: "I'll put her away." Mitty got out of the car. "Hey, better leave the key." "Oh," said Mitty, handing the man the ignition key. The attendant vaulted into the car, backed it up with insolent skill, and put it where it belonged.

They're so damn cocky, thought Walter Mitty, walking along Main Street; they think they know everything. Once he had tried to take his chains off, outside New Milford, and he had got them wound around the axles. A man had had to come out in a wrecking car and unwind them, a young, grinning garageman. Since then Mrs. Mitty always made him drive to a garage to have the chains taken off. The next time, he thought, I'll wear my right arm in a sling; they won't grin at me then. I'll have my right arm in a sling and they'll see I couldn't possibly take the chains off myself. He kicked at the slush on the sidewalk. "Overshoes," he said to himself, and he began looking for a shoe store.

When he came out into the street again, with the overshoes in a box under his arm, Walter Mitty began to wonder what the other thing was his wife had told him to get. She had told him, twice, before they set out from their house for Waterbury. In a way he hated these weekly trips to town—he was always getting something wrong. Kleenex, he thought, Squibbs, razor blades? No. Toothpaste, toothbrush, bicarbonate, carborundum, initiative and referendum? He gave it up. But she would remember it. "Where's the what's-its-name?" she would ask. "Don't tell me you forgot the what's-its-name." A newsboy went by shouting something about the Waterbury trial.

..."Perhaps this will refresh your memory." The District Attorney suddenly thrust a heavy automatic at the quiet figure on the witness stand. "Have you ever seen this before?" Walter Mitty took the gun and examined it expertly. "This is my Webley-Vickers 50.80," he said calmly. An excited buzz ran around the courtroom. The Judge rapped for order. "You are a crack shot with any sort of firearms, I believe?" said the District Attorney, insinuatingly. "Objection!" shouted Mitty's attorney. "We have shown that the defendant could not have fired the shot. We have shown that he wore his right arm in a sling on the night of the fourteenth of July." Walter Mitty raised his hand briefly and the bickering attorneys were stilled. "With any known make of gun," he said evenly, "I could have killed Gregory Fitzhurst at three hundred feet with my left hand." Pandemonium broke loose in the courtroom. A woman's scream rose above the bedlam and suddenly a lovely, dark-haired girl was in Walter Mitty's arms. The District Attorney struck at her savagely. Without rising from his chair, Mitty let the man have it on the point of the chin. "You miserable cur!"

"Puppy biscuit," said Walter Mitty. He stopped walking and the buildings of Waterbury rose up out of the misty courtroom and surrounded him again. A woman who was passing laughed. "He said 'Puppy biscuit,'" she said to her companion. "That man said 'Puppy biscuit' to himself." Walter Mitty hurried on. He went into an A & P, not the first one he came to but a smaller one farther up the street. "I want some biscuit for small, young dogs," he said to the clerk. "Any special brand, sir?" The greatest pistol shot in the world thought a moment. "It says 'Puppies Bark for It' on the box," said Walter Mitty.

His wife would be through at the hairdressers in fifteen minutes, Mitty saw in looking at his watch, unless they had trouble drying it; sometimes they had trouble drying it. She didn't like to get to the hotel first; she would want him to be there waiting for her as usual. He found a big leather chair in the lobby, facing a window, and he put the overshoes and the puppy biscuit on the floor beside it. He picked up an old copy of Liberty and sank down into the chair. "Can Germany Conquer the World Through the Air?" Walter Mitty looked at the pictures of bombing planes and of ruined streets.

..."The cannonading has got the wind up in young Raleigh, sir," said the sergeant. Captain Mitty looked up at him through tousled hair. "Get him to bed," he said wearily. "With the others. I'll fly alone." "But you can't sir," said the sergeant anxiously. "It takes two men to handle that bomber and the Archies are pounding hell out of the air. Von Richtman's circus is between here and Saulier." "Somebody's got to get that ammunition dump," said Mitty. "I'm going over. Spot of brandy?" He poured a drink for the sergeant and one for himself. War thundered and whined around the dugout and battered at the door. There was a rending of wood and splinters flew through the room. "A bit of a near thing," said Captain Mitty carelessly. "The box barrage is closing in," said the sergeant. "We only live once, Sergeant," said Mitty, with his faint, fleeting smile. "Or do we?" He poured another brandy and tossed it off. "I never seen a man could hold his brandy like you, sir," said the sergeant. "Begging your pardon, sir." Captain Mitty stood up and strapped on his huge Webley-Vickers automatic. "It's forty kilometers through hell, sir," said the sergeant. Mitty finished one last brandy. "After all," he said softly, "what isn't?" The pounding of the cannon increased; there was the rat-tat-tatting of machine guns, and from somewhere came the menacing pocketa-pocketa-pocketa of the new flame-throwers. Walter Mitty walked to the door of the dugout humming "Auprés de Ma Blonde." He turned and waved to the sergeant. "Cheerio!" he said....

Something struck his shoulder. "I've been looking all over this hotel for you," said Mrs. Mitty. "Why do you have to hide in this old chair? How did you expect me to find you?" "Things close in," said Walter Mitty vaguely. "What?" Mrs. Mitty said. "Did you get the what's-its-name? The puppy biscuit? What's in that box?" "Overshoes," said Mitty. "Couldn't you have put them on in the store?" "I was thinking," said Walter Mitty. "Does it ever occur to you that I am sometimes thinking?" She looked at him. "I'm going to take your temperature when I get you home," she said.

They went out through the revolving doors that made a faintly derisive whistling sound when you pushed them. It was two blocks to the parking lot. At the drugstore on the corner she said, "Wait here for me. I forgot something. I won't be a minute." She was more than a minute. Walter Mitty lighted a cigarette. It began to rain, rain with sleet in it. He stood up against the wall of the drugstore, smoking.... He put his shoulders back and his heels together. "To hell with the handkerchief," said Walter Mitty scornfully. He took one last drag on his cigarette and snapped it away. Then, with that faint, fleeting smile playing about his lips, he faced the firing squad; erect and motionless, proud and disdainful, Walter Mitty the Undefeated, inscrutable to the last.

OFFLOADING FOR MRS. SCHWARTZ

by George Saunders

Elizabeth always thought the fake stream running through our complex was tacky. Whenever I'd sit brooding beside it after one of our fights, she'd hoot down on me from the balcony. Then I'd come in and we'd make up. Oh would we. I think of it. I think of it and think of it. Finally in despair, I call GuiltMasters. GuiltMasters are Jean and Bob Fleen, a brother/sister psychiatric practice. In their late-night TV ads, they wear cowls and capes and stand on either side of a sobbing neurotic woman in sweater and slacks. By the end of the bit, she's romping through a field of daisies. I get Jean Fleen. I tell her I've done a bad thing I can't live with. She says I've called the right place. She says there's nothing so shameful it can't be addressed by GuiltMasters. I take a deep breath and spill my guts. There's a silence from Jean's end. Then she asks can I hold. Upbeat Muzak comes on. Several minutes later Bob comes on and asks can they call me back. I wait by the phone. One hour, two hours, all night. Nothing. The sun comes up. Brad from Complex Grounds turns on the bubbler and the whitewater begins to flow. I don't shower. I don't shave. I put on the same pants I had on before. It's too much. Three years since her death and still I'm a wreck. I think of fleeing the city. I think of working on a shrimper, or setting myself on fire downtown. Instead I go to work.

In spite of my problems, personal interactive holography marches on. All morning I hopefully dust. Nobody comes in. At noon I work out a little tension by running amok in one of my modules. I choose Bowling With the Pros. A holographic smoothie in a blazer greets me and affably asks if I'm as tired as he is of perennially overhooking the ball when what I really need is to consistently throw strikes. I tell him fuck off. In a more sophisticated module, he'd ask why the hostility, but my equipment is outdated and instead he looks confused and tries to shake my hand. What crappy verisimilitude. No wonder I'm in the red. No wonder my rent's overdue. He asks isn't bowling a lovely recreation? I tell him I'm in mourning. He says the hours spent in a bowling alley with friends certainly make for some fantastic memories years down the line. I tell him my life's in the crapper. He grins and says let's bowl, let's go in and bowl, let's go in and bowl a few frames—with the Pros! I take him by the throat. Of course he Dysfunctions. Of course I'm automatically unbooted. I doff my headset and dismount the treadmill. Once again it's just me and my failing shop. Once again the air reeks of microwaved popcorn. Once again I am only who I am.

Wonderful, I think, you've fouled your own four-hundred-dollar module. And I have. So I trash it. I write it off to grief management. I go to lunch. I opt for an autodispensed Freight-Furter. Of course, I overmicrowave and the paper cowcatcher melds with the bun and the little engineer's face runs down his overalls. It's even more inedible than unusual. I chuck it. I can't afford another. I chuck it and go wait for my regulars.

At two Mr. Bomphil comes in looking guilty and as always requests Violated Prom Queen, then puts on high heels and selects Treadmill Three. Treadmill Three is behind a beam, so he's free to get as worked up as he likes, which is very. I try not to hear him moan. I try not to hear him call each football-team member by name. He's followed by Theo Kiley, an appliance salesman, who lays down a ream of Frigidaire specs and asks for Legendary American Killers Stalk You. I strap on his headset. I insert his module. For twenty minutes he hems and haws with Clyde Barrow. Finally he slips up and succumbs to a burst of machine-gun fire, then treats himself to a Sprite. "Whew," he says. "Next time I'll know to avoid the topic of his mom." I remind him he's got an outstanding bill. He says thanks. He says his bill and his ability to match wits with great criminals are the only outstanding things he's got. We laugh. We laugh some more. He shakes his head and leaves. I curse him under my breath, then close up early and return to my lonely home.

Next day Mrs. Gaither from Corporate comes to town. Midway through my Significant Accomplishments Assessment, armless Mr. Feltriggi comes to the door and as usual rings the bell with his face. I let him in and he unloads his totebag of cookbooks for sale. Today it's "Crazy Cajun Carnival" and "Going Bananas with Bananas: A Caribbean Primer." But I know what he really wants. With my eyes I tell him wait. Finally Gaither finishes raking my sub-par Disbursement Ledger over the coals and goes across the mall to O My God for some vintage religious statuary. I slip the headset on Feltriggi and run Youth Roams Kansas Hometown, 1932. It's all homemade bread and dirt roads and affable dogcatchers. What a sweet grin appears. How he greets each hometowner with his ghost limbs and beams at the chirping of the holographic birds. He kneels awhile in Mrs. Lawler's larder, sniffing spices that remind him of his mother elbow-deep in flour. He drifts out to the shaded yard and discusses Fascism with the iceman near some swaying wheat. His posture changes for the better. He laughs aloud. He's young again and the thresher has yet to claim his arms.

Gaither comes back with a St. Sebastian cookie jar. I nudge Feltriggi and tell him that's all for today. He takes off the headset and offers me a cookbook in payment. I tell him forget it. I tell him that's what friends are for. It's seventy bucks a session and he knows it. He rams his head into my chest as a sign of affection.

"That type of a presence surely acts to deflate revenues," Gaither says primly as Feltriggi goes out.

"No lie," I say. "That's why I nearly beat him up everytime he comes in here."

"I'm not sure that's appropriate," she says.

"Me neither," I say. "That's why I usually don't really do it."

"I see," she says. "Let's talk briefly about personal tragedy. No one's immune. But at what point must mourning cease? In your case, apparently never."

I think: You never saw Elizabeth lanky and tan and laughing in Napa.

"I like your cookie jar," I say.

"Very well," she says, "Seal your own doom."

She says she's shocked at the dryness of my treadmill bearings and asks if I've ever heard of oil. She sighs and gives me her number at the Quality Inn in case I think of anything that might argue against Franchise Agreement Cancellation. Then out she goes, sadly shaking her head.

It's only my livelihood. It's only every cent Elizabeth left me. I load up my mobil pack. I select my happiest modules. Then I go off to my real job, my penance, my albatross.

Rockettown's our ghetto. It's called Rockettown because long ago they put up a building there in which to build rockets. But none were built and the building's now nothing, which is what it's always been, except for a fenced-off dank corner that was once used to store dilapidated fireplugs and is now a filthy daycare for the children of parents who could care less. All around Rockettown little houses went up when it was thought the building would soon be full of people making rockets and hauling down impressive wages. They're bad little houses, put up quick, and now all the people who were young and had hoped to build rockets are old and doddering and walk by the empty building mumbling why why why.

In the early days of my grief, Father Luther told me to lose myself in service by contacting ElderAid, Inc. I got Mrs. Ken Schwartz. Mrs. Ken Schwartz lives in Rockettown. She lives in Rockettown remembering Mr. Ken Schwartz and cursing him for staying so late at Menlo's TenPin on nights when she forgets he's been dead eighteen years. Mrs. Ken Schwartz likes me and my happy modules. Especially she likes Viennese Waltz. Boy does she. She's bedridden and lonely and sometimes in her excitement bruises her arms on her headboard when the orchestra starts to play. Tonight she says she's feeling weak. She says she used to be a different person and wishes she could go back to the days when she was loved. She mourns Fat Patrice and their jovial games of Old Maid. She mourns the front-yard oak the city felled without asking her. Mostly she mourns Mr. Ken Schwartz.

I pull out all the stops. I set Color on high contrast. I tape sensors to her lips and earlobes. I activate the Royalty Subroutine. Soon the prince is lavishing her with praise. Soon they're sneaking off from the ball for some tender words and a kiss or two on a stone bench beside the Danube. Soon I'm daubing her eyes with tissue while she weeps at the beauty of the fishermen bowing from their little boats as they realize it's the prince himself trying to retrieve her corsage from the river. I make tea. I read my magazine. Finally I stroke her forehead while humming Strauss and slowly fading the volume.

"You," she says, smiling sweetly when she's all the way back. "You're too good to me."

"No one could be too good to you," I say.

"Oh you," she says. "You're a saint."

No, I think, I'm a man without a life, due to you. Then I feel ashamed and purposely bash my shin against the bedframe while tucking her in. I get her some juice. I check her backdoor lock. All around the room are dirty plates I've failed to get to the sink and old photos of Mr. Ken Schwartz assessing the condition of massive steamboilers while laughing confidently.

Out on the street it's cold and a wino's standing in a dumpster calling a stray cat Uncle Chuck. I hustle directly to my Omni, fearing for my gear. I drive through frightening quarters of the city, nervously toggling my defrost lever, thinking of Mrs. Ken Schwartz. The last few months she's gone badly downhill. She's unable to feed herself or autonomously use the bathroom. Talk about losing yourself in service to a greater extent than planned. I'm over there night and day and still it's not enough. She needs a live-in but they don't come cheap, and my shop hasn't turned a profit in months. What to do? I think and think. I think so much I lose track of where I am and blunder by The Spot. You fool, I think, you ass, how much additional pain would you like? Here a drunk named Tom Clifton brought his Coupe De Ville onto the sidewalk as Elizabeth shopped for fruit on the evening of a day when we'd fought like hell. On the evening of a day when I'd called her an awful name. What name? I can't say the word. I even think it and my gut burns. I'm a saint.

The fight started when I accused her of flirting with our neighbor Len Kobb by bending low on purpose. I was angry and implied that she couldn't keep her boobs in her top to save her life. If I could see her one last time I'd say: thanks very much for dying at the worst possible moment and leaving me holding the bag of guilt. I'd say: if you had to die, couldn't you have done it when we were getting along? I madly flee The Spot. There are boat lights in the harbor and a man in a tux inexplicably jogging through the park. There's a moon bobbing up between condemned buildings. There's the fact that tomorrow I'm Lay Authority Guest at the Lyndon Baines Johnson School for Precocious Youth. I'm slated to allow interested kids to experience the module entitled Hop-Hop the Bunny Masters Fractions. Frankly I fear I'll be sneered at. How interested could a mob of gifted kids be in a rabbit and a lisping caterpillar subdividing acorns ad nauseam? But I've promised the principal, Mrs. Briff. And I'm not in a position to decline any revenue source. So at an hour of the night when other men my age are rising from their beds to comfort screaming newborns I return to the mall for my Hop-Hop module. I use my pass key. Something's strange. Modules are strewn everywhere. The cashbox sits on the fax machine. One of my treadmills lies on its side.

"How is all of this fancy equipment used?" someone asks from behind me, pressing a sharp knife to my throat, "More specifically, which of it is worth the most? And remember sir, you're answering for your life."

He sounds old but feels strong. I tell him it's hard to explain. I offer to demonstrate.

He says do so, but slowly. I fit him with a headset. I gently guide him to a treadmill, then run Sexy Nurses Scrub You Down. Immediately his lips get moist. Immediately he pops a mild bone and loosens his grip on the knife and I'm able to coldcock him with the FedEx tape gun. He drops drooling to my nice carpet. A man his age should be a doting grandfather, not a crook threatening me with death. I feel violated. Such a man was Tom Clifton, past his prime and bitter. How does someone come to this?

I strap him down and set my console for Scan.

It seems his lousy name is Hank. I hear his portly father calling it out across a cranberry bog. I know the smell of his first baseball cap. Through his eyes I see the secret place under the porch where he hid whenever his fat kissing aunt came. Later I develop a love for swing. It seems he was a Marine at

Iwo who on his way to bootcamp saw the aging Ty Cobb at a depot. I sense his panic on the troop transport, then quickly doff my headset as he hits the beach and the bullets start to fly.

To my horror, I see that his eyelids are fluttering and his face is contorting. My God, I think, this is no Scan, this is a damn Offload. I check the console, and sure enough, via one incorrect switch setting, I've just irrevocably transferred a good third of his memories to my hard drive.

When he comes to, he hops off the table looking years younger, suddenly happy-go-lucky, asks where he is, and trots blithely out the door, free now of bootcamp, free of Iwo, free of all memory of youthful slaughter, free in fact of any memory at all of the first twenty years of his life. I'm heartsick. What have I done? On the other hand, it stopped him from getting up and trying to kill me. On the other hand, it appears he left here a happier man, perhaps less inclined to felony.

I grab my Hop-Hop module. On the cover is Hop-Hop, enthusiastically giving the thumbs-up to an idealized blond boy lifting an enormous 4 into a numerator. As if being robbed weren't enough, first thing tomorrow morning a roomful of genius kids is going to eat me alive.

Then, crossing the deserted Food Court, I get a brainstorm. I hustle back to the shop and edit out Hank's trysts with starving women in Depression-era hobo camps and his one homo fling with his cousin Julian. I edit the profanity out of Iwo. I edit out the midnight wanks, the petty thefts, the unkind words, all but the most inoffensive of the bodies of his buddies on the pale sand beach.

Next morning I herd kid after kid behind my white curtain and let them experience Hank's life. They love it. They leave jabbering knowledgeably about the Pacific Theater and the ultimate wisdom of using the Bomb. They leave humming "American Patrol." They leave praising Phil Rizzuto's fielding and cursing the Brown Shirts. They pat old Mr. Panchuko, the geriatric janitor, on the back and ask him what caliber machine gun he operated at the Bulge. He stands scratching his gut, stunned, trying to remember. The little Klotchkow twins jitterbug. Andy Pitlin, all of three feet tall, hankers aloud for a Camel.

Mrs. Briff is more than impressed. She asks what else do I have. I ask what else does she want. She says for starters how about the remainder of the century. I tell her I'll see what I can do.

The kids come out of it with a firsthand War Years experience and I come out of it with a check for five hundred dollars, enough to hire a temporary live-in for Mrs. Ken Schwartz. Which I gladly do. A lovely Eurasian named Wei, a student of astrophysics who, as I'm leaving them alone for the first time, is brushing out Mrs. Ken Schwartz's hair and humming "Let Me Call You Sweetheart."

"Will you stay forever?" I ask her.

"With all due respect," she replies, "I will stay as long as you can pay me."

Two weeks later, Briff's on my tail for more modules and Wei's on my tail for her pay. I tell Mrs. Ken Schwartz all, during one of her fifteen-minute windows of lucidity. When lucid she's shrewd and bright. She understands her predicament. She understands the limitations of my gear. She understands that I can't borrow her memories, only take them away forever.

She says she can live without the sixties.

I haul my stuff over to her place and take what I need. I edit out her mastectomy, Ken Schwartz's midlife crisis and resulting trip to Florida, and her constant drinking in his absence. I stick to her walking past a protest and counseling a skinny girl on acid to stay in school. It's not great but I've got a deadline. I call it America in Tumult—The Older Generation Looks On In Dismay.

I have it couriered over to Briff, dreading her response. But to my amazement she sends a cash bonus. She reports astounding increases in grandparental bonding. She reports kids identifying a Mercury Cougar with no prompting and disgustedly calling each other Nixon whenever a trust is betrayed.

Thereafter I retain Wei on a weekly basis by whittling away at Mrs. Schwartz's memories. I submit Pearl Harbor—Week Prior to Infamy. I submit The Day the Music Died—Buddy Holly Remembered, which unfortunately is merely Mrs. Schwartz hearing the news on a pink radio, then disinterestedly going back to cleaning her oven. Finally Briff calls, hacked off. She says she wants some real meat. She asks how about the entire twenties, a personal favorite of hers. She's talking flappers. She's talking possible insights on Prohibition. I stonewall. I tell her give me a few days to exhaustively check my massive archive. I call Mrs. Ken Schwartz. She says during the twenties she was a lowly phone operator in Pekin, Illinois. She sounds disoriented, and wearily asks where her breasts are. Clearly this has gone far enough.

I call Briff and tell her no more modules. She ups her offer to three thousand a decade. She's running for school board and says my modules are the primary arrow in her quiver. But what am I supposed to do? Turn Mrs. Schwartz into a well-cared-for blank slate? Start kidnapping and offloading strangers? I say a little prayer:

God, I've botched this life but good. I've failed you in all major ways. You gave me true love and I blew it. I'm nothing. But what have you got against Mrs. Ken Schwartz? Forgive me. Help me figure this out.

And then in a flash I figure it out.

I lock the shop. On the spine of a blank module I write 1951–1992—Baby Boomers Come Into Their Own. At three thousand a decade that's twelve grand. I address an envelope to Briff and enclose an invoice. I write out some instructions and rig myself up.

Memories shmemories, I think, I'll get some new ones. These old ones give me no peace.

Then I let it rip. It all goes whizzing by: Anthony Newburg smacking me. Mom on the dock. An Agnew Halloween mask at a frat house. Bev Malloy struggling with my belt. The many seasons. The many flags, dogs, paths, the many stars in skies of many hues.

My sweet Elizabeth.

Holding hands we gape at an elk in Estes Park. On our knees in a bed of tulips I kiss her cheek. The cold clear water of Nacogdoches. The birthday banner she made of scarves in our little place on Ellington. The awful look on her face as I called her what I called her. Her hair, trailing fine and light behind her as she stormed out to buy fruit.

The grave, the grave, my sad attempt to become a franchisee.

Then I'm a paunchy guy in a room, with a note pinned to his sleeve: "You were alone in the world," it says, "and did a kindness for someone in need. Good for you. Now post this module, and follow this map to the home of Mrs. Ken Schwartz. Care for her with some big money that will come in the mail. Find someone to love. Your heart has never been broken. You've never done anything unforgivable or hurt anyone beyond reparation. Everyone you've ever loved you've treated like gold."

JEALOUS HUSBAND RETURNS IN FORM OF PARROT

by Robert Olen Butler

I never can quite say as much as I know. I look at other parrots and I wonder if it's the same for them, if somebody is trapped in each of them, paying some kind of price for living their life in a certain way. For instance, "Hello," I say, and I'm sitting on a perch in a pet store in Houston and what I'm really thinking is Holy shit. It's you. And what's happened is I'm looking at my wife.

"Hello," she says, and she comes over to me, and I can't believe how beautiful she is. Those great brown eyes, almost as dark as the center of mine. And her nose, I don't remember her for her nose, but its beauty is clear to me now. Her nose is a little too long, but it's redeemed by the faint hook to it.

She scratches the back of my neck.

Her touch makes my tail flare. I feel the stretch and rustle of me back there. I bend my head to her and she whispers, "Pretty bird."

For a moment, I think she knows it's me. But she doesn't, of course. I say "Hello" again and I will eventually pick up "pretty bird." I can tell that as soon as she says it, but for now I can only give her another "Hello." Her fingertips move through my feathers, and she seems to know about birds. She knows that to pet a bird you don't smooth his feathers down, you ruffle them.

But, of course, she did that in my human life, as well. It's all the same for her. Not that I was complaining, even to myself, at that moment in the pet shop when she found me like I presume she was supposed to. She said it again "Pretty bird,"and this brain that works the way it does now could feel that tiny little voice of mine ready to shape itself around these sounds. But before I could get them out of my beak, there was this guy at my wife's shoulder, and all my feathers went slick-flat to make me small enough not to be seen, and I backed away. The pupils of my eyes pinned and dilated, and pinned again.

He circled around her. A guy that looked like a meat packer, big in the chest and thick with hair, the kind of guy that I always sensed her eyes moving to when I was alive. I had a bare chest, and I'd look for little black hairs on the sheets when I'd come home on a day with the whiff of somebody else in the air. She was still in the same goddam rut.

A "hello" wouldn't do, and I'd recently learned "good night," but it was the wrong suggestion altogether, so I said nothing and the guy circled her, and he was looking at me with a smug little smile, and I fluffed up all my feathers, made myself about twice as big, so big he'd see he couldn't mess with me. I waited for him to draw close enough for me to take off the tip of his finger.

But she intervened. Those nut-brown eyes were before me, and she said, "I want him."

And that's how I ended up in my own house once again. She bought me a large black wrought-iron cage, very large, convinced by some young guy who clerked in the bird department and who took her aside and made his voice go much too soft when he was doing the selling job. The meat packer didn't like it. I didn't either. I'd missed a lot of chances to take a bite out of this clerk in my stay at the shop, and I regretted that suddenly.

But I got my giant cage, and I guess I'm happy enough about that. I can pace as much as I want. I can hang upside down. It's full of bird toys. That dangling thing over there with knots and strips of rawhide and a bell at the bottom needs a good thrashing a couple of times a day, and I'm the bird to do it. I look at the very dangle of it, and the thing is rough, the rawhide and the knotted rope, and I get this restlessness back in my tail, a burning, thrashing feeling, and it's like all the times where I was sure there was a man naked with my wife. Then I go to this thing that feels so familiar and I bite and bite, and it's very good.

I could have used the thing the last day I went out of this house as a man. I'd found the address of the new guy at my wife's office. He'd been there a month, in the shipping department, and three times she'd mentioned him. She didn't even have to work with him, and three times I heard about him, just dropped into the conversation. "Oh," she'd say when a car commercial came on the television, "that car there is like the one the new man in shipping owns. Just like it." Hey, I'm not stupid. She said another thing about him and then another, and right after the third one I looked myself in the bathroom, because I couldn't rage about this anymore. I felt like a damn fool whenever I actually said anything about this kind of feeling and she looked at me as though she could start hating me real easy, and so I was working on saying nothing, even if it meant locking myself up. My goal was to hold my tongue about half the time. That would be a good start.

But this guy from shipping. I found out his name and his address, and it was one of her typical Saturday afternoons of vague shopping. So I went to his house, and his car that was just like the commercial was outside. Nobody was around in the neighborhood, and there was this big tree in back of the house going up to a second-floor window that was making funny little sounds. I went up. The shade was drawn but not quite all the way. I was holding on to a limb with my arms and legs wrapped around it like it was her in those times when I could forget the others for a little while. But the crack in the shade was just out of view, and I crawled on till there was no limb left, and I fell on my head. When I think about that now, my wings flap and I feel myself lift up, and it all seems so avoidable. Though I know I'm different now. I'm a bird.

Except I'm not. That what's confusing. It's like those times when she would tell me she loved me and I actually believed her and maybe it was true and we clung to each other in bed and at times like that I was different. I was the man in her life. I was whole with her. Except even at that moment, as I held her sweetly, there was this other creature inside me who knew a lot more about it and couldn't quite put all the evidence together to speak.

My cage sits in the den. My pool table is gone, and the cage is sitting in that space, and if I come all the way down to one end of my perch I can see through the door and down the back hallway to the master bedroom. When she keeps the bedroom door open, I can see the space at the foot of the bed but not the bed itself. I can sense it to the left, just out of sight. I watch the men go in and I hear the sounds, but I can't quite see. And they drive me crazy.

I flap my wings and I squawk and I fluff up and I slick down and I throw seed and I attack that dangly, too, as if it was the guy's balls, but it does no good. It never did any good in the other life, either, the thrashing around I did by myself. In that other life I'd have given anything to be standing in this den with her doing this thing with some other guy just down the hall, and all I had to do was walk down there and turn the corner and she couldn't deny it anymore.

But now all I can do is try to let it go. I sidestep down to the opposite end of the cage and I look out the big sliding glass doors to the backyard. It's a pretty yard. There are great, placid live oaks with good places to roost. There's a blue sky that plucks at the feathers on my chest. There are clouds. Other birds. Fly away. I could just fly away.

I tried once, and I learned a lesson. She forgot and left the door to my cage open, and I climbed beak and foot, beak and foot, along the bars and curled around to stretch sideways out the door, and the vast scene of peace was there, at the other end of the room. I flew.

And a pain flared through my head, and I fell straight down, and the room whirled around, and the only good thing was that she held me. She put her hands under my wings and lifted me and clutched me to her breast, and I wish there hadn't been bees in my head at the time, so I could have enjoyed that, but she put me back in the cage and wept awhile. That touched me, her tears. And I looked back to the wall of sky and trees. There was something invisible there between me and that dream of peace. I remembered, eventually, about glass, and I knew I'd been lucky; I knew that for the little, fragile-boned skull I was doing all this thinking in, it meant death.

She wept that day, but by night she had another man. A guy with a thick Georgia-truck-stop accent and pale white skin and an Adams apple big as my seed ball. This guy has been around for a few weeks, and he makes a whooping sound down the hallway, just out of my sight. At times like that I want to fly against the bars of the cage, but I don't. I have to remember how the world has changed.

She's single now, of course. Her husband, the man that I was, is dead to her. She does not understand all that is behind my "hello." I know many words, for a parrot. I am a yellow-name Amazon, a handsome bird, I think, green with a splash of yellow at the back of my neck. I talk pretty well, but none of my words are adequate. I can't make her understand.

And what would I say if I could? I was jealous in life. I admit it. I would admit it to her. But it was because of my connection to her. I would explain that. When we held each other, I had no past at all, no present but her body, no future but to lie there and not let her go. I was an egg hatched beneath her crouching body, I entered as a chick into her wet sky of a body, and all that I wished was to sit on her shoulder and fluff my feathers and lay my head against her cheek, with my neck exposed to her hand. And the glances that I could see in her troubled me deeply: the movement of her eyes in public to other men, the laughs sent across a room, the tracking of her mind behind her blank eyes, pursuing images of others, her distraction even in our bed, the ghosts that were there of men who'd touched her, perhaps even that very day. I was not part of all those other men who were part of her. I didn't want to connect to all that. It was only her that I would fluff for, but these others were there also, and I couldn't put them aside. I sensed them inside her, and so they were inside me. If I had the words, these are the things I would say.

But half an hour ago, there was a moment that thrilled me. A word we all knew in the pet shop, was just the right word after all. This guy with his cowboy belt buckle and rattlesnake boots and his pasty face and his twanging words of love trailed after my wife through the den, past my cage, and I said, "Cracker." He even flipped his head back a little at this in surprise. He'd been called that before to his face, I realized. I said it again, "Cracker." But to him I was a bird, and he let it pass. "Cracker," I said. "Hello, cracker." That was even better. They were out of sight through the hall doorway, and I hustled along the perch and I caught a glimpse of them before they made the turn to the bed and I said, "Hello, cracker," and he shot me one last glance.

It made me hopeful. I eased away from that end of the cage, moved toward the scene of peace beyond the far wall. The sky is chalky-blue today, blue like the brow of the blue-front Amazon who was on the perch next to me for about a week at the store. She was very sweet, but I watched her carefully for a day or two when she first came in. And it wasn't long before she nuzzled up to a cockatoo named Willy, and I knew she'd break my heart. But her color now, in the sky, is sweet, really. I left all those feelings behind me when my wife showed up. I am a faithful man, for all my suspicions. Too faithful, maybe. I am ready to give too much, and maybe that's the problem.

The whooping began down the hall, and I focussed on a tree out there. A crow flapped down, his mouth open, his throat throbbing, though I could not hear his sound. I was feeling very odd. At least I'd made my point to the guy in the other room. "Pretty bird," I said, referring to myself. She called me "pretty bird, and I believed her and I told myself again, "Pretty bird."

But then something new happened, something very difficult for me. She appeared in the den naked. I have not seen her naked since I fell from the tree and had no wings to fly. She always had a certain tidiness in things. She was naked in the bedroom, clothed in the den. But now she appears from the hallway, and I look at her, and she is still slim and she is beautiful, I think, at least I clearly remember, that as her husband I found her beautiful in this state. Now, though, she seems too naked. Plucked. I find that a sad thing. I am sorry for her, and she goes by me and she disappears into the kitchen. I want to pluck some of my own feathers, the feathers from my chest, and give them to her. I love her more in that moment, seeing her terrible nakedness, than I ever have before.

And since I had success in the last few minutes with words, when she comes back I am moved to speak. "Hello," I say, meaning, You are still connected to me, I still want only you. "Hello," I say again. Please listen to this tiny heart that beats fast at all times for you.

And she does indeed stop, and she comes to me and bends to me. "Pretty bird," I say, and I am saying, You are beautiful, my wife, and your beauty cries out for protection. "Pretty." I want to cover you with my own nakedness. "Bad bird," I say. If there are others in your life, even in your mind, then there is nothing I can do. "Bad." Your nakedness is touched from inside by the others. "Open," I say. How can we be whole together if you are not empty in the place that I am to fill?

She smiles at this, and she opens the door to my cage. "Up," I say, meaning, Is there no place for me in this world where I can be free of this terrible sense of others?

She reaches in now and offers her hand, and I climb onto it and I tremble and she says, "Poor baby." "Poor baby," I say. You have yearned for wholeness, too, and somehow I failed you. I was not enough. "Bad bird," I say. I'm sorry.

And then the cracker comes around the corner. He wears only his rattlesnake boots. I take one look at his miserable, featherless body and shake my head. We keep our sexual parts hidden, we parrots, and this man is a pitiful sight. "peanut," I say. I presume that my wife simply has not noticed. But that's foolish, of course. This is, in fact, what she wants. Not me. And she scrapes me off her hand onto the open cage door and she turns her naked back to me and embraces this man, and they laugh and stagger in their embrace around the corner.

For a moment, I still think I've been eloquent. What I've said only needs repeating for it to have its transforming effect. "Hello," I say, "Hello. Pretty bird. Pretty. Bad bird. Bad. Open. Up. Poor baby. Bad bird." And I am beginning to hear myself as I really sound to her. "Peanut." I can never say what is in my heart to her. Never.

I stand on my cage door now, and my wings stir. I look at the corner to the hallway, and down at the end the whooping has begun again. I can fly there and think of things to do about all this.

But I do not. I turn instead, and I look at the trees moving just beyond the other end of the room. I look at the sky the color of the brown of a blue-front Amazon. A shadow of birds spanks across the lawn. And I spread my wings. I will fly now. Even though I know there is something between me and that place where I can be free of all these feelings, I will fly. I will throw myself there again and again. Pretty bird. Bad bird. Good night.

PAUL'S CASE
by Willa Cather

A skillful author seldom relies on one mode of characterization. To accept the characters as real, we must see them as well as hear about them. Therefore, an author usually combines methods of presentation, selecting variously the one most appropriate to the demands of the plot, the role of a particular character, and the central idea of the story.

Since the central idea of a story may be the portrayal of a certain kind of person, characterization and character types are extremely important to analysis and understanding.

"Paul's Case" tells of a boy who is seeking satisfaction in a society that denies it to him. His character is revealed to us in a variety of ways through the words of his father and his teachers and through his own thoughts. These thoughts reveal a side of the boy unknown to anyone else. Understanding this character is crucial to the central idea of the story.

As you read the story, consider these aspects:

- *Paul is obviously unhappy, but why? What would make him happier and how does that tie in with the central idea?*
- *Pay close attention to what we know of what others in the story think of Paul.*
- *Would you say Paul is "normal" or "average" for his age? If not, identify what is different about him from most other boys his age and why the author made him different.*
- *The theatre represents something special to Paul; it also provides a clue to Paul's unhappiness.*
- *Cather chose the title of the story intentionally; it's not "Paul's Story," it's "Paul's Case."*

It was Paul's afternoon to appear before the faculty of the Pittsburgh High School to account for his various misdemeanors.

He had been suspended a week ago, and his father had called at the Principal's office and confessed his perplexity about his son.

Paul entered the faculty room suave and smiling. His clothes were a trifle outgrown, and the tan velvet on the collar of his open overcoat was frayed and worn; but for all that there was something of a dandy about him, and he wore an opal pin in his neatly knotted black four-in-hand, and a red carnation in his buttonhole. This latter adornment the faculty somehow felt was not properly significant of the contrite spirit befitting a boy under the ban of suspension.

Paul was tall for his age and very thin, with high, cramped shoulders and a narrow chest. His eyes were remarkable for a certain hysterical brilliancy, and he continually used them in a conscious, theatrical sort of way, peculiarly offensive in a boy. The pupils were abnormally large, as though he were addicted to belladonna, but there was a glassy glitter about them which that drug does not produce.

When questioned by the Principal as to why he was there, Paul stated, politely enough, that he wanted to come back to school. This was a lie, but Paul was quite accustomed to lying; found it, indeed, indispensable for overcoming friction. His teachers were asked to state their respective charges against him, which they did with such a rancor and aggrievedness as evinced that this was not a usual case. Disorder and impertinence were among the offences named, yet each of his instructors felt that it was scarcely possible to put into words the real cause of the trouble, which lay in a sort of hysterically defiant manner of the boy's; in the contempt which they all knew he felt for them, and which he seemingly made not the effort to conceal.

Once, when he had been making a synopsis of a paragraph at the blackboard, his English teacher had stepped to his side and attempted to guide his hand. Paul had started back with a shudder and thrust his hands violently behind him. The astonished woman could scarcely have been more hurt and embarrassed had he struck at her. The insult was so involuntary and definitely personal as to be unforgettable. In one way and another, he had made all his teachers, men and women alike, conscious of the same feeling of physical aversion. In one case he habitually sat with his hand shading his eyes; in another had made a running commentary on the lecture, with humorous intent.

His teachers felt this afternoon that his whole attitude was symbolized by his shrug and his flippantly red carnation flower, and they fell upon him without mercy, his English teacher leading the pack. He stood through it smiling, his pale lips parted over his white teeth. (His lips were continually twitching, and he had a habit of raising his eyebrows that was contemptuous and irritating to the last degree.) Older boys than Paul had broken down and shed tears under that ordeal, but his set smile did not once desert him, and his only sign of discomfort was the nervous trembling of the fingers that toyed with the buttons of his overcoat, and an occasional jerking of the other hand which held his hat. Paul was always smiling, always glancing about him, seeming to feel that people might be watching him and trying to detect something. This conscious expression, since it was as far as possible from boyish mirthfulness, was usually attributed to insolence or smartness.

As the inquisition proceeded, one of his instructors repeated an impertinent remark of the boy's, and the Principal asked him whether he thought that a courteous speech to make to a woman. Paul shrugged his shoulders slightly and his eyebrows twitchcd.

"I don't know," he replied. "I didn't mean to be polite or impolite, either. I guess it's a sort of way I have, of saying things regardless."

The Principal asked him whether he didn't think that a way it would be well to get rid of. Paul grinned and said he guessed so. When he was told that he could go, he bowed gracefully and went out. His bow was like a repetition of the scandalous red carnation.

His teachers were in despair, and his drawing-master voiced the feeling of them all when he declared there was something about the boy which none of them understood. He added: "I don't really believe that smile of his comes altogether from insolence; there's something sort of haunted about it. The boy is not strong for one thing. There is something wrong about the fellow."

Paul, one saw only his white teeth and the forced animation of his smile. The drawing-master had come to realize that, in looking at his eyes. One warm afternoon the boy had gone to sleep at his drawing-board, and his master had noted with amazement what a white, blue-veined face it was; drawn and wrinkled like an old man's about the eyes, the lips twitching even in his sleep.

His teachers left the building dissatisfied and unhappy; humiliated to have felt so vindictive toward a mere boy, to have uttered this feeling in cutting terms, and to have set each other on, as it were, in the gruesome game of intemperate reproach. One of them remembered having seen a miserable street cat set at bay by a ring of tormentors.

As for Paul, he ran down the hill whistling the Soldiers' Chorus from Faust, looking behind him now and then to see whether some of his teachers were not there to witness his lightheartedness. As it was now late in the afternoon and Paul was on duty that evening as usher at Carnegie Hall, he decided that he would go home to supper.

When he reached the concert hall, the doors were not yet open. It was chilly outside, and he decided to go up into the picture gallery always deserted at this hour where there were some of Raffelli's gay studies of Paris streets and an airy blue Venetian scene or two that always exhilarated him. He was delighted to find no one in the gallery but the old guard, who sat in the corner, a newspaper on his knee, a black patch over one eye and the other closed. Paul possessed himself of the place and walked confidently up and down, whistling under his breath. After a while he sat down before a blue Rico and lost himself. When he bethought him to look at his watch, it was after seven o'clock, and he rose with a start and ran downstairs, making a face at Augustus Caesar, peering out from the cast-room, and an evil gesture at the Venus of Milo as he passed her on the stairway. When Paul reached the ushers' dressing-room, half a dozen boys were there already, and he began excitingly to tumble into his uniform. It was one of the few that at all approached fitting, and Paul thought it very becoming though he knew the tight, straight coat accentuated his narrow chest, about which he was exceedingly sensitive. He was always excited while he dressed, twanging all over to the tuning of the strings and the preliminary flourishes of the horns in the music-room; but tonight he seemed quite beside himself, and he teased and plagued the boys until, telling him that he was crazy, they put him down on the floor and sat on him.

Somewhat calmed by his suppression, Paul dashed out to the front of the house to seat the early comers. He was a model usher. Gracious and smiling he ran up and down the aisles. Nothing was too much trouble for him; he carried messages and brought programs as though it were his greatest pleasure in life, and all the people in his section thought him a charming boy, feeling that he remembered and admired them. As the house filled, he grew more and more vivacious and animated, and the color came to his cheeks and lips. It was very much as though this were a great reception and Paul were the host. Just as the musicians came out to take their places, his English teacher arrived with checks for the seats which a prominent manufacturer had taken for the season. She betrayed some embarrassment when she handed Paul the tickets, and a hauteur which subsequently made her feel very foolish. Paul was startled for a moment, and had the feeling of wanting to put her out; what business had she here among all these fine people and gay colors? He looked her over and decided that she was not appropriately dressed and must be a fool to sit downstairs in such togs. The tickets had probably been sent her out of kindness, he reflected, as he put down a seat for her, and she had about as much right to sit there as he had.

When the symphony began, Paul sank into one of the rear seats with a long sigh of relief, and lost himself as he had done before the Rico. It was not that symphonies, as such, meant anything in particular to Paul, but the first sight of the instruments seemed to free some hilarious spirit within him; something that struggled there like the genie in the bottle found by the Arab fisherman. He felt a sudden zest of life; the lights danced before his eyes and the concert hall blazed into unimaginable splendor. When the soprano soloist came on, Paul forgot even the nastiness of his teacher's being there, and gave himself up to the peculiar intoxication such personages always had for him. The soloist chanced to be a German woman, by no means in her first youth, and the mother of many children; but she wore a satin gown and a tiara, and she had that indefinable air of achievement, that world-shine upon her, which always blinded Paul to any possible defects. After a concert was over, Paul was often irritable and wretched until he got to sleep and tonight he was even more than usually restless. He had the feeling of not being able to let down; of its being impossible to give up his delicious excitement which was the only thing that could be called living at all. During the last number he withdrew and, after hastily changing his clothes in the dressing-room, slipped out to the side door where the singer's carriage stood. Here he began pacing rapidly up and down the walk, waiting to see her come out. Over yonder the Schenley, in its vacant stretch, loomed big and square through the fine rain, the windows of its twelve stories glowing like those of a lighted cardboard house under a Christmas tree. All the actors and singers of any importance stayed there when they were in Pittsburgh, and a number of the big manufacturers of the place lived there in the winter. Paul had often hung about the hotel, watching the people go in and out, longing to enter and leave schoolmasters and dull care behind him forever.

At last the singer came out, accompanied by the conductor, who helped her into her carriage and closed the door with a cordial auf wiedersehen which set Paul to wondering whether she were not an old sweetheart of his. Paul followed the carriage over to the hotel, walking so rapidly as not to be far from the entrance when the singer alighted and disappeared behind the swinging glass doors which were opened by a Negro in a tall hat and a long coat. In the moment that the door was ajar, it seemed to Paul that he, too, entered. He seemed to feel himself go after her up the steps, into the warm, lighted building, into an exotic, a tropical world of shiny, glistening surfaces and basking ease. He reflected upon the mysterious dishes that were brought into the dining room, the green bottles in buckets of ice, as he had seen them in the supper-party pictures of the Sunday supplement. A quick gust of wind brought the rain down with sudden vehemence, and Paul was startled to find that he was still outside in the slush of the gravel driveway; that his boots were letting in the water and his scanty overcoat was clinging wet about him; that the lights in front of the concert hall were out, and that the rain was driving in sheets between him and the orange glow of the windows above him. There it was, what he wanted tangibly before him, like the fairy world of a Christmas pantomime; as the rain beat in his face. Paul wondered whether he were destined always to shiver in the black night outside, looking up at it.

He turned and walked reluctantly toward the car tracks. The end had to come sometime; his father in his night clothes at the top of the stairs, explanations that did not explain, hastily improvised fictions that were forever tripping him up, his upstairs room and its horrible yellow wallpaper, the creaking bureau with the greasy plush collar-box, and over his painted wooden bed the pictures of George Washington and John Calvin, and the framed motto, 'Feed my Lambs,' which had been worked in red worsted by his mother, whom Paul could not remember. Half an hour later, Paul alighted from the Negley Avenue car and went slowly down one of the side streets off the main thoroughfare. It was a highly respectable street, where all the houses were exactly alike, and where business men of moderate means begot and reared large families of children, all of whom went to Sabbath School and learned the shorter catechism, and were interested in arithmetic; all of whom were as exactly alike as their homes, and of a piece of the monotony in which they lived. Paul never went up Cordelia Street without a shudder of loathing. His home was next to the house of the Cumberland minister. He approached it tonight with the nerveless sense of defeat, the hopeless feeling of sinking back forever into ugliness and commonness that he had always had when he came home. The moment he turned into Cordelia Street he felt the waters close above his head. After each of these orgies of living, he experienced all the physical depression which follows a debauch; the loathing of respectable beds, of common food, of a house permeated by kitchen odors; a shuddering repulsion for the flavorless, colorless mass of every-day existence; a morbid desire for cool things and soft lights and fresh flowers.

The nearer he approached the house, the more absolutely unequal Paul felt to the sight of it all; his ugly sleeping chamber; the old bathroom with the grimy zinc tub, the cracked mirror, the dripping spigots; his father, at the top of the stairs, his hairy legs sticking out from his nightshirt, his feet thrust into carpet slippers. He was so much later than usual that there would certainly be enquiries and reproaches. Paul stopped short before the door. He felt that he could not be accosted by his father tonight; that he could not toss again on that miserable bed. He would not go in. He would tell his father that he had no carfare, and it was raining so hard he had gone home with one of the boys and stayed out all night.

Meanwhile, he was wet and cold. He went around to the back of the house and tried one of the basement windows, found it open, and raised it cautiously, and scrambled down the cellar wall to the floor. There he stood, holding his breath, terrified by the noise he had made; but the floor above him was silent, and there was no creak on the stairs. He found a soap-box, and carried it over to the soft ring of light that streamed from the furnace door, and sat down. He was horribly afraid of rats, so he did not try to sleep, but sat looking distrustfully at the dark, still terrified lest he might have awakened his father.

In such reactions, after one of the experiences which made days and nights out of the dreary blanks of the calendar, when his senses were deadened, Paul's head was always singularly clear. Suppose his father had heard him getting in at the window and had come down and shot him for a burglar? Then, again, suppose his father had come down, pistol in hand, and he had cried out in time to save himself, and his father had been horrified to think how nearly he had killed him? Then, again, suppose a day should come when his father would remember that night, and wish there had been no warning cry to stay his hand? With this last supposition Paul entertained himself until daybreak.

The following Sunday was fine; the sodden November chill was broken by the last flash of autumnal summer. In the morning Paul had to go to church and Sabbath School, as always. On seasonable Sunday afternoons the burghers of Cordelia Street usually sat out on their front stoops, and talked to their neighbors on the next stoop, or called to those across the street in neighborly fashion. The men sat placidly on gay cushions placed upon the steps that led down to the sidewalk, while the women, in their Sunday waists, sat in rockers on the cramped porches, pretending to be greatly at their ease. The children played in the streets; there were so many of them that the place resembled the recreation grounds of a kindergarten. The men on the steps, all in their shirt-sleeves, their vests unbuttoned, sat with their legs well apart, their stomachs comfortably protruding, and talked of the prices of things, or told anecdotes of the sagacity of their various chiefs and overlords. They occasionally looked over the multitude of squabbling children, listened affectionately to their high-pitched, nasal voices, smiling to see their own proclivities reproduced in their offspring, and interspersed their legends of the iron kings with remarks about their sons' progress at school, their grades in arithmetic, and the amounts they had saved in their toy banks. On this last Sunday of November, Paul sat all afternoon on the lowest step of his stoop, staring into the street, while his sisters, in their rockers, were talking to the minister's daughters next door about how many shirtwaists they had made in the last week, and how many waffles someone had eaten at the last church supper. When the weather was warm, and his father was in a particularly jovial frame of mind, the girls made lemonade, which was always brought out in a red-glass pitcher, ornamented with forget-me-nots in blue enamel. This the girls thought very fine, and the neighbors joked about the suspicious color of the pitcher.

Today, Paul's father, on the top step, was talking to a young man who shifted a restless baby from knee to knee. He happened to be the young man who was daily held up to Paul as a model, and after whom it was his father's dearest hope that he would pattern. This young man was a ruddy complexion, with a compressed, red mouth, and faded, nearsighted eyes, over which he wore thick spectacles, with gold bows that curved about his ears. He was clerk to one of the magnates of a great steel corporation, and was looked upon in Cordelia Street as a young man with a future. There was a story that, some five years ago he was now barely twenty-six he had been a trifle dissipated, but in order to curb his appetites and save the loss of time and strength that a sowing of wild oats might have entailed, he had taken his chief's advice, oft reiterated to his employees, and at twenty-one had married the first woman whom he could persuade to share his fortunes. She happened to be an angular schoolmistress, much older than he, who also wore thick glasses, and who had now borne him four children, all nearsighted like herself. The young man was relating how his chief, now cruising in the Mediterranean, kept in touch with all the details of the business, arranging his office hours on his yacht just as though he were at home, and knocking off work enough to keep two stenographers busy. His father told, in turn, the plan his corporation was considering, of putting in an electric railway plant at Cairo. Paul snapped his teeth; he had an awful apprehension that they might spoil it all before he got there. Yet he rather liked to hear these legends of the iron kings, that were told and retold on Sundays and holidays; these stories of palaces in Venice, yachts on the Mediterranean, and high play at Monte Carlo appealed to his fancy, and he was interested in the triumphs of cash-boys who had become famous, though he had no mind for the cash-boy stage.

After supper was over, and he had helped to dry the dishes, Paul nervously asked his father whether he could go to George's to get some help in his geometry, and still more nervously asked for carfare. This latter request he had to repeat, as his father, on principle, did not like to hear requests for money, whether much or little. He asked Paul whether he could not go to some boy who lived nearer, and told him that he ought not to leave his school work until Sunday; but he gave him the dime. He was not a poor man, but he had a worthy ambition to come up in the world. His only reason for allowing Paul to usher was that he thought a boy ought to be earning a little.

Paul bounded upstairs, scrubbed the greasy odor of the dishwater from his hands with the ill-smelling soap he hated, and then shook over his fingers a few drops of violet water from the bottle he kept hidden in his drawer. He left the house with his geometry conspicuously under his arm, and the moment he got out of Cordelia Street and boarded a downtown car, he shook off the lethargy of two deadening days, and began to live again. The leading juvenile of the permanent stock company which played at one of the downtown theatres was an acquaintance of Paul's, and the boy had been invited to drop in at the Sunday night rehearsals whenever he could. For more than a year Paul had spent every available moment loitering about Charley Edward's dressing room. He had won a place among Edward's following not only because the young actor, who could not afford to employ a dresser, often found him useful, but because he recognized in Paul something akin to what churchmen term vocation. It was at the theater and at Carnegie Hall that Paul really lived; the rest was but a sleep and a forgetting. This was Paul's fairy tale, and it had for him all the allurement of a secret love. The moment he inhaled the gassy, painty, dusty odor behind the scenes, he breathed like a prisoner set free, and felt within him the possibility of doing or saving splendid, brilliant things. The moment the cracked orchestra beat out the overture from Martha, or jerked at the serenade from Rigoletto, all stupid and ugly things slid from him, and his senses were deliciously, yet delicately fired.

Perhaps it was because, in Paul's world, the natural nearly always wore the guise of ugliness, that a certain element of artificiality seemed to him necessary in beauty. Perhaps it was because his experience of life elsewhere was so full of Sabbath School picnics, petty economies, wholesome advice as to how to succeed in life, and the unescapable odors of cooking, that he found this existence so alluring, these smartly clad men and women so attractive, that he was so moved by these starry apple orchards that bloomed perennially under the limelight. It would be difficult to put it strongly enough how convincingly the stage entrance of the theater was for Paul, the actual portal of romance. Certainly none of the company ever suspected it, least of all Charley Edwards. It was very like the old stories that used to float about London of fabulously rich Jews, who had subterranean halls, with palms, and fountains, and soft lamps, and richly apparelled women who never saw the disenchanting light of London day. So, in the midst of that smoke-palled city, enamored of figures and grimy oil, Paul had his secret temple, his wishing-carpet, his bit of blue-and-white Mediterranean shore bathed in perpetual sunshine. Several of Paul's teachers had a theory that his imagination had been perverted by garish fiction; but the truth was he scarcely ever read at all. The books at home were not such as would either tempt or corrupt a youthful mind, and as for reading the novels that some of his friends urged upon him well, he got what he wanted much more quickly from music; any sort of music, from an orchestra to a barrel-organ. He needed only the spark, the indescribable thrill that made his imagination master of his senses, and he could make plots and pictures enough of his own. It was equally true that he was not stage-struck—not, at any rate, in the usual acceptation of the expression. He had no desire to become an actor, any more than he had to become a musician. He felt no necessity to do any of these things; what he wanted was to see, to be in the atmosphere, float on the wave of it, to be carried out, blue league after league, away from everything.

After a night behind the scenes, Paul found the schoolroom more than ever repulsive; the bare floors and naked walls; the prosy men who never wore frock coats, or violets in their buttonholes; the women with their dull gowns, shrill voices, and pitiful seriousness about pretensions that govern the dative. He could not bear to have the other pupils think, for a moment, that he took these people seriously; he must convey to them that he considered it all trivial, and was there only by way of a joke, anyway. He had autographed pictures of all the members of the stock company which he showed his classmates, telling them the most incredible stories of his familiarity with these people, of his acquaintance with the soloists who came to Carnegie Hall, his suppers with them and the flowers he sent them. When these stories lost their effect, and his audience grew listless, he would bid all the boys goodbye, announcing that he was going to travel for a while; going to Naples, to California, to Egypt. Then, next Monday, he would slip back, conscious and nervously smiling; his sister was ill, and he would have to defer his voyage until spring.

Matters went steadily worse with Paul at school. In the itch to let his instructors know how heartily he despised them, and how thoroughly he was appreciated elsewhere, he mentioned once or twice that he had no time to fool with theorems; adding with a twitch of the eyebrows and a touch of that nervous bravado which so perplexed them that he was helping the people down at the stock company; they were old friends of his.

The upshot of the matter was that the Principal went to Paul's father, and Paul was taken out of school and put to work.

The manager at Carnegie Hall was told to get another usher in his stead; the doorkeeper at the theater was warned not to admit him to the house; and Charley Edwards remorsefully promised the boy's father not to see him again.

The members of the stock company were vastly amused when some of Paul's stories reached them, especially the women. They were hard-working women, most of them supporting indolent husbands or brothers, and they laughed rather bitterly at having stirred the boy to such fervid and florid inventions. They agreed with the faculty and with his father, that Paul's was a bad case.

The east-bound train was plowing through a January snowstorm; the dull dawn was beginning to show grey when the engine whistled a mile out of Newark. Paul started up from the seat where he had lain curled in uneasy slumber, rubbed the breath-misted window glass with his hand, and peered out. The snow was whirling in curling eddies above the white bottom lands, and the drifts lay already deep in the fields and along the fences, while here and there the tall dead grass and dried weed stalks protruded black above it. Lights shone from the scattered houses, and a gang of laborers who stood beside the track waved their lanterns. Paul had slept very little, and he felt grimy and uncomfortable. He had made the all-night journey in a day coach because he was afraid if he took a Pullman he might be seen by some Pittsburgh business man who had noticed him in Denny and Carson's office. When the whistle woke him, he clutched quickly at his breast pocket, glancing about him with an uncertain smile. But the little, clay-bespattered Italians were still sleeping, the slatternly women across the aisle were in open-mouthed oblivion, and even the crumby, crying babies were for the time stilled. Paul settled back to struggle with his impatience as best he could. When he arrived at the Jersey City station, he hurried through his breakfast, manifestly ill at ease and keeping a sharp eye about him. After he reached the Twenty-Third Street station, he consulted a cabman, and had himself driven to a men's furnishing establishment which was just opening for the day. He spent upward of two hours there, buying, buying with endless reconsidering and great care. His new street suit he put on in the fitting-room; the frock coat and dress clothes he had bundled into the cab with his new shirts. Then he drove to a hatter's and a shoe house. His next errand was at Tiffany's, where he selected silver-mounted brushes and a scarf pin. He would not wait to have his silver marked, he said. Lastly, he stopped at a trunk shop on Broadway, and had his purchases packed into various traveling bags.

It was a little after one o'clock when he drove up to the Waldorf, and, after settling with the cabman, went into the office. He registered from Washington; said his mother and father had been abroad, and that he had come down to await the arrival of their steamer. He told his story plausibly and had no trouble, since he offered to pay for them in advance, in engaging his rooms; a sleeping-room, sitting-room, and bath.

Not once, but a hundred times Paul had planned his entry into New York. He had gone over every detail of it with Charley Edwards, and in his scrapbook at home there were pages of description about New York hotels, cut from the Sunday papers.

When he was shown to his sitting-room on the eighth floor, he saw at a glance that everything was as it should be; there was but one detail in his mental picture that the place did not realize, so he rang for the bellboy and sent him down for flowers. He moved about nervously until the boy returned, putting away his new linen and fingering it delightedly as he did so. When the flowers came, he put them hastily into water, and then tumbled into a hot bath. Presently he came out of his white bathroom, resplendent in his new silk underwear, and playing with the tassels of his red robe. The snow was whirling so fiercely outside his windows that he could scarcely see across the street, but within, the air was deliciously soft and fragrant. He put the violets and jonquils on the taboret beside the couch, and threw himself down with a long sigh, covering himself with a Roman blanket. He was thoroughly tired; he had been in such haste, he had stood up to such a strain, covered so much ground in the last twenty-four hours, that he wanted to think how it had all come about. Lulled by the sound of the wind, the warm air, and the cool fragrance of the flowers, he sank into deep, drowsy retrospection. It had been wonderfully simple; when they had shut him out of the theater and concert hall, when they had taken away his bone, the whole thing was virtually determined. The rest was a mere matter of opportunity. The only thing that at all surprised him as his own courage for he realized well enough that he had always been tormented by fear, a sort of apprehensive dread which, of late years, as the meshes of the lies he had told closed about him, had been pulling the muscles of his body tighter and tighter. Until now, he could not remember a time when he had not been dreading something. Even when he was a little boy, it was always there behind him, or before, or on either side. There had always been the shadowed corner, the dark place into which he dared not look, but from which something seemed always to be watching him and Paul had done things that were not pretty to watch, he knew.

But now he had a curious sense of relief, as though he had at last thrown down the gauntlet to the thing in the corner.

Yet it was but a day since he had been sulking in the traces; but yesterday afternoon that he had been sent to the bank with Denny and Carson's deposit, as usual but this time he was instructed to leave the book to be balanced. There was above two thousand dollars in checks, and nearly a thousand in the bank notes which he had taken from the book and quietly transferred to his pocket. At the bank he had made out a new deposit slip. His nerves had been steady enough to permit of his returning to the office, where he had finished his work and asked for full day's holiday tomorrow, Saturday, giving a perfectly reasonable pretext. The bank book, he knew, would not be returned before Monday or Tuesday, and his father would be out of town for the next week. From the time he slipped the bank notes into his pocket until he boarded the night train for New York, he had not known a moment's hesitation.

How astonishingly easy it had all been; here he was, the thing done; and this time there would be no awakening, no figure at the top of the stairs. He watched the snowflakes whirling by his window until he fell asleep. When he awoke, it was four o'clock in the afternoon. He bounded up with a start; one of his precious days gone already! He spent nearly an hour in dressing, watching every stage of his toilet carefully in the mirror. Everything was quite perfect; he was exactly the kind of boy he had always wanted to be.

When he went downstairs, Paul took a carriage and drove up Fifth Avenue toward the Park. The snow had somewhat abated; carriages and tradesmen's wagons were hurrying soundlessly to and fro in the winter twilight; boys in woolen mufflers were shoveling off the doorsteps; the Avenue stages made fine spots of color against the white street. Here and there on the corners whole flower gardens blooming behind glass windows, against which the snowflakes stuck and melted; violets, roses, carnations, lilies-of-the-valley somehow vastly more lovely and alluring that they blossomed thus unnaturally in the snow. The Park itself was a wonderful stage, a winterpiece. When he returned, the pause of the twilight had ceased, and the tune of the streets had changed. The snow was falling faster, lights streamed from the hotels that reared their many stories fearlessly up into the storm, defying the raging Atlantic winds. A long, black stream of carriages poured down the Avenue, intersected here and there by other streams, tending horizontally. There were a score of cabs about the entrance of his hotel, and his driver had to wait. Boys in livery were running in and out of the awning stretched across the sidewalk, up and down the red velvet carpet laid from the door to the street. Above, about, within it all, was the rumble and roar, the hurry and toss of thousands of human beings as hot for pleasure as himself, and on every side of him towered the glaring affirmation of the omnipotence of wealth.

The boy set his teeth and drew his shoulders together in a spasm of realization; the plot of all dramas, the text of all romances, the nerve-stuff of all sensations was whirling about him like the snowflakes. He burnt like a fagot in a tempest. When Paul came down to dinner, the music of the orchestra floated up the elevator shaft to greet him. As he stepped into the thronged corridors, he sank back into one of the chairs against the wall to get his breath. The lights, the chatter, the perfumes, the bewildering medley of color he had, for a moment, the feeling of not being able to stand it. But only for a moment; these were his own people, he told himself. He went slowly about the corridors, through the writing rooms, smoking rooms, reception rooms, as through he were exploring the chambers of an enchanted palace, built and peopled for him alone.

When he reached the dining room he sat down at a table near a window. The flowers, the white linen, the many-colored wine glasses, the gay toilettes of the women, the low popping of corks, the undulating repetitions of the Blue Danube from the orchestra, all flooded Paul's dream with bewildering radiance. When the roseate tinge of his champagne was added that cold, precious, bubbling stuff that creamed and foamed in his glass Paul wondered that there were honest men in the world at all. This was what all the world was fighting for, he reflected; this was what all the struggle was about. He doubted the reality of his past. Had he ever known a place called Cordelia Street, a place where fagged-looking business men boarded the early car? Mere rivets in a machine they seemed to Paul, sickening men, with combings of children's hair always hanging to their coats, and the smell of cooking in their clothes. Cordelia Street. Ah, that belonged to another time and country! Had he not always been thus, had he not sat here night after night, from as far back as he could remember, looking pensively over just such shimmering textures, and slowly turning the stem of a glass like this one between his thumb and middle finger? He rather thought he had.

He was not in the least abashed or lonely. He had no special desire to meet or to know any of these people; all he demanded was the right to look on and conjecture, to watch the pageant. The mere stage properties were all he contended for. Nor was he lonely later in the evening, in his loge at the Opera. He was entirely rid of his nervous misgivings, of his forced aggressiveness, of the imperative desire to show himself different from his surroundings. He felt now that his surroundings explained him. Nobody questioned the purple; he had only to wear it passively. He had only to glance down at his dress coat to reassure himself that here it would be impossible for anyone to humiliate him.

He found it hard to leave his beautiful sitting room to go to bed that night, and sat long watching the raging storm from his turret window. When he went to sleep, it was with the lights turned on in his bedroom; partly because of his old timidity, and partly so that, if he should wake in the night, there would be no wretched moment of doubt, no horrible suspicion of yellow wallpaper, or of Washington and Calvin above his bed.

On Sunday morning the city was practically snowbound. Paul breakfasted late, and in the afternoon he fell in with a wild San Francisco boy, a Freshman at Yale, who said he had run down for a little flyer over Sunday. The young man offered to show Paul the night side of town, and the two boys went off together after dinner, not returning to the hotel until seven o'clock the next morning. They had started out in the confiding warmth of a champagne friendship, but their parting in the elevator was singularly cool. The freshman pulled himself together to make his train, and Paul went to bed. He awoke at two o'clock in the afternoon, very thirsty and dizzy, and rang for ice water, coffee, and the Pittsburgh papers. On the part of the hotel management, Paul excited no suspicion. There was this to be said for him, that he wore his spoils with dignity and in no way made himself conspicuous. His chief greediness lay in his ears and eyes, and his excesses were not offensive ones. His dearest pleasures were the grey winter twilights in his sitting room; his quiet enjoyment of his flowers, his clothes, his wide divan, his cigarette, and his sense of power. He could not remember a time when he had felt so at peace with himself. The mere release from the necessity of petty lying, lying every day and every day, restored his self respect. He had never lied for pleasure, even at school; but to make himself noticed and admired, to assert his difference from other Cordelia Street boys; and he felt a good deal more manly, more honest, even, now that he had no need for boastful pretensions, now that he could, as his actor friends used to say, dress the part. It was characteristic that remorse did not occur to him. His golden days went by without a shadow, and he made each as perfect as he could.

On the eighth day of his arrival in New York, he found the whole affair exploited in the Pittsburgh papers, exploited with a wealth of detail which indicated that local news of a sensational nature was at a low ebb. The firm of Denny and Carson announced that it had no intention of prosecuting. The Cumberland minister had been interviewed, and expressed his hope of yet reclaiming the motherless lad, and Paul's Sabbath School teacher declared that she would spare no effort to that end. The rumor had reached Pittsburgh that the boy had been seen in a New York hotel, and his father had gone East to find him and bring him home. Paul had just come in to dress for dinner; he sank into the chair, weak in the knees, and clasped his head in his hands. It was to be worse than jail, even; the tepid waters of Cordelia Street were to close over him finally and forever. The grey monotony stretched before him in hopeless, unrelieved years. Sabbath School, Young People's Meeting, the yellow-papered room, the damp dish towels; it all rushed back upon him with sickening vividness. He had the old feeling that the orchestra had suddenly stopped, the sinking sensation that the play was over. The sweat broke out on his face, and he sprang to his feet, looked about him with his white, conscious smile, and winked at himself in the mirror. With something of the childish belief in miracles with which he had so often gone to class, all his lessons unlearned, Paul dressed and dashed whistling down the corridor to the elevator. He had no sooner entered the dining room and caught the measure of the music than his remembrance was lightened by his old elastic power of claiming the moment, mounting with it, and finding it all-sufficient. The glare and glitter about him, the mere scenic accessories had again, and for the last time, their old potency. He would show himself that he was game, he would finish the thing splendidly. He doubted, more than ever, the cxistence of Cordelia Street, and for the first time he drank his wine recklessly. Was he not, after all, onc of these fortunate beings? Was he not still himself, and in his own place? He drummed a nervous accompaniment to the music and looked about him, telling himself over and over that it had paid. He reflected drowsily, to the swell of the violin and the chill sweetness of his wine, that he might have done it more wisely. He might have caught an outbound steamer and been well out of their clutches before now. But the other side of the world had seemed too far away and too uncertain then; he could not have waited for it; his need had been too sharp. If he had to choose over again, he would do the same thing tomorrow. He looked affectionately about the dining room, now gilded with a soft mist. Ah, it had paid indeed!

Paul was awakened next morning by a painful throbbing in his head and feet. He had thrown himself across the bed without undressing, and had slept with his shoes on. His limbs and hands were lead-heavy, and his tongue and throat were parched. There came upon him one of those fateful attacks of clear-headedness that never occurred except when he was physically exhausted and his nerves hung loose. He lay still and closed his eyes and let the tide of realities wash over him. His father was in New York; stopping at some joint or other, he told himself. The memory of successive summers on the front stoop fell upon him like a weight of black water. He had not a hundred dollars left; and he knew now, more than ever, that money was everything, the wall that stood between all he loathed and all he wanted. The thing was winding itself up; he had thought of that on his first glorious day in New York, and had even provided a way to snap the thread. It lay on his dressing table now; he had got it out last night when he came blindly up from dinner but the shiny metal hurt his eyes, and he disliked the look of it, anyway. He rose and moved about with a painful effort, succumbing now and again to attacks of nausea. It was the old depression exaggerated; all the world had become Cordelia Street. Yet somehow he was not afraid of anything, was absolutely calm; perhaps because he had looked into the dark corner at last, and knew. It was bad enough, what he saw there; but somehow not so bad as his long fear of it had been. He saw everything clearly now. He had a feeling that he had made the best of it, that he had lived the sort of life he was meant to live, and for half an hour he sat staring at the revolver. But he told himself that was not the way, so he went downstairs and took a cab to the ferry.

When Paul arrived at Newark, he got off the train and took another cab, directing the driver to follow the Pennsylvania tracks out of town. The snow lay heavy on the roadways and had drifted deep in the open fields. Only here and there the dead grass or dried weed stalks projected, singularly black, above it. Once well into the country, Paul dismissed the carriage and walked, floundering along the tracks, his mind a medley of irrelevant things. He seemed to hold in his brain an actual picture of everything he had seen that morning. He remembered every feature of both his drivers, the toothless old woman from whom he had bought the red flowers in his coat, the agent from whom he had got his ticket, and all of his fellow-passengers on the ferry. His mind, unable to cope with vital matters near at hand, worked feverishly and deftly at sorting and grouping these images. They made for him a part of the ugliness of the world, of the ache in his head, and the bitter burning on his tongue. He stooped and put a handful of snow into his mouth as he walked, but that, too, seemed hot. When he reached a little hillside, where the tracks ran through a cut some twenty feet below him, he stopped and sat down.

The carnations in his coat were drooping with cold, he noticed; their red glory over. It occurred to him that all the flowers he had seen in the show windows that first night must have gone the same way, long before this. It was only one splendid breath they had, in spite of their brave mockery at the winter outside the glass. It was a losing game in the end, it seemed, this revolt against the homilies by which the world is run. Paul took one of the blossoms carefully from his coat and scooped a little hole in the snow, where he covered it up. Then he dozed awhile, from his weak condition, seeming insensible to the cold.

The sound of an approaching train woke him and he started to his feet, remembering only his resolution, and afraid lest he should be too late. He stood watching the approaching locomotive, his teeth chattering, his lips drawn away from them in a frightened smile; once or twice he glanced nervously sidewise, as though he were being watched. When the right moment came, he jumped. As he fell, the folly of his haste occurred to him with merciless clearness, the vastness of what he had left undone. There flashed through his brain, clearer than ever before, the blue Adriatic water, the yellow of Algerian sands.

He felt something strike his chest, his body being thrown swiftly through the air, on and on, immeasurably far and fast, while his limbs gently relaxed. Then, because the picture-making mechanism was crushed, the disturbing visions flashed into black, and Paul dropped back into the immense design of things.

RIDING THE RAP
by Elmore Leonard

Ocala Police picked up Dale Crowe Junior, two o'clock in the morning, for weaving, crossing the center line, and having a busted tail-light. Then while Dale was blowing a point-one-nine they put his name and date of birth into the national crime computer and learned he was a fugitive felon, wanted on a three-year-old charge of Unlawful Flight to Avoid Incarceration. A few days later Raylan Givens, with the Marshal's Service, came up from Palm Beach County to take Dale back, and the Ocala Police wondered about Raylan.

How come if he was a federal officer and Dale Crowe Junior was wanted on a state charge.... He told them he was with FAST, the Fugitive Apprehension Strike Team, assigned to the Sheriff's Office in West Palm. And that was pretty much all this marshal said. They wondered, too, since he was alone, how he'd be able to drive and keep an eye on his prisoner. Dale Crowe Junior had been convicted of a third-degree five-year felony, Battery of a Police Officer, and was looking at additional time on the fugitive warrant. Dale Junior might feel he had nothing to lose on this trip south. He was a rangy kid with the build of a college athlete, bigger than this marshal in his blue suit and cowboy boots—the marshal calm, though, not appearing to be the least apprehensive. He said the West Palm strike team was shorthanded at the moment, the reason he was alone, but he believed he would manage.

And when he put his hat on and drove off with Dale Junior in the confiscated two-year-old Cadillac he was using, a dark-blue one, an Ocala officer said, "He believes he'll manage...."

Another officer said, "Don't you know who that is? He's the one the Mafia guy drew on last winter in Miami Beach—the two of them sitting at the same table, and this marshal shot him dead. Yeah, Raylan Givens. It was in the paper."

"That why he didn't give us the time of day? I doubt he said five words. Shows us his star...."

The one who had read about Raylan Givens said, "I didn't get that impression. I saw him as all business, the kind goes by the book."

He said to Dale Crowe Junior, "I know you think you can drive when you've had a few. How good are you when you're sober?"

This marshal not sounding like the usual hard-ass lawman; Dale Junior was glad of that. He said, "I had a Caddy myself one time, till I sold it for parts and went to work at Disney's. You know what I tried out for? Play Goofy. Mickey Mouse's friend? Only you had to water-ski, and I couldn't get the hang of it. Sir, I like to mention that these three years since I took off? I been clean. I never even left the state of Florida all that time, not wanting to be too far away from my folks, my old mom and dad, except I never did get to see them."

The marshal, Raylan Givens, said, "If you're gonna talk I'll put you in the trunk and I'll drive."

So neither of them said another word until they were south of Orlando on the Turnpike, a hundred and sixty miles to West Palm, Dale Junior staring straight ahead at the highway, flat and straight through Florida scrub, boring, holding it right around sixty so as to make the trip last, give him time to think of a move he might try on the marshal. The man didn't appear to be much to handle, had a slim build and looked like a farmer—sounded like one, too—forty years old or so; he sat against his door, seat belt fastened, turned somewhat this way. He had on one of those business cowboy hats, but broken in; it looked good on him, the way he wore it cocked over one eye.

Dale Junior would feel him staring, though when he glanced over, the marshal was usually looking out at the road or the countryside, patient, taking the ride as it came. Dale Junior decided to start feeling him out.

"Can I say something?"

The marshal was looking at him now.

"What's that?"

"There's a service plaza coming up. I wouldn't mind stopping, get something to eat?"

The man shook his head and Dale Junior made a face, giving the marshal an expression of pain.

"I couldn't eat that jail food they give you. Some kind of potatoes and imitation eggs cold as ice." He waited as long as he could, almost a minute, and said, "I don't see why we can't talk some. Pass the time."

The marshal said, "I don't care to hear any sad stories, all the bad luck and bum deals life's handed you."

Dale Junior showed him a frown. "Don't it mean anything I got nothing on my sheet the past three years, that I've been clean all that time?"

The marshal said, "Not to me it doesn't. Son, you're none of my business."

Dale Junior shook his head, giving himself a beat look now, without hope. He said, "I'll tell you, I thought more'n once of giving myself up. You know why?"

The marshal waited, not helping any.

"So I could see my folks. So I'd know they was O.K. I didn't dare write, knowing the mails would be watched." When the marshal didn't comment, Dale Junior said, "They do that, don't they?"

"What?"

"Watch the mails?"

"I doubt it."

Dale Junior said, "Oh, well," paused, and said, "My old dad lost one of his legs, had it bit off by a alligator this time he's fishing the rim canal, by Lake Okeechobee? I sure wish I could see him before we get to Gun Club. That's where were going, huh—the Gun Club jail?"

"You're going to the county lockup," the marshal said, "to await a sentence hearing."

"Yeah, well, that's what they call it, account of it's off Gun Club Road. So you're not from around there, huh—West Palm?"

The marshal didn't answer, seeming more interested in the sky, clouds coming in from way out over the ocean.

"Where you from, anyway?"

"I live down in Miami."

"I been there once or twice. Man, all the spics, huh? My dad's never been to Palm Beach or seen the ocean. Never got any closer'n Twenty Mile Bend. You believe it? Spent his whole life over there around Belle Glade, Canal Point, Pahokee...." He waited, eyes on the road, before saying, "You know, if we was to get off near Stuart we could take 76 over to the lake, run on down to Belle Glade—it wouldn't be more'n a few miles out of the way and I'd get to see my folks. I mean just stop and say hi, kiss my old mom...." Dale Junior turned to look at the marshal. "What would you say to that?" He waited and said, "Not much, huh?"

"Your old dad's never been to Palm Beach or seen the ocean," the marshal said, "but he's been up to Starke, hasn't he? He's seen the Florida State Prison. You have an uncle came out of there, Elvin Crowe, and another one did his time at Lake Butler. I think we'll skip visiting any of your kin this trip."

Dale Junior said, "My uncles're both dead."

And the marshal said, "By gunshot, huh? You understand how I see your people?"

Now he said, "You can speed it up some."

Dale Junior looked over at him. "You want me to break the law?"

Raylan didn't answer, staring at the open vista of flat land to the east, what he imagined the plains of Africa might be like.

"We could use some gas."

"We'll make it," Raylan said.

"Fort Drum Service Plaza's coming up."

Raylan didn't say anything to that.

"Aren't you hungry?"

This time Raylan said, "I'll see you get something at the jail."

"I ain't had a regular meal," Dale Junior said, "since the day I was arrested, and you know what it was? A hamburger and fries, some onion rings. That night for supper I had potato chips. See, all day I was out looking for work. I had a job, working for a paint contractor? Scraped down and sanded this entire goddam two-story house and the guy lets me go. That's what they do, they use you. My trade, I drove a big goddam cane truck from the fields to the sugar house—back before I had that trouble and had to take off. Now, the way the system works, what's known as the free-enterprise system? They're free to use you on some dirt job nobody wants, and when you get done they fire you. Four dollars an hour, man—that's the system, as good as it gets."

Raylan watched him as he spoke, Dale Junior staring straight ahead, rigid, arms extended, hands gripping the top arc of the steering wheel. Big hands with bony white knuckles. Raylan turned a little more in the seat-belt harness to face him and raised his left leg a few inches to rest it against the edge of the seat. He could feel his service pistol, a Beretta 9, holstered to his right hip, wedged in there against the door. Handcuffs were hooked to his belt. A shotgun, an MP5 machine gun, his vest, a sledgehammer, and several more pairs of cuffs were in the trunk. He had left the Palm Beach County Sheriff's Office about nine this morning. Almost five hours up to Ocala, then had to wait around an hour for the paperwork before getting his prisoner. By then it was after three. Now, more than halfway back, it was starting to get dark.

"The night I got stopped," Dale Junior said, "I had like four beers and the potato chips while I shot some pool, that's all. O.K., driving home, this place where I been staying with a friend, I'm minding my own fucking business, not doing anything wrong, I get pulled over. Listen to this. On account of one of my tail-lights ain't working. The cops get me out of the car, tell me to walk the line, touch my fucking nose, they give me all this shit and take me in for the breath test. O.K., I want to know who says it's fair. I'm clean three years, been working on and off when I could find a job, and now I'm gonna get sent up to F.S.P.?" Dale Junior said. "Do five years, maybe even more'n that on account of a busted tail-light?"

Raylan got ready.

Dale Junior said, "Bull shit!" Turned his head and strained against his seat belt as he swung at Raylan backhand to club him with his fist, and Raylan brought his leg up under the arm coming at him and punched the heel of his cowboy boot hard into Dale Junior's face. The car swerved left, hit the grassy median, and swerved back into the double lanes, Dale Junior hunched over the wheel holding on. By this time Raylan was out of his seat belt, had his Beretta in his right hand, and was holding it in Dale Junior's face, waiting for him to look over.

When he did, Raylan said, "Pull off the road." He waited until they were parked on the shoulder before reaching around to get his handcuffs. He said to Dale Junior, "Here, put one on your left wrist and snap the other one to the wheel."

Dale Junior, blood leaking from his nose, stunned but still irate, in Raylan's judgment, said, "I can't drive handcuffed to the steering wheel."

Raylan held up his free hand for Dale Junior to look at and began rubbing the tips of his thumb and index finger together. He said, "You know what this is? It's the world's smallest violin. A fella did that in a movie where these six scudders wearing black suits go and rob a jewelry store and they all get killed. You see it? It was a good one?"

They drove on toward West Palm with darkness spreading over the land, Dale Junior getting used to the handcuffs, looking over as the marshal said, "Put your lights on." Saying then, "Everybody's got problems, huh? Different kinds for different people. Account of you think you're tough you're going up to State Prison where you'll have to prove it."

Dale Junior said, "You gonna report what I did, get me another couple of years up there?" and had to wait.

The marshal taking a few moments before he said, "Last month I went to Brunswick, Georgia, to visit my sons. One's ten, the other's four and a half, living up there with their mom and a real-estate man she married name of Gary, has a little cookie-duster mustache. Winona calls the boys punkins, always has. But this Gary calls them punks. I told him not to do it, my sons aren't punks. He says it's short for 'punkin,' that's all. I told him, 'I don't care for it, O.K.? So don't call them that.' If I'd known about you then I could've told Gary your story and said, 'That's what a punk is, a person refuses to grow up.'"

"I asked you," Dale Junior said, "if you're gonna bring me up on a charge."

"You hear your tone of voice?" the marshal said, sitting over there in the dark. "I'm not your problem."

It was quiet in the car following the headlights along the Turnpike, neither of them saying another word until they came to the toll booth and the marshal paid the man and they got off on Okeechobee Boulevard in West Palm. The marshal told him to go east to Military Trail and turn right, and Dale Junior told him he knew the way to Gun Club, O.K.?

Now there were street lights and signs and stores lit up, back in civilization.

"Your problem," the marshal said, "you can't accept anyone telling you what to do."

Dale Junior only grunted, feeling another sermon coming.

The marshal saying now, "If you can't live with it, don't ever get into law enforcement."

"If I can't live with what?"

"Being told what to do, having superiors."

Dale Junior said, "Oh," slowing down and braking for a yellow light turning red, thinking, Jesus, what he always wanted to do, get into law enforcement.

It was as they coasted to the intersection and stopped they got rammed from behind.

Raylan felt himself pressed against the seat harness, his head snapping back and forward again. He heard Dale Junior say "God damn!" and saw him gripping the wheel, looking up at the rearview mirror now. Raylan got his seat belt undone before looking around to see the headlights of a pickup truck close behind the Cadillac's rear deck. Now it was backing up a few feet, the driver making sure the bumpers weren't locked together.

"Goddam jig," Dale Junior said.

Two of them, young black guys, coming from the pickup now as Raylan got out and walked back toward them: the one on the driver's side wearing a crocheted skullcap, the other one, his hair done in cornrows, holding something in his right hand Raylan took to be a pistol, holding it against his leg, away from a few cars going past just then—all the traffic Raylan could see coming for the next few blocks. They were by a vacant lot; stores across the street appeared closed except for a McDonald's.

The pickup truck's bumper, higher than the Cadillac's, had plowed into the sheet metal, smashing the tail-lights on the left side and popping the trunk, the lid creased and raised a few inches.

Raylan recognized the revolver the guy held, a .357 mag with a six-inch barrel; he had one at home just like it, Smith & Wesson. Raylan kept his mouth shut, not wanting to say something that might get these guys upset. This was a car-jacking, the guys were no doubt wired, and that .357 could go off for no reason. Raylan looked at the damaged trunk again, studying it to be occupied.

The one with cornrows and the gun against his leg said, "You see what I got here?"

Raylan looked him in the eye for the first time and nodded.

The one in the crocheted skullcap walked up to the driver's side of the Cadillac. The one with cornrows said to Raylan, "We gonna trade, let you have a pickup truck for this here. You see a problem with that?"

Raylan shook his head.

The one in the crocheted skullcap glanced back this way as he said, "Come here, look at this."

The moment the one with the cornrows turned and moved away Raylan raised the trunk lid. He brought out his Remington 12-gauge, then had to wait for a car to pass before stepping away from the trunk. Raylan put the shotgun on the two guys looking at Dale Junior handcuffed to the steering wheel and did something every lawman knew guaranteed attention and respect. He racked the pump on the shotgun, back and forward, and that hard metallic sound, better than blowing a whistle, brought the two guys around to see they were out of business.

"Let go of the pistol," Raylan said. "Being dumb don't mean you want to get shot."

He used two pairs of cuffs from the trunk to link the car-jackers together—had them do it left wrist to left wrist and right wrist to right wrist—side by side and had them slide into the front seat next to Dale Junior.

Would he have shot them? Dale Junior kept quiet wondering about it. One of the cops back in Ocala had told him he'd better behave while in this marshal's care, but he hadn't thought about it until now. He could feel the shoulder of the car-jacker sitting next to him, the one with cornrows, pressing against his arm. Now the marshal, back there in the dark with his shotgun, was saying, "Fellas, this is Dale Crowe Junior, another one believes it's the system's fault he's ill-tempered and feels it's O.K. to assault people."

Saying then, after a minute, "I know a fella sixty-seven years old, got rich off our economic system running a sports book, has more money'n he can ever spend. But this man, with all his advantages, doesn't know what to do with himself. Mopes around, drinks too much, gets everybody upset and worried so they'll feel sorry for him."

The car-jacker next to Dale Junior said, "You was to lemme go, I'll see the man don't bother you no more."

Dale Junior thought the marshal would tell him to keep his mouth shut, maybe poke him with the shotgun. But nothing happened like that, and there was a silence, no sound from back there in the dark until the marshal said, "You miss the point. This friend of mine isn't bothering me any, he's his own problem. Same as you fellas. I don't take what you did personally. You understand? Want to lean on you. Or wish you any more state time'n you deserve. What you'll have to do now is ride the rap, as they say. It's all anybody has to do."

SON IN THE AFTERNOON
by John A. Williams

It was hot. I tend to be a bitch when it's hot. I goosed the little Ford over Sepulveda Boulevard toward Santa Monica until I got stuck in the traffic that pours from L.A. into the surrounding towns. I'd had a very lousy day at the studio. I was, still am, a writer and this studio had hired me to check scripts and films with Negroes in them to make sure the Negro moviegoer wouldn't be offended. The signs were already clear; one day the whole of American industry would be racing pellmell to get a Negro, showcase a spade. I was kind of a pioneer. I'm a Negro writer, you see. The day had been tough because of a couple of verbs slink and walk. One of those Hollywood hippies had done a script calling for a Negro waiter to slink away from the table where a dinner party was glaring at him. I said the waiter should walk, not slink, because later on he becomes a hero. The Hollywood hippie, who understood it all because he had some colored friends, said that it was essential to the plot that the waiter slink. I said you don't slink one minute and become a hero the next; there has to be some consistency. The Negro actor I was standing up for said nothing either way. He had played Uncle Tom roles so long that he had become Uncle Tom. But the director agreed with me.

Anyway…hear me out now. I was on my way to Santa Monica to pick up my mother, Nora. It was a long haul for such a hot day. I had planned a quiet evening: a nice shower, fresh clothes, and then I would have dinner at the Watkins and talk with some of the musicians on the scene for a quick taste before they cut to their gigs. After, I was going to the Pigalle down on Figueroa and catch Earl Grant at the organ, and still later, if nothing exciting happened, I'd pick up Scottie and make it to the Lighthouse on the Beach or to the Strollers and listen to some of the white boys play. I liked the long drive, especially while listening to Sleepy Stein's show on the radio. Later, much later of course, it would be home, back to Watts. So you see, this picking up Nora was a little inconvenient. My mother was a maid for the Couchmans. Ronald Couchman was an architect, a good one I understood from Nora who has a fine sense for this sort of thing; you don't work in some hundred-odd houses during your life without getting some idea of the way a house should be laid out. Couchman's wife, Kay, was a playgirl who drove a white Jaguar from one party to another. My mother didn't like her too much; she didn't seem to care much for her son, Ronald, junior. There's something wrong with a parent who can't really love her own child, Nora thought. The Couchmans lived in a real fine residential section, of course. A number of actors lived nearby, character actors, not really big stars.

Somehow it is very funny. I mean that the maids and butlers knew everything about these people, and these people knew nothing at all about the help. Through Nora and her friends I knew who was laying whose wife; who had money and who really had money; I knew about the wild parties hours before the police, and who smoked marijuana, when, and where they got it.

To get to Couchman's driveway I had to go three blocks up one side of a palm-planted center strip and back down the other. The driveway bent gently, then swept back out of sight of the main road. The house, sheltered by slim palms, looked like a transplanted New England Colonial. I parked and walked to the kitchen door, skirting the growling Great Dane who was tied to a tree. That was the route to the kitchen door.

I don't like kitchen doors. Entering people's houses by them, I mean. I'd done this thing most of my life when I called at places where Nora worked to pick up the patched or worn sheets or the half-eaten roasts, the battered, tarnished silver, the fringe benefits of a housemaid. As a teen-ager I'd told Nora I was through with that crap; I was not going through anyone's kitchen door. She only laughed and said I'd learn. One day soon after, I called for her and without knocking walked right through the front door of this house and right on through the living room. I was almost out of the room when I saw feet behind the couch. I leaned over and there was Mr. Jorgensen and his wife making out like crazy. I guess they thought Nora had gone and it must have hit them sort of suddenly and they went at it like the hell-bomb was due to drop any minute. I've been that way too, mostly in the spring. Of course, when Mr. Jorgensen looked over his shoulder and saw me, you know what happened. I was thrown out and Nora right behind me. It was the middle of winter, the old man was sick and the coal bill three months overdue. Nora was right about those kitchen doors. I learned.

My mother saw me before I could ring the bell. She opened the door. "Hello," she said. She was breathing hard, like she'd been running or something. "Come in and sit down. I don't know where that Kay is. Little Ronald is sick and she's probably out gettin' drunk again." She left me then and trotted back through the house, I guess to be with Ronnie. I hated the combination of her white nylon uniform, her dark brown face and the wide streaks of gray in her hair. Nora had married this guy from Texas a few years after the old man had died. He was all right. He made out okay. Nora didn't have to work, but she just couldn't be still; she always had to be doing something. I suggested she quit work, but I had as much luck as her husband. I used to tease her about liking to be around those white folks. It would have been good for her to take an extended trip around the country visiting my brothers and sisters. Once she got to Philadelphia, she could go right out in the cemetery and sit awhile with the old man.

I walked through the Couchman home. I liked the library. I thought if I knew Couchman I'd like him. The room made me feel like that. I left it and went into the big living room. You could tell that Couchman had let his wife do that. Everything in it was fast, dart-like, with no sense of ease. But on the walls were several of Couchman's conceptions of buildings and homes. I guess he was a disciple of Wright. My mother walked rapidly through the room without looking at me and said, "Just be patient, Wendell. She should be here real soon."

"Yeah," I said, "with a snootful." I had turned back to the drawings when Ronnie scampered into the room, his face twisted with rage.

"Nora!" he tried to roar, perhaps the way he'd seen the parents of some of his friends roar at their maids. I'm sure Kay didn't shout at Nora, and I don't think Couchman would. But then no one shouts at Nora. "Nora, you come right back here this minute!" the little bastard shouted and stamped and pointed to a spot on the floor where Nora was supposed to come to roost. I have a nasty temper. Sometimes it lies dormant for ages and at other times, like when the weather is hot and nothing seems to be going right, it's bubbling and ready to explode. "Don't talk to my mother like that, you little…!" I said sharply, breaking off just before I cursed. I wanted him to be large enough for me to strike. "How'd you like me to talk to your mother like that?"

The nine-year-old looked up at me in surprise and confusion. He hadn't expected me to say anything. I was just another piece of furniture. Tears rose in his eyes and spilled out onto his pale cheeks. He put his hands behind him, twisted them. He moved backwards, away from me. He looked at my mother with a "Nora, come help me" look. And sure enough, there was Nora, speeding back across the room, gathering the kid in her arms, tucking his robe together. I was too angry to feel hatred for myself.

Ronnie was the Couchman's only kid. Nora loved him. I suppose that was the trouble. Couchman was gone ten, twelve hours a day. Kay didn't stay around the house any longer than she had to. So Ronnie had only my mother. I think kids should have someone to love, and Nora wasn't a bad sort. But somehow when the six of us, her own children, were growing up we never had her. She was gone, out scuffling to get those crumbs to put into our mouths and shoes for our feet and praying for something to happen so that all the space in between would be taken care of. Nora's affection for us took the form of rushing out into the morning's five o'clock blackness to wake some silly bitch and get her coffee; took form in her trudging five miles home every night instead of taking the streetcar to save money to buy tablets for us, to use at school, we said. But the truth was that all of us liked to draw and we went through a writing tablet in a couple of hours every day. Can you imagine? There's not a goddamn artist among us. We never had the physical affection, the pat on the head, the quick, smiling kiss, the "gimmee a hug" routine. All of this Ronnie was getting.

Now he buried his little blond head in Nora's breast and sobbed. "There, there now," Nora said, "Don't you cry, Ronnie. Ol' Wendell is just jealous, and he hasn't much sense either. He didn't mean nuthin'."

I left the room. Nora had hit it of course, hit it and passed on. I looked back. It didn't look so incongruous, the white and black together. I mean. Ronnie was still sobbing. His head bobbed gently on Nora's shoulder. The only time I ever got that close to her was when she trapped me with a bear hug so she could whale the daylights out of me after I put a snowball through Mrs. Grant's window. I walked outside and lit a cigarette. When Ronnie was in the hospital the month before, Nora got me to run her way over to Hollywood every night to see him. I didn't like that worth a damn. All right, I'll admit it: it did upset me. All that affection I didn't get nor my brothers and sisters going to that little white boy who, without a doubt, when away from her called her the names he'd learned from adults. Can you imagine a nine-year-old kid calling Nora a "girl," "our girl?" I spat at the Great Dane. He snarled and then I bounced a rock off his fanny. "Lay down, you bastard," I muttered. It was a good thing he was tied up.

I heard the low cough of the Jaguar slapping against the road. The car was throttled down, and with a muted roar it swung into the driveway. The woman aimed it for me. I was evil enough not to move. I was tired of playing with these people. At the last moment, grinning, she swung the wheel over and braked. She bounded out of the car like a tennis player vaulting over a net.

"Hi," she said tugging at her shorts.

"Hello."

"You're Nora's boy?"

"I'm Nora's son." Hell, I was as old as she was; besides, I can't stand "boy."

"Nora tells us you're working in Hollywood. Like it?"

"It's all right."

"You must be pretty talented."

We stood looking at each other while the dog whined for her attention. Kay had a nice body and it was well tanned. She was high, boy, was she high. Looking at her, I could feel myself going into my sexy bastard routine; sometimes I can swing it great. Maybe it had to do with the business inside. Kay took off her sunglasses and took a good look at me. "Do you have a cigarette?"

I gave her one and lit it. "Nice tan," I said. Most white people I know think it's a great big deal if a Negro compliments them on their tans. It's a large laugh. You have all this volleyball about color and come summer you can't hold the white folks back from the beaches, anyplace where they can get some sun. And of course the blacker they get, the more pleased they are. Crazy. If there is ever a Negro revolt, it will come during the summer and Negroes will descend upon the beaches around the nation and paralyze the country. You can't conceal cattle prods and bombs and pistols and police dogs when you're showing your birthday suit to the sun.

"You like it?" she asked. She was pleased. She placed her arm next to mine.

"Almost the same color," she said.

"Ronnie isn't feeling well," I said.

"Oh, the poor kid. I'm so glad we have Nora. She's such a charm. I'll run right in and look at him. Do have a drink in the bar. Fix me one too, will you?" Kay skipped inside and I went to the bar and poured out two strong drinks. I made hers stronger than mine. She was back soon. "Nora was trying to put him to sleep and she made me stay out." She giggled. She quickly tossed off her drink. "Another, please?" While I was fixing her drink she was saying how amazing it was for Nora to have such a talented son. What she was really saying was that it was amazing for a servant to have a son who was not also a servant. "Anything can happen in a democracy," I said. "Servants' sons drink with madames and so on."

"Oh, Nora isn't a servant," Kay said. "She's part of the family."

Yeah, I thought. Where and how many times had I heard that before?

In the ensuing silence, she started to admire her tan again. "You think it's pretty good, do you? You don't know how hard I worked to get it." I moved close to her and held her arm. I placed my other arm around her. She pretended not to see or feel it, but she wasn't trying to get away either. In fact she was pressing closer and the register in my brain that tells me at the precise moment when I'm in, went off. Kay was very high. I put both arms around her and she put both hers around me. When I kissed her, she responded completely.

"Mom!"

"Ronnie, come back to bed," I heard Nora shout from the other room. We could hear Ronnie running over the rug in the outer room. Kay tried to get away from me, push me to one side, because we could tell that Ronnie knew where to look for his Mom: he was running right for the bar, where we were. "Oh, please," she said, "don't let him see us."

I wouldn't let her push me away.

"Stop!" she hissed. "He'll see us!" We stopped struggling just for an instant, and we listened to the echoes of the word see. She gritted her teeth and renewed her efforts to get away.

Me? I had the scene laid right out. The kid breaks into the room, see, and sees his mother in this real wriggly clinch with this colored guy who's just shouted at him, see, and no matter how his mother explains it away, the kid has the image of the colored guy and his mother for the rest of his life, see?

That's the way it happened. The kid's mother hissed under her breath, "You're crazy" and she looked at me as though she were seeing me or something about me for the very first time. I'd released her as soon as Ronnie, romping into the bar, saw us and came to a full, open-mouthed halt. Kay went to him. He looked first at me, then at his mother. Kay turned to me, but she couldn't speak.

Outside in the living room my mother called, "Wendell, where are you? We can go now."

I started to move past Kay and Ronnie. I felt many things, but I made myself think mostly, There you little bastard, there.

My mother thrust her face inside the door and said, "Goodbye, Mrs. Couchman. See you tomorrow. 'Bye, Ronnie."

"Yes," Kay said, sort of stunned. "Tomorrow." She was reaching for Ronnie's hand as we left, but the kid was slapping her hand away. I hurried quickly after Nora, hating the long drive back to Watts.

THE STAR
by Arthur C. Clarke

Even popular or escape fiction may have a thematic basis; it may make a comment about some aspect of the human condition. Although escapist literature (like the following science fiction story) is written primarily for entertainment, it can also broaden our own awareness of ourselves and our lives. The best stories achieve a balance between enlightenment and entertainment, skillfully blending the theme and the elements. "The Star" makes a strong statement about human nature by blending literary elements like character, setting, and conflict with an entertaining narrative. Although the story is set in the future, Clarke's realistic characters still behave like people you may know. But their behavior is spurred by an event that is both familiar and puzzling.

Here are some things to keep in mind as you read.

- *The main character in this story is a Jesuit monk, a member of the Society of Jesus (a Catholic religious order founded by Ignatius Loyola in 1534).*
- *Jesuits devote their lives to missionary and educational work and are also known as the intellectuals of the church.*
- *The story makes a reference to a painting by Paul Rubens (1577–1640), a Flemish artist who painted a well-known picture of Loyola.*
- *The story mentions two Latin phrases. The first, AD MAJOREM DEI GLORIUM, means "For the greater glory of God." The second is the Exercitia Spiritualia, which means "Spiritual Exercises," a book written by Loyola, which the Jesuits use for guidance.*

Everything that happens in this story—the actions and words of the characters, the setting, the slow-but-sure progress to the surprise ending—points to a central idea which is a statement about the relationship we each have to God; it's a concern that is as old as human nature itself.

It is three thousand light years to the Vatican. Once, I believed that space could have no power over faith, just as I believed that the heavens declared the glory of God's handiwork. Now I have seen that handiwork, and my faith is sorely troubled. I stare at the crucifix that hangs on the cabin wall above the Mark VI Computer, and for the first time in my life I wonder if it is no more than an empty symbol.

I have told no one yet, but the truth cannot be concealed. The facts are there for all to read, recorded on the countless miles of magnetic tape and the thousands of photographs we are carrying back to Earth. Other scientists can interpret them as easily as I can, and I am not one who would condone that tampering with the truth which often gave my order a bad name in the olden days.

The crew are already sufficiently depressed: I wonder how they will take this ultimate irony. Few of them have any religious faith, yet they will not relish using this final weapon in their campaign against me—that private, good-natured, but fundamentally serious, war which lasted all the way from Earth. It amused them to have a Jesuit as chief astrophysicist: Dr. Chandler, for instance, could never get over it (Why are medical men such notorious atheists?). Sometimes he would meet me on the observation deck, where the lights are always low so that the stars shine with undiminished glory. He would come up to me in the gloom and stand staring out of the great oval port, while the heavens crawled slowly around us as the ship turned end over end with the residual spin we had never bothered to correct.

"Well, Father," he would say at last, "it goes on forever and forever, and perhaps Something made it. But how you can believe that Something has a special interest in us and our miserable little world—that just beats me." Then the argument would start, while the stars and nebulae would swing around us in silent, endless arcs beyond the flawlessly clear plastic of the observation port.

It was, I think, the apparent incongruity of my position that caused most amusement to the crew. In vain I would point to my three papers in the Astrophysical Journal, my five in the Monthly Notices of the Royal Astronomical Society. I would remind them that my order has long been famous for its scientific works. We may be few now, but ever since the eighteenth century we have made contributions to astronomy and geophysics out of all proportion to our numbers. Will my report on the Phoenix Nebula end our thousand years of history? It will end, I fear, much more than that.

I do not know who gave the nebula its name, which seems to me a very bad one. If it contains a prophecy, it is one that cannot be verified for several billion years. Even the word nebula is misleading: this is a far smaller object than those stupendous clouds of mist—the stuff of unborn stars—that are scattered throughout the length of the Milky Way. On the cosmic scale, indeed, the Phoenix Nebula is a tiny thing—a tenuous shell of gas surrounding a single star.

Or what is left of a star....

The Ruben's engraving of Loyola seems to mock me as it hangs there above the spectrophotometer tracings. What would you, Father, have made of this knowledge that has come into my keeping, so far from the little world that was all the universe you knew? Would your faith have risen to the challenge, as mine has failed to do?

You gaze into the distance, Father, but I have traveled a distance beyond any that you could have imagined when you founded our order a thousand years ago. No other survey ship has been so far from Earth: we are at the very frontiers of the explored universe. We set out to reach the Phoenix Nebula, we succeeded, and we are homeward bound with our burden of knowledge. I wish I could lift that burden from my shoulders, but I call to you in vain across the centuries and the light years that lie between us.

On the book you are holding the words are plain to read. AD MAJOREM DEI GLORIAM, the message runs, but it is a message I can no longer believe. Would you still believe it, if you could see what we have found?

We knew, of course, what the Phoenix Nebula was. Every year, in our galaxy alone, more than a hundred stars explode, blazing for a few hours or days with thousands of times their normal brilliance before they sink back into death and obscurity. Such are the ordinary novae—the commonplace disasters of the universe. I have recorded the spectrograms and light curves of dozens since I started working at the Lunar Observatory.

But three or four times in every thousand years occurs something beside which even a nova pales into total insignificance.

When a star becomes a supernova, it may for a little while outshine all the massed suns of the galaxy. The Chinese astronomers watched this happen in A.D. 1054, not knowing what it was they saw. Five centuries later, in 1572, a supernova blazed in Cassiopeia so brilliantly that it was visible in the daylight sky. There have been three more in the thousand years that have passed since then.

Our mission was to visit the remnants of such a catastrophe, to reconstruct the events that led up to it, and, if possible, to learn its cause. We came slowly in through the concentric shells of gas that had been blasted out six thousand years before, yet were expanding still. They were immensely hot, radiating even now with a fierce violet light, but were far too tenuous to do us any damage. When the star had exploded, its outer layers had been driven upward with such speed that they had escaped completely from its gravitational field. Now they formed a hollow shell large enough to engulf a thousand solar systems, and at its center burned the tiny, fantastic object which the star had now become—a White Dwarf, smaller than the Earth, yet weighing a million times as much.

The glowing gas shells were all around us, banishing the normal night of interstellar space. We were flying into the center of a cosmic bomb that had detonated millennia ago and whose incandescent fragments were still hurtling apart. The immense scale of the explosion, and the fact that the debris already covered a volume of space many billions of miles across, robbed the scene of any visible movement. It would take decades before the unaided eye could detect any motion in these tortured wisps and eddies of gas, yet the sense of turbulent expansion was overwhelming.

We had checked our primary drive hours before, and were drifting slowly toward the fierce little star ahead. Once it had been a sun like our own, but it had squandered in a few hours the energy that should have kept it shining for a million years. Now it was a shrunken miser, hoarding its resources as if trying to make amends for its prodigal youth.

No one seriously expected to find planets. If there had been any before the explosion, they would have been boiled into puffs of vapor, and their substance lost in the greater wreckage of the star itself. But we made the automatic search, as we always do when approaching an unknown sun, and presently we found a single small world circling the star at an immense distance. It must have been the Pluto of this vanished solar system, orbiting on the frontiers of the night. Too far from the central sun ever to have known life, its remoteness had saved it from the fate of all its lost companions.

The passing fires had seared its rocks and burned away the mantle of frozen gas that must have covered it in the days before the disaster. We landed, and we found the Vault.

Its builders had made sure that we would. The monolithic marker that stood above the entrance was now a fused stump, but even the first long-range photographs told us that here was the work of intelligence. A little later we detected the continent-wide pattern of radioactivity that had been buried in the rock. Even if the pylon above the Vault had been destroyed, this would have remained, an immovable and all but eternal beacon calling to the stars. Our ship fell toward this gigantic bull's-eye like an arrow into its target.

The pylon must have been a mile high when it was built, but now it looked like a candle that had melted down into a puddle of wax. It took us a week to drill through the fused rock, since we did not have the proper tools for a task like this. We were astronomers, not archaeologists, but we could improvise. Our original purpose was forgotten: this lonely monument, reared with such labor at the greatest possible distance from the doomed sun, could have only one meaning. A civilization that knew it was about to die had made its last bid for immortality.

It will take us generations to examine all the treasures that were placed in the Vault. They had plenty of time to prepare, for their sun must have given its first warnings many years before the final detonation. Everything that they wished to preserve, all the fruit of their genius, they brought here to this distant world in the days before the end, hoping that some other race would find it and that they would not be utterly forgotten. Would we have done as well, or would we have been too lost in our own misery to give thought to a future we could never see or share?

If only they had had a little more time! They could travel freely enough between the planets of their own sun, but they had not yet learned to cross the interstellar gulfs, and the nearest solar system was a hundred light-years away. Yet even had they possessed the secret of the Transfinite Drive, no more than a few millions could have been saved. Perhaps it was better thus.

Even if they had not been so disturbingly human as their sculpture shows, we could not have helped admiring them and grieving for their fate. They left thousands of visual records and the machines for projecting them, together with elaborate pictorial instructions from which it will not be difficult to learn their written language. We have examined many of these records, and brought to life for the first time in six thousand years the warmth and beauty of a civilization that in many ways must have been superior to our own. Perhaps they only showed us the best, and one can hardly blame them. But their words were very lovely, and their cities were built with a grace that matches anything of man's. We have watched them at work and play, and listened to their musical speech sounding across the centuries. One scene is still before my eyes—a group of children on a beach of strange blue sand, playing in the waves as children play on Earth. Curious whiplike trees line the shore, and some very large animal is wading in the shadows yet attracting no attention at all.

And sinking into the sea, still warm and friendly and life-giving, is the sun that will soon turn traitor and obliterate all this innocent happiness.

Perhaps if we had not been so far from home and so vulnerable to loneliness, we should not have been so deeply moved. Many of us had seen the ruins of ancient civilizations on other worlds, but they had never affected us so profoundly. This tragedy was unique. It is one thing for a race to fail and die, as nations and cultures have done on Earth. But to be destroyed so completely in the full flower of its achievement, leaving no survivors—how could that be reconciled with the mercy of God?

My colleagues have asked me that, and I have given what answers I can. Perhaps you could have done better, Father Loyola, but I have found nothing in the Exercitia Spiritualia that helps me here. They were not an evil people: I do not know what gods they worshiped, if indeed they worshiped any. But I have looked back at them across the centuries, and have watched while the loveliness they used their last strength to preserve was brought forth again into the light of their shrunken sun. They could have taught us much: why were they destroyed?

I know the answers that my colleagues will give when they get back to Earth. They will say that the universe has no purpose and no plan, that since a hundred suns explode every year in our galaxy, at this very moment some race is dying in the depths of space. Whether that race has done good or evil during its lifetime will make no difference in the end: there is no divine justice, for there is no God.

Yet, of course, what we have seen proves nothing of the sort. Anyone who argues thus is being swayed by emotion, not logic. God has no need to justify His actions to man. He who built the universe can destroy it when He chooses. It is arrogance—it is perilously near blasphemy—for us to say what He may or may not do.

This I could have accepted, hard though it is to look upon whole worlds and peoples thrown into the furnace. But there comes a point when even the deepest faith must falter, and now, as I look at the calculations lying before me, I know I have reached that point at last.

We could not tell, before we reached the nebula, how long ago the explosion took place. Now, from the astronomical evidence and the record in the rocks of that one surviving planet, I have been able to date it very exactly. I know in what year the light of this colossal conflagration reached our Earth. I know how brilliantly the supernova whose corpse now dwindles behind our speeding ship once shone in terrestrial skies. I know how it must have blazed low in the east before sunrise, like a beacon in that oriental dawn.

There can be no reasonable doubt: the ancient mystery is solved at last. Yet, oh God, there were so many stars you could have used. What was the need to give these people to the fire, that the symbol of their passing might shine above Bethlehem?

TEN MILES WEST OF VENUS
by Judy Troy

After Marvelle Lyle's husband, Morgan, committed suicide—his body being found on an April evening in the willows that grew along Black Creek—Marvelle stopped going to church. Franklin Sanders, her minister at Venus United Methodist, drove out to her house on a Sunday afternoon in the middle of May to see if he could coax her back. Her house was ten miles west of Venus—seven miles on the highway and three on a two-lane road that cut through the open Kansas wheat fields and then wound back through the forest preserve. The woods at this time of year were sprinkled with white blooming pear trees.

Franklin had his radio tuned to Gussie Dell's weekly "Neighbor Talk" program. Gussie was a member of his congregation, and Franklin wanted to see what embarrassing thing she would choose to say today. The week before, she had told a story about her grandson, Norman, drawing a picture of Jesus wearing high heels. "I have respect for Norman's creativity," she had said, "I don't care if Norman puts Jesus in a garter belt."

Today, though, she was on the subject of her sister, whom Franklin had visited in the hospital just the day before. "My sister has cancer," Gussie said. "She may die or she may not. My guess is she won't. I just wanted to say that publicly."

Franklin pulled into Marvelle's driveway and turned off the radio too soon to hear whatever Gussie was going to say next; he imagined it was something unfavorable about her sister's husband, who, for years now, had been sitting outside in his chicken shed, watching television. "One of these days I'm going to dynamite him out of there," Gussie liked to say. She was generally down on marriage, which Franklin couldn't argue with—his own marriage being unhappy, and that fact not a secret among his parishioners.

Franklin parked his new Ford Taurus between Marvelle's old pickup and the ancient Jeep Morgan had driven. Hanging from the Jeep's rearview mirror were Morgan's military dog tags. He'd been in the Vietnam War, though Franklin had never known any details about it. Morgan Lyle had never been forthcoming about himself, and the few times Franklin had seen him at church Morgan had spent the length of the sermon and most of the service smoking outside. "You have to accept him as he is," Marvelle had once told Franklin. "Otherwise, well, all I'm saying is he doesn't mean anything by what he says and does."

Also in the driveway—just a big gravel clearing, really, between the house and the garage where Morgan had had his motorcycle repair shop—was the dusty van their son, Curtis, drove. He was thirty-one and still living at home. Franklin, who was sixty-three, could remember Curtis as the blond-headed child who had once, in Sunday School, climbed out of a window in order to avoid reciting the Lord's Prayer. Now the grownup Curtis, in faded pants and no shirt, his thinning hair pulled back into a ponytail, opened the door before Franklin had a chance to knock. "Well, come on in, I guess," Curtis said. Behind him, Marvelle appeared in the kitchen doorway.

The house was built haphazardly into a hill, and was so shaded with oak and sweetgum trees that the inside—in spring and summer, anyway—was dark during the day. The only light in the room was a small lamp on a desk in the corner, shining down on iridescent feathers and other fly-tying materials. Curtis sat down at the desk and picked up a hook.

"I'll make coffee," Marvelle told Franklin, and he followed her into the kitchen, which was substantially brighter. An overhead light was on, and the walls were painted white. "I thought Sunday afternoons were when you visited the sick," Marvelle said.

"It was, but I do that on Saturdays now. I find other reasons to get out of the house on Sundays." Franklin sat at the kitchen table and watched her make coffee. She was a tall, muscular woman, and she'd lost weight since Morgan's death. Her jeans looked baggy on her; her red hair was longer than it used to be, and uncombed. "You could stand to eat more," Franklin told her.

"You men complain when we're fat and then worry when we're thin."

"When did I ever say you were fat?" Franklin said.

Marvelle turned toward him with the coffeepot in her hand. "You're right. You never did."

Franklin looked down at the table. This afternoon, with his mind on Morgan, and not on himself or his marriage, he'd managed to push aside the memory of an afternoon years ago, when he and Marvelle had found themselves kissing in the church kitchen. "Found themselves" was just how it had seemed to him. It was, like this day, a Sunday afternoon in spring; Marvelle and his wife and two other parishioners had been planting flowers along the front walk. Marvelle had come into the kitchen for coffee just when he had. He wasn't so gray-haired then or so bottom-heavy, and they walked toward each other and kissed passionately, as if they had planned it for months.

"You've always been an attractive woman," he said quietly.

"Don't look so guilty. It was a long time ago." Marvelle sat down across from him as the coffee brewed. "The amazing thing is that it only happened once."

"No," Franklin said, "it's that I allowed it to happen at all."

"Where was God that day? Just not paying attention?" Marvelle asked.

"That was me not paying attention to God," Franklin told her.

Curtis had turned on the radio in the living room, and Franklin could faintly hear a woman singing. Louder was the sound of the coffee brewing. The kitchen table was next to a window that overlooked a sloping wooded hill and a deep ravine. These woods, too, Franklin noticed, had their share of flowering pear trees. "It looks like snow has fallen in a few select places," he said.

"Doesn't it? I saw two deer walking down there this morning. For a moment, I almost forgot about everything else."

Franklin looked at her face, which was suddenly both bright and sad.

"That's interesting," he said carefully, "because that's what church services do for me."

"Sure they do. Otherwise, you'd lose your place," Marvelle said.

"You don't realize something," Franklin told her. "I'd rather not be the one conducting them. I feel that more and more as I get older. I'd like to sit with the congregation and just partake."

"Would you? Well, I wouldn't. I wouldn't want to do either one." She got up and poured coffee into two mugs and handed one to Franklin. "How do you expect me to feel?" she asked him, standing next to the window. "Do you see God taking a hand in my life? There are people in that congregation who didn't want to see Morgan buried in their cemetery."

"You're talking about two or three people out of a hundred and twenty."

"I bet you felt that way yourself," Marvelle told him.

"You know me better than to think that," Franklin said.

Marvelle sat down and put her coffee on the table in front of her. "All right, I do. Just don't make me apologize."

"When could anybody make you do anything you didn't want to do?" Franklin said to her.

Franklin left late in the afternoon, saying goodbye to Curtis after admiring Curtis's fly-tying abilities. Marvelle accompanied him to his car walking barefoot over the gravel. "You'll be walking over coals next," Franklin said, joking.

"Are you trying to sneak God back into the conversation?" Marvelle asked him. She had her hand on his car door as he got in, and she closed the door after him.

"I'm talking about the toughness of your feet," Franklin said through the open window. "I don't expect that much from God. Maybe I used to. But the older I get, the easier I am on him. God's getting older, too, I figure."

"Then put on your seat belt," Marvelle said. She stepped back into a patch of sunlight, so the last thing he saw as he drove away was the sun on her untidy hair and on her pale face and neck.

The woods he passed were gloomier now, with the sun almost level with the tops of the tallest oaks; it was a relief to him to drive out of the trees and into the green wheat fields.

The radio was broadcasting a Billy Graham sermon, which Franklin found he couldn't concentrate on. He was wondering about Gussie's sister and if she'd live, and for how long, and what her husband might be thinking, out in that chicken shed. When Franklin was at the hospital the day before, Gussie's sister hadn't mentioned her husband. She'd wanted to know exactly how Franklin's wife had redecorated their bedroom.

"Blue curtains and a flowered bedspread," he had told her, and that was all he could remember—nothing about the new chair or the wallpaper or the lamps, all of which he took note of when he went home afterward.

He was also thinking, less intentionally, about Marvelle, who was entering his thoughts as erratically as the crows flying down into the fields he was passing. She was eight or nine years older than when he'd kissed her, but those years had somehow changed into days. When Franklin tried to keep his attention on her grief, it wandered off to her hair, her dark eyes—to every godless place it could. It wasn't until he heard Billy Graham recite, "He maketh me to lie down in green pastures: He leadeth me beside the still waters," that Franklin's mind focussed back on Morgan lying in the willows. From that point on he paid attention to the words, falling apart a little when he heard, "Surely goodness and mercy shall follow me all the days of my life," because he didn't know anything more moving, except maybe love, which he didn't feel entitled to; he never had.